Evolution
of the
SYNAGOGUE

Evolution
of the
SYNAGOGUE

Problems and Progress

Edited by
Howard Clark Kee
and Lynn H. Cohick

TRINITY PRESS INTERNATIONAL
Harrisburg, Pennsylvania

Trinity Press International, P.O. Box 1321, Harrisburg, PA 17105

Trinity Press International is a division of the Morehouse Group.

Cover design: Corey Kent

Cover image: The forecourt of the fourth–fifth-century synagogue in the Ancient City of Sardis, courtesy of Marianne Bonz

Library of Congress Cataloging-in-Publication Data

Evolution of the synagogue : problems and progress / edited by Lynn H. Cohick and Howard Clark Kee.
    p. cm.
    Includes bibliographical references and index.
    ISBN 1-56338-296-2 (pa. : alk. paper)
    1. Synagogues – History. 2. Jews – Antiquities. 3. Judaism – History – Talmudic period, 10–425. I. Cohick, Lynn H. II. Kee, Howard Clark.
BM653 .E86 1999
296.6′5′09015 – dc21   99-044917

Printed in the United States of America

99 00 01 02 03 04   10 9 8 7 6 5 4 3 2 1

Contents

Abbreviations

AJA	*American Journal of Archaeology*
ANRW	*Aufstieg und Niedergang der römischen Welt*
BAR	*Biblical Archaeology Review*
BASOR	*Bulletin of the American Schools of Oriental Research*
BJS	Brown Judaic Studies
BSP	Black Sea Project
CBQ	*Catholic Biblical Quarterly*
CIG	*Corpus inscriptionum graecarum*
CIJ	*Corpus inscriptionum judaicarum*
CIL	*Corpus inscriptionum latinarum*
CIRB	*Corpus inscriptionum regni bosporani* (Moscow: Academia Scientiarum, 1965)
CPJ	*Corpus papyrorum judaicorum*
CSEL	*Corpus scriptorum ecclesiasticorum latinorum*
DJD	Discoveries in the Judaean Desert
FRLANT	Forschungen zur Religion und Literatur des Alten und Neuen Testaments
GCS	Griechischen christlichen Schriftsteller
GDI	Sammlung der griechischen Dialektinschriften (Göttingen: Vandenhoeck & Ruprecht, 1899)
GV	Griechische Vers-Inschriften. Bd. 1: Grabepigramme (ed. W. Peek, Berlin, 1955)
HSCP	*Harvard Studies in Classical Philology*
HTR	*Harvard Theological Review*

ICC	International Critical Commentary
IEJ	*Israel Exploration Journal*
JAC	*Jahrbuch für Antike und Christentum*
JBL	*Journal of Biblical Literature*
JJP	*Journal of Juristic Papyrology*
JJS	*Journal of Jewish Studies*
JQR	*Jewish Quarterly Review*
JRS	*Journal of Roman Studies*
JSNTSup	Journal for the Study of the New Testament Supplement Series
JSQ	*Jewish Studies Quarterly*
JTS	*Journal of Theological Studies*
LCL	Loeb Classical Library
NTS	*New Testament Studies*
NovTSup	Novum Testamentum, Supplements
POXY	Oxyrhynchus Papyri. Ed. A. S. Hunt
RevSR	*Revue de sciences religieuses*
RHE	*Revue d'histoire ecclésiastique*
SNTSMS	Society for New Testament Studies Monograph Series
TDNT	*Theological Dictionary of the New Testament*
VDI	*Vestnik drevnei istorii*
ZNW	*Zeitschrift für die neutestamentliche Wissenschaft*

Introduction

Howard Clark Kee

During the past twenty years archaeological excavations in Israel combined with insightful reexamination of the ancient writings of Judaism and early Christianity have resulted in radical reassessment of scholarly understanding of the origins and development of the synagogue in postbiblical Judaism. The assumption that the social, organizational, and physical structures of the synagogue as reflected in the rabbinic sources and as evident from archaeological remains of synagogues from the third and fourth century C.E. were already operative in the period before and immediately following the start of the Common Era has been basically discredited.

A major factor in this radical change has been the work of scholars such as Jacob Neusner, who have employed the methods of historical criticism in the analysis of rabbinic sources, and have shown the clear but unwarranted scholarly tendency to read later developments in the rabbinic movement back into earlier times. Since the publication more than twenty years ago of his book tracing the development of Pharisaism with the revealing title *From Politics to Piety*,[1] Neusner's hundreds of books and articles have provided historical and literary analysis of the profound reshaping of Judaism in the period from the Fall of the Temple to the emergence of the rabbinic systems and structures of thought. In a more recent study, *Judaism in the Matrix of Christianity*, he has insightfully analyzed the links between the conceptual and institutional development of the synagogue and of the Christian church in the Constantinian period.[2] The evidence that the oldest physical structures adapted for primary use as meeting places for Jewish worship

---

1. Jacob Neusner, *From Politics to Piety: The Emergence of Pharisaic Judaism* (Englewood Cliffs, N.J.: Prentice-Hall, 1973).

2. Second printing, with new preface and introduction, South Florida Studies in the History of Judaism 8 (Atlanta: Scholars Press, 1991).

1

date from the third century and subsequently is equally important.[3] The development within Judaism from housing meetings in private homes or general purpose public halls to erecting formal structures designed for worship and study has been traced by L. Michael White in *The Social Origins of Christian Architecture,* vol. 1.[4] The essays included in *The Galilee in Late Antiquity* edited by Lee I. Levine trace other aspects of these developments both conceptually and architecturally.[5] As a result of archaeological excavations of buildings that are unmistakably synagogues, it has become clear that residential structures, or those designed for group gatherings, were in the third century adapted and modified to serve the primary purpose of a Jewish place of worship. We have had this knowledge since the 1930s, when the excavation of Dura-Europos showed that, in a residential quarter of this city in Syria, three residential structures were given major modifications in order to serve as the sites for gathering and worship — one for Jews, one for Christians, and one for devotees of Mithra.[6] These excavations have continued down to the present in Galilee and in the Crimea.[7] They enable scholars to trace the evolution of the synagogue from a meeting in whatever space was available and suitable to the construction of increasingly complex worship centers.

In light of these archaeological excavations and research, the Philadelphia Seminar in Christian Origins, which convenes at the University of Pennsylvania and is supported by the Department of Religious Studies, appropriately chose the theme of the development of the synagogue for the presentations and discussion of the seminar in the academic year 1995–96. The papers, which represent a range of views on the subject of the Evolution of the Synagogue, have been collected and edited by H. C. Kee and Lynn Cohick. Other scholars who have been investigating the develop-

3. The evidence is sketched in my essay "Defining the First Century Synagogue," *NTS* 41, no. 4 (October 1995): 493–97.

4. Subtitle, *Building God's House in the Roman World: Architectural Adaptation among Pagans, Jews and Christians* (Baltimore and London: Johns Hopkins University Press, 1990; Valley Forge, Pa.: Trinity Press International, 1996). See also his *The Social Origins of Christian Architecture,* vol. 2, subtitle *Texts and Monuments for the Christian Domus Ecclesiae in Its Environment* (Valley Forge, Pa.: Trinity Press International, 1997).

5. New York and Jerusalem: Jewish Theological Seminary of America; distributed by Harvard University Press (Cambridge, Mass., 1992).

6. See the analysis of these sites in C. H. Kraeling, *The Synagogue,* Final Report VII, Part 1, of *The Excavations at Dura-Europos,* ed. A. R. Bellinger, F. E. Brown, A. Perkins, and C. B. Welles (New York: KTAV, 1979).

7. See additional bibliography below, p. 175.

ment of the synagogue have also been invited to submit papers on this theme. This collection of essays is offered as a contribution to the ongoing discussion of this question, which has important implications for historical understanding of both rabbinic Judaism and early Christianity.

Part One

THE ORIGINS
OF THE SYNAGOGUE
IN THE LAND
OF ISRAEL

CHAPTER ONE

Defining the
First-Century C.E. Synagogue

Problems and Progress

Howard Clark Kee

Boston University and the University of Pennsylvania

The basic assumptions of many New Testament scholars about the
nature of the *synagōgē* in the first century prior to the First Jewish Revolt continue to match those enunciated by Lee Levine in
his introduction to *Ancient Synagogues Revealed*.[1] The features in
his description are (1) regular prayers, (2) study, (3) sacred meals,
(4) repository for communal funds, (5) law courts, (6) general assembly hall, (7) hostel, (8) and residence for synagogue officials.
Although he refers to Josephus, Acts and Ezra as sources for this
historical reconstruction, the primary basis for his assumptions is
the familiar Theodotus inscription, found by the French archaeologist Raimond Weill in the course of excavations in the so-called
City of David section of the southeastern hill of Jerusalem from
November 1913 to March 1914.

Information about this find was made accessible to New Testament scholars chiefly through Adolf Deissmann in the fourth edition
of *Light from the Ancient East* (1922).[2] Deissmann refers to Weill's

---

1. Lee J. Levine, *Ancient Synagogues Revealed* (Jerusalem: Israel Exploration
Society, 1981). His analysis of the synagogue was developed and expanded in his
introduction, especially in relation to diaspora synagogues, in a series of essays by
various scholars in *The Synagogue in Late Antiquity* (Philadelphia: American Schools
of Oriental Research, 1987). Recently Levine's understanding of the synagogue in the
early Roman period has been significantly altered, and now more nearly resembles
the historical view set forth in this essay.

2. *Light from the Ancient East: The New Testament Illustrated by Recently Discovered Texts of the Graeco-Roman World*, trans. Lionel R. M. Strachan (New York:
G. H. Doran, 1927), Appendix V, 439–41.

report on his excavations of Roman baths and specifically to the inscription found in a cistern, which "[Weill] assigns, no doubt correctly, to the period before the destruction of Jerusalem"; that is, before 70. Although in the years immediately following the discovery other scholars suggested a later date for the inscription, Deissmann asserted that "the question of its age is not at all complicated," since "it may be said of any and every Jewish inscription that turns up in the rubbish heaps of Jerusalem, if it is in Greek and in characters of the early Roman period, that it must have been written before 70 A.D." He adopted the theory of Emil Schürer that after 70 no Jew could settle in Jerusalem, much less build any structure there.[3] He goes on to say that the testimony of the inscription to "an undisturbed stream of pilgrims and an unbroken continuity of the congregation's office-bearers" proves that it comes from the pre-70 period. Seventy years later, the same bland assumption about the date of this inscription and some of the same set of historical inferences are drawn by Lester Grabbe in his *Judaism from Cyrus to Hadrian,* who proceeds on the basis of this inscription to offer generalizations similar to Levine's earlier hypothesis about the construction of pre-70 synagogues in Palestine.[4] A more cautious use of the inscription is to be found in the revised edition of Schürer, however, where mention is made of the discovery of the Theodotus inscription, and the date assigned is "the beginning of the first century A.D.," but without comment the only activities mentioned as associated with the first-century C.E. synagogue are "the reading of the law and the teaching of the precepts."[5] Lodgings, dining rooms, or other facilities for visitors from foreign lands are not mentioned in the inscription.

When the Theodotus inscription was first found, archaeologists knowledgeable about Palestinian finds initially assessed it to be from the later Roman imperial period, as Deissmann himself notes.[6] Estimates of the date of the inscription by a number of distinguished epigraphers whom I consulted informally converged on the period from the mid-second to the late third century C.E. But the scholarly opinion about the date that has predominated since Deissmann's

---

3. He adopted the theory from the original edition: Emil Schürer, *Geschichte des jüdischen Volkes,* 1:649, 703.

4. 2 vols. (Minneapolis: Fortress, 1992), 2:541.

5. Emil Schürer, *The History of the Jewish People in the Age of Jesus Christ (175 B.C.–A.D. 135)* 2, new English version rev. and ed. Geza Vermes, Fergus Millar, and Matthew Black (Edinburgh: T. & T. Clark, 1979), 425.

6. Deissmann, *Light,* 439, n. 2.

publication of the text continues to be based on inferences about simple continuities between Palestinian Judaism before and after the two Jewish revolts. Chiefly through the brilliant work of Jacob Neusner,[7] however, there is growing awareness that the diversity of modes of Jewish identity and practice in the pre-70 C.E. period declined following the failure of the Second Jewish Revolt, and that there began the process toward orthodoxy and orthopraxis, culminating in the emergence and role-definition of the rabbinic leadership in the period from the second to the fifth century, as evident in the Mishnah and the Talmud. Just as the traditional pious and scholarly assumptions about "normative Judaism" have been challenged by scholars investigating postbiblical Judaism, so current analytical archaeological methods demand a careful assessment of this discovery of an inscribed stone slab in a junk-filled cistern that was part of a Roman bath complex. Metaphorically, on this single inscribed stone has been erected a highly dubious scholarly construct: the supposed architectural and institutional synagogue of the first century C.E.

None of the essential criteria for assigning a date — location in a closed locus with datable contemporary evidence (coins and pottery) — was available for determining the age of the Theodotus inscription, nor was any of the other material also found in the cistern dated. Accordingly, the pre-70 date assigned to it is evidently pure conjecture. The fact that a Roman bath system such as the one that was the locus of the discovery of the inscription was built in the older part of Jerusalem known as the City of David makes most sense if the construction were to be dated some time after the city was rebuilt by Hadrian as Aelia Capitolina. In this period an elaborate Roman-type pool was built on the site of the Pool of Siloam in the area where the ancient water supply system of the city was developed. On purely inferential grounds, the finding of the inscription among rubbish in the bottom of the cistern increases the probability that it is from a date later than the second- or third-century Roman bath complex in which it was found. The inscription may have been dumped there in the fourth century at the time that the city was being rebuilt in the post-Constantinian period, when anti-Jewish sentiment and activities soared. But the inquiry need not be limited to conjectures. Three concrete lines of investigation must

---

7. Neusner's thesis about the transformation of Judaism in this period is effectively summarized in the preface and introduction to the second printing of his *Judaism in the Matrix of Christianity*, South Florida Studies in the History of Judaism 8 (Atlanta: Scholars Press, 1991).

be explored in deciding on the probable date of the Theodotus inscription, and thus on the import of this find for our understanding of the history of the synagogue: (1) linguistic analyses of the terms used for gatherings of pious Jews in the centuries just before and after the turn of the eras; (2) archaeological studies that have been made in recent decades of the remains of ancient meeting places in Palestine, including comparative analyses of the range of evidence; (3) historical studies of Judaism in the period from Herod to the Byzantine period.

Before turning to these analyses, however, it may be useful to offer a translation and brief analysis of the inscription:

> Theodotus, son of Vettenus and ruler of the synagogue, son of a ruler of the synagogue and grandson of a ruler of the synagogue, built the synagogue for the reading of the Law (*anagnōsin*) and instruction (*didachēn*) in the commandments; also the strangers' lodgings (*kzenōma*) and dining rooms (*dōmata*) and water facilities (*ta chrēstēria*) and hostel (*kātaluna*) for the use of those from foreign lands (kzenēs). The foundation of this his fathers and the elders (*presbyteroi*) and Simonides laid.

The father of Theodotus is identified as Vettenus, which is an instance of the distinctive Roman mode of designating his clan: *gens*. Since Rome did not seize power in Palestine until Pompey's invasion in 63 B.C.E., it is highly unlikely that this Roman mode of group identity by *gens* would have been popular among devout Jews in the opening decades of the first century C.E. when (on the basis of Deissmann's date for the inscription) Theodotus's father would have been at his maturity, much less in the preceding generation of his grandfather.

While there is an abundance of evidence that pious Jews met regularly in Palestine and throughout the Diaspora from the early Roman period on for reading and instruction in the Law from as early as the second century B.C.E. onward, we have no evidence (see below) for the existence of distinctive buildings erected for this purpose or facilities to carry out the auxiliary functions and facilities such as ablutions and to provide housing and food for pious visitors from other parts of the world. The reference to laying the foundations may allude to the literal structural antecedents of the synagogue building erected by the earlier generations of Theodotus's family, or as seems more likely, it may simply point to the earlier stages of the organization for the synagogue as a community, with the elders (or presbyters) as those who shared the leadership of the group. Before addressing more specifically the question of its date, we must consider the terminology for the places where Jews gathered in the Roman period and functions carried out in such places.

The Ancient Linguistic Evidence for the Meaning of *Synagōgē*

Careful analysis of the use of the term, *synagōgē*, in Greek literature and in Jewish writings of the post-Maccabean period shows that its dominant meaning is "assembly" or "community." Schrage, in the article on *synagōgē* in *TDNT*,[8] notes that in both secular Greek literature and in pre-70 C.E. Jewish writings (including the Septuagint and the so-called Apocrypha) the term means "gathering" — of books, boats or people. The assemblies may be for social, political or military purposes. Not noted by Schrage, but relevant for our inquiry, are occurrences of the term *synagōgē* in Greek literature with reference to the collecting of troops (Thucydides 2.18) or simply to a meeting (Plato, *Theocritus* 150a). The corresponding verb, *synagō*, likewise means simply "to bring together." Not adequately taken into account by Schrage and others is the fact that the LXX uses *synagōgē* to translate eighteen different Hebrew words for gathering, and that what is gathered includes monsters (Prov 21:16), waters (Gen 1:9; Lev 11:36) and stones (Job 8:17). Surprisingly, the term for the whole assembly of Israel in 1 Sam 17:47 is *ekklēsia*. A revealing example of the connotations of this terminology in Greek literature occurs in Xenophon's *Anabasis* (1.3.9) where Cyrus assembled a meeting of his own soldiers: *synegagen ekklēsian tōn stratiōtōn*. Here also, the cognate verb, *synagō*, is directly linked with the term that became dominant for the early Christian community, *ekklēsia*. Schrage does note that in the LXX *synagōgē* alternates with *ekklēsia* as translations of *qahal* and *edhah* (802).

Schrage does also note that the term was used broadly in secular Greek literature for gathering people or things (books, laws, letters, crops, military troops), and in the LXX for communities and assemblies (on national, legal or cultic bases), as well as for bodies of water. These gatherings included Gentile peoples and nations,[9]

---

8. 7:799–814.
9. Zeph 3:8; Gen 28:3; 35:11; 48:4; Jer 50:9.

gatherings of the wicked,[10] or the whole congregation of Israel,[11] as well as the assemblies of the pious.[12] One should also note that in the so-called Old Testament Apocrypha *synagōgē* means an assembly of people. At times it is simply the whole community (Sir 4:7), but it can also refer to a group of sinners (Sir 16:6; 21:9), or to a distinctive segment of the Jewish people, such as the Chasidim (1 Macc 2:42) or the scribes (1 Macc 7:12). In Susanna *synagōgē* is a recurrent term for the entire Jewish community (Sus 28, 42, 52, 60).[13] In noncanonical writings such as *The Testaments of the Twelve Patriarchs, synagōgē* is used for the assembly of God's people, both Jewish and Gentile, rather than for an institutional or architectural structure.[14] On the other hand, where the focus is on the actual structure or facility to accommodate a large gathering of people, the LXX term is *parembolē*.

Schrage's chief interest in the meaning of *synagōgē* is on "a community gathered for common action" rather than on the simple fact that "the community is in assembly" (803). Terms used in the literature of this period for the gathering places of pious Jews include *proseuchē*,[15] *proseutērion, eucheion, sabbataiou, hagios topos, hieron, ho oikos, didaskaleion.* Yet when Schrage offers his complete sketch of the synagogue, he builds his case not only on this earlier material (including the LXX, the apocrypha, Philo, Josephus and the New Testament) but also on the rabbinic evidence from the second to the sixth century C.E. to make his case. Not surprisingly, therefore, he accepts as important evidence for the first-century C.E. synagogue the inscription of Theodotus, from which he infers that a regular feature of a synagogue was a hospice (814). He divides the New Testament evidence into two groups: synagogue as congregation and synagogue as building, but declares that "In the

---

10. In Ps 85:14 a lawless, powerful band (*synagōgē*) attacks God's people.

11. Ex 16:1, 4, 6; Num 14:17, 27, 35.

12. Ex 12:6; Lev 9:5; Num 8:9; Ps 111:1.

13. Although Schrage tries to make the point that Susanna 28 is the one passage in the LXX which refers to the building where the people gather as *synagōgē*, it is clear that the gathering takes place in the private home of her husband, Joakim.

14. *T. Levi* 11:5, the congregation of Israel; *T. Benj* 11:2–3. the gathering of the Gentiles through the testimony of the messiahs of Levi and Judah.

15. Detailed and fully documented analysis of *proseuchē* in relation to synagogue has been done by Martin Hengel "Proseuche und Synagoge: Jüdische Gemeinde, Gotteshaus und Gottesdienst in der Diaspora und in Palästina," in *Tradition und Glaube: Das frühe Christentum in seiner Umwelt*, Festschrift für K. G. Kühn, ed. G. Jeremias, H. Kühn, and H. Stegemann (Göttingen: Vandenhoeck & Ruprecht, 1971), 157–83; repr. in *The Synagogue: Studies in Origins, Archaeology and Architecture*, ed. J. Gutmann (New York: KTAV, 1975), 27–54.

overwhelming majority of instances in the New Testament, *synagōgē* means the Jewish building.[16] A careful analysis of the occurrences of this term and of the cognate verb, *synago,* shows, however, that this generalization is not only unwarranted but overlooks the evidence within the New Testament of the process of the development of the synagogue toward its considerably later institutional forms.

The most useful sources for documentation of the use of *synagōgē* among Jews of the first century C.E. are the writings of Philo and Josephus. One of the most clearly indicative passages in Josephus is found in his autobiography (*Life,* 277). When he was attempting to halt the insurrection against Rome, his encounters with various groups in Galilee included a town meeting in Tiberias where "everyone" came together (συνάγονται ἅπαντες *synagontai hapantes*), and that took place in a *proseuchē,* described by him as a very large *oikēma,* "able to accommodate a great crowd." The term *oikēma* likewise has a range of meanings in Greek literature from "dwelling" to "storehouse" to "brothel" and "animal cage."[17] Clearly the central feature is the gathering itself, not the facility where the meeting occurs. The most revealing passage in Josephus as to the precise connotation of *synagōgē* is obscured by the translation in the Loeb edition of the *Antiquities* (XIX.299–307). There the Roman legate, Petronius, during the reign of Claudius wrote a letter of protest to the leading men of Dora who had defiled the synagogue of the Jews in that city by setting up in it an image of Caesar. Petronius declared that these desecrators had prevented the Jews from *being* (*einai*) a synagogue by their action of transferring this object into the Jewish place of gathering (*en tō tēs synagōgēs topo*), where the group had a right to be in charge of their own place.

In the extensive writings of Philo, the standard term for the place where Jews gather for study of the law is *proseuchē.* In his treatise on *Special Laws* (2:62) Philo observes that "each seventh day in every city there stand wide open thousands of *didaskaleia* [institutes of instruction] in good sense, temperance, courage, justice and all the virtues. They sit in them quietly and in order, with ears alert and with full attention, so much do they thirst for the drink which the teacher's words supply." In his work, *On Dreams,* Philo quotes an Egyptian official who scornfully describes the Jews in that country as those who "sit in your little conclaves (*synagogiois,*

---

16. *Synagōgē* in *TDNT* 7:830.
17. Examples of these meanings are found: "dwelling," Plato *Phaedrus* 116a, Herodotus 1.17; "storehouse," Demosthenes 42.6, 19; "animal cage," Herodotus 7.119; "brothel," Herodotus 2.121; Plato *Charmides* 163b.

a diminutive form of *synagōgē*), gather your usual group (*thiason*) and in safety read your holy books, expounding anything that may not be clear, and with verbosity and no regard for time, expatiating on your ancestral philosophy" (2:127). In his *Embassy to Gaius* Philo discusses in detail the *proseuchai,* which he says are located in every part of the city of Alexandria (20:132), how they were attacked by hostile mobs and some were seized by Agrippa (346). All his references to the structures that came to be called the synagogue buildings employ the term *proseuchē*. Appealing to the precedents of the Hellenistic rulers of Egypt and of Caesar Augustus, he notes that they never made changes with regard to the function of the *proseuchas* in Alexandria (23:152). Augustus, he declares (155–56) knew of the large district across the Tiber owned by Jews, that they had not changed their ancestral customs, and that they met every sabbath in their proseuchas to "receive public instruction in their national philosophy." Caesar did not "expel them from Rome or deprive them of their Roman citizenship" nor did he prevent them from meeting (*synagesthai*) in their *proseuchas* for "the exposition of their laws."[18]

Returning to the use of the terms for synagogues in the works of Josephus, in *War* 2.285 — which may have achieved its present form in the last decade of the first century C.E.[19] — we find his description of the attempt by Jews in Caesarea who "had a synagogue" (*synagōgēn echontes*) to buy a plot where they could erect a building. The owner of the adjacent space built on it in such a way as to make access extremely difficult for the Jews, and someone sacrificed birds at the entrance to their meeting prior to their assembling there for the sabbath session. Here the phrase *eis tēn syagōgēn* almost certainly means "into the meeting," but it cannot be completely excluded that following the destruction of the temple in 70 C.E., the term *synagōgē,* which earlier had been used with reference to the Jewish group meetings, began to be used to refer as well to the structure where they met.

Examination of the use of the term *synagōgē* in the Gospels and Acts shows that in nearly every case, a translation of the word with the connotation of "meeting" or "gathering" makes perfect sense. From the first report of Jesus entering a synagogue in our oldest

---

18. Text and translation of Philo's *Legatio ad Gaium* edited and annotated by E. Mary Smallwood, *Philonis Alexandrini: Legatio ad Gaium* (Leiden: Brill, 1970).

19. The thesis that there was a later modest revision and expansion of the *Wars* was offered by Robert Eisler and adopted by H. St. J. Thackeray in the Loeb edition of Josephus (Cambridge, Mass.: Harvard University Press, 1957), vii–xii.

Gospel (Mark 1:21–29)[20] the important factor is that Jesus took part in a meeting for the purpose of study. The informality of the activity is indicated by the contrast between the effectiveness and power of Jesus' teaching and the official interpretations of the law by the scribes (1:22). Jesus extends this synagogue teaching activity "throughout all Galilee" (1:39),[21] in spite of his obvious lack of credentials or formal authorization. Similarly, the account of his teaching in a synagogue "in his own hometown" (Mark 6:1–2)[22] gives no hint of formal structure or even formal proceedings, since this local laborer's son is permitted to teach on the sabbath. The objections are to his words, not to having a lay member of the local town speak out in this gathering. The launching of the plot to destroy Jesus (Mark 3:6) is based on his having violated the sabbath law against work and then having defended his action in a local gathering (3:1 5), rather than on any infraction by him of formal synagogue procedure. Jesus' teaching activity is not limited to synagogue gatherings, but takes place in crowds gathered "beside the sea" (2:13) and in his own house (2:15–17) where "scribes of the Pharisees" have come to listen and to challenge his interpretation of the Jewish legal traditions,

Some scholars have inferred that reference to scribes claiming "the best seats in the synagogues" (Mark 12:39)[23] implies a formal physical structure for the meeting place. But it can mean only the most visible location in the gathering taking place in a home or public meeting hall. In his description of the Essenes,[24] Philo notes that on the sabbath they "proceed to sacred spots which they call synagogues. There, arranged in rows, according to their ages, the younger below the elder, they sit decorously as befits the occasion with attentive ears." In the Community Rule from Qumran (1QS 6:8–9) when the congregation assembles, "each man shall sit in his place: the priests shall sit first, and the elders second, and all the rest of the people according to their rank." Nothing in this rule indicates special architectural features, but simply seating order in a room or an assembly hall.

Two revealing details about the subsequent institutional development of the synagogues do appear in Mk 1:39 and 13:9, however.

---

20. Cf. Luke 4:31–37.
21. Cf. Matt 4:23–25; Luke 4:44.
22. Cf. Matt 13:53–58. Greatly expanded and altered in Luke 4:16–30; see below.
23. Cf. Matt 23:6; Luke 11:20.
24. In *Every Good Man Is Free* 81, trans. F. H. Colson, LCL 9 (Cambridge, Mass.: Harvard University Press, 1941).

The first is mention of "*their* synagogues," which of course implies that Jesus and his followers have their own synagogues. Luke uses this phrase only once (4:15), but Matthew repeats Mark's term (Matt 12:9) and makes the same distinction in 13:54 and 23:34. The clear implication is that in the later first-century Jews and Christians are in process of developing their own versions of this tradition for gatherings of their respective clienteles for study of scripture and worship in a community of sharing. The process of establishing authoritative synagogue leadership and procedures is implicit in Mark 13:9, where Jesus warns his followers to expect persecution at the hands of "councils" (*synedria*) and "synagogues." Both Matthew (10:17) and Luke (12:11) repeat this warning, but Luke adds "prisons" as a mode of punishment by the Jewish authorities (21:12). Matthew alone in the Gospel tradition reports a saying of Jesus about a role of authority in the interpretation of Torah to the people gathered in the synagogue: Moses' seat (Matt 23:2),[25] but there is no evidence that this seat was a physical feature in the oldest excavated synagogues.

Two unique features of Luke's adaptation of the Gospel tradition imply development of the synagogue in still other directions than those in Mark and Matthew. The first of these is the implication of a degree of formality and due process that characterizes the synagogue meeting in Luke 4:16–30, in contrast with the earlier version in Mark 6:1–6. Luke's phrase "according to custom" with reference to Jesus' going to the synagogue on the sabbath makes the intentional character of this formalization explicit. The procedure is further implied in Jesus' standing to read the scripture, the attendant's choice of Isaiah as the reading for the day, the return of the scroll to the attendant, and Jesus' taking of the seat to offer the exposition. These details likely reflect practice in synagogal worship in the later first or early second century when Luke was writing his two-volume work. The second unique Lukan detail in relation to the synagogue is the identification in Luke 7:5 of the centurion who brought his servant to Jesus to be healed as one who "loves our nation and built us our synagogue." Here is the one unambiguous reference in the New Testament to *synagōgē* as a building. In the survey of archaeological evidence concerning the synagogue we shall return to this feature in the development of this institution. The Gospel of John has only two references to *synagōgē* (6:59; 18:20),

---

25. Discussion and bibliography on Moses' seat in Schürer, rev. ed., 2:442, n. 66).

both of which can be understood as referring to a gathering rather than a structure.

In Acts the many references to synagogue may be grouped under two categories: (1) those that simply mention where Paul and his associates went to engage the Jews, and (2) those that depict Paul and others as expounding scripture and/or debating with Jewish leaders. In 6:9 the two synagogues specified are differentiated by the various social and geographical origins of their members — that of the "Freedmen," and that of the "Cyrenaicans and Alexandrians," both of which are of north African origin — with no reference to distinct and separate physical structures. Other synagogues are identified simply in terms of location by city: Damascus (9:2, 20), Pisidian Antioch (13:14), Iconium (14:1), Beroea (17:6). The major activity of Paul and his colleagues in the synagogues is the exposition of scripture and the consequent arguments for interpretations that point to Jesus as the Messiah: in Cyprus (13:5), in Pisidian Antioch (13:14), where the *archisynagōges* requests a hortatory interpretation of the scripture; in Thessalonica (17:1); in Athens (17:17); in Corinth (18:4); in Ephesus (18:19, 26; 19:8). In the synagogue at Pisidian Antioch, Paul is asked by the *archisynagōgos* to offer a word of exhortation to the people. In all these passages, the focus is on the group gathered (including Gentile converts; 18:4) and on the exposition of scripture that takes place on the sabbath. In his final apologies before Jewish and Roman authorities, Paul makes the point that his activity in the synagogues was the exposition of the scriptures (22:19; 24:12). The conflict between the new movement and the Jews is highlighted in Paul's defense before Agrippa that his associates have been "often punished in all the synagogues." In all these cases the emphasis is on the gathered group and the major enterprise carried out there: the interpretation of scripture.

Three passages in Acts point more directly to this interpretation of *synagōgē* as a meeting rather than a distinct building. The first is that, as a consequence of conflict in the synagogue at Corinth over Jesus as the Messiah expected in the Jewish scriptures, those who are persuaded by Paul move to the house next door (18:7), which probably means that the Jewish meetings were in a house as well.[26] The clearest evidence of the connotation of the term in Acts is in 13:43, where we read that, following Paul's exposition of scripture

---

26. The assumption by Schrage and others that the fragmented inscription from Corinth which presumably reads [*synagōgē heraiōn*] dates from the first century (art. Συναγωγή, *TDNT* 7:812) is now widely discredited, since the find has no datable archeological links.

in Antioch-in-Pisidia, *lutheisēs de tēs sunagōgēs:* the meeting was dissolved. Translators of this passage feel obliged to render the Greek as "the meeting of the synagogue broke up," apparently assuming that the omission of the explicit reference to the synagogue would imply that a seismic disturbance had wrecked the building. I know of no translations that here assume demolition of a physical structure. That the synagogue meetings are perceived as taking place in convenient facilities rather than in special structures is further confirmed by the report in Acts 19:8–9 that, when hostility arose in the Ephesus synagogue where Paul had been "speaking boldly, arguing and pleading about the kingdom of God," he withdrew and moved the gathering of disciples to the (school or lecture hall) of Tyrannus, which the apostle may have used after the regular daily instruction was finished.[27] The locus of these gatherings, Jewish and Christian, was flexible and was determined by space available and suitable for the attendees, ranging from a private house to a public hall.

This analysis of the New Testament evidence shows that in the great majority of occurrences, *synagōgē* means simply an assembly or a gathering of people. In Mark 13:9 and parallels the warning by Jesus to his followers that they will be summoned before "councils and beaten in synagogues" implies two different kinds of assemblies, not different kinds of buildings. The only reference in the Gospels or Acts that unambiguously indicates synagogue as an edifice is Luke 7:5, as noted above, where the centurion in Capernaum is commended by the Jewish presbyters because "he loves our nation, and he built us our synagogue." On the other hand, Acts bears evidence that the synagogues met in homes or public halls, a practice matched by that of the early Christians. This is explicit in Acts 2–5, where the apostles meet "from house to house." In Ephesus, as Paul reports (1 Cor 16:19), the church meets in the house of Aquila and Priscilla, with whom Paul had stayed in Corinth, according to Acts 18:3, and later in their house in Rome (Rom 16:5). Both New Testament texts and archaeological evidence confirm that Christians first gathered in houses.[28] It seems highly probable that synagogues began in the same way as did the subsequent assembling of early Christians: as house-based gatherings of pious Jews, which moved to public meeting-halls as the growth of the movement

27. Suggested by K. Lake and H. J. Cadbury in *The Beginnings of Christianity,* repr. (Grand Rapids: Baker, 1965), Part One, 4:239.

28. L. Michael White, *Building God's House in the Roman World: Architectural Adaptation among Pagans, Jews and Christians* (Baltimore and London: Johns Hopkins University Press, 1990), 102–39.

required, until in the second or third century — with the temple destroyed and no prospect of its being rebuilt — they reached the stage of building their own distinctive structures to meet the community needs for study and worship. Thus, as we noted in Acts 18:1–8, when Paul withdrew from his sessions with the Jews in Corinth, he moved his operation to "the house next door to the synagogue," which probably means that the synagogue itself was a meeting in a house rather than a special building. This inference is confirmed by the simplicity of the act by which Crispus, the ruler of the synagogue, is converted, together with his entire household. Hints of development toward formalization of procedure and organization of the synagogue community are most evident in Luke-Acts, where the ruler of the synagogue is mentioned (Luke 8:41), and (as noted above) set procedures seem to be followed when Jesus speaks in the synagogue at Nazareth (Luke 4:16, 20, 28). But all other references to synagogue in the Gospels and Acts may be understood as depictions of assemblies of the seeking and the committed in the cities of Palestine and the wider Greco-Roman world with no reference, implicit or explicit, to the specific structure in which the meeting occurred. Mark 12:38–39 conveys the primary sense of *synagōgē* by its collocation with other *loci* for informal social groupings: in the market place, at feasts, and in the meetings (*en tais synagogais*).

This inference concerning *synagōgē* is confirmed by an analysis of the cognate verb, *synagō*, in the Gospels and Acts. Images of the new community include the two or three *gathered* in Jesus' name (Matt 18:20) and the parable of the Wedding Feast, where the diverse guests are *gathered* (Matt 22:10). Similarly, in the assembling of the Pharisees to oppose Jesus this verb is used (Matt 22:34, 41). The groups *gather* to learn from him (Mark 2:2; 4:1; 5:21), as do the "apostles" following the mission of the twelve (Mark 6:7, 30). John describes Jesus as "gathering into one" the children of God (John 11.52), and the same term is used for the assembling of the disciples (18:2; 20:19). It is in Acts, however, that the verb *synagō* is used in a virtually technical sense to describe the gathering of God's people, both traditional Israel (4:6, 26, 27) and the new community, beginning with the apostles, who share their possessions, the Spirit, and their commitment (4:31), and continuing with the enlarging new people of God in Antioch (14:27), in Jerusalem (15:6), in Antioch (15:30) and at Troas (20:8). Most significant is the terminology in Acts 11:26 about the gathering (*synachthēnai*) of a great crowd in the *ekklēsia* in Antioch, where they were first called Christians. These cognates, verb and noun, refer to the assembling of the group, not to a building specially constructed for worship purposes.

Thus one must conclude that, with the single exception of Luke 7:5, the synagogue is depicted in the New Testament and in pre-70 Jewish writings as a gathering rather than as a distinctive type of religious structure. We turn now to the archaeological evidence for this phenomenon.

The Archaeological Evidence for *Synagōgē* as a Building

Three recent surveys of archaeological remains, though differing in detail, unite in their reconstruction of the stages by which the synagogue as a distinctive architectural structure emerged in Galilee and Judea in the latter half of the second century C.E. The first of these surveys is that by Eric Meyers in the *Anchor Bible Dictionary*.[29] He lists only three synagogues as "early" — from the pre-70 C.E. period: those from Gamla, Masada, and Herodium. All three of these structures are small and rectangular, with internal columns supporting the roof and stepped benches around the sides, presumably for seating those gathered in the room. Wholly lacking are the Torah shrines, which were to become central and essential for the later synagogue structures. Gamla, on a mountain northeast of the Sea of Galilee, was under Roman siege during the First Jewish Revolt.[30] and is the only likely first-century C.E. candidate in Palestine for a structure designed as a place of Jewish community assembly. This function may be inferred from the stepped rows of stone benches that surround the building, with aisles behind and a rectangular apse supported by stone columns. There is, however, no equipment or decoration that implies a religious function, although most scholars refer to it as a "Second Temple synagogue."[31] Joseph Gutmann asserts that the so-called synagogues at Masada and Herodium are merely meeting halls, and that "there is no proof of piety or of a

---

29. Ed. David Noel Freedman (New York: Doubleday, 1992), 6:251–60.

30. Josephus, *War* 4.1ff.

31. So S. Gutmann, the excavator, in "The Synagogue at Gamla" and Z. Ma'oz, in "The Synagogue at Gamla and the Typology of Second Century Synagogues." Both essays are in *Ancient Synagogues Revealed*, ed. Lee I. Levine (Jerusalem: Israel Exploration Society, 1981), 30–34, 35–41. Ma'oz acknowledges that the only other pre-70 "synagogues" on which he bases his typology are those at Herodium and Masada. None of them in fact has any of the distinctive features of the later synagogues.

definite place of worship other than the wishful thinking [of the excavators].[32]

In a declaration with fundamental implications for our study, Meyers calls for a clear distinction between synagogue as "a social and religious institution" and "as a distinct and discrete architectural entity," and concludes that "in the first centuries [C.E.] large private houses were used as places of worship alongside other buildings that could be utilized for worship and other matters requiring public assembly. In Palestine, it would seem, it was about a hundred years after the destruction of the Temple that the synagogue *as building* began to emerge as a central feature of Jewish communal life." This distinctive type of building first took root in Galilee (255). Unfortunately, some scholars today continue to investigate the subject of the synagogue in the early centuries of the Common Era without taking into account the important distinction that Meyers has called for between the synagogue as social institution and the architectural entity that subsequently emerged.[33] Curiously, however, Meyers opens his survey of the synagogue by quoting a translation of the Theodotus inscription, and dating it to the first century C.E., although he passes over any programmatic features of the synagogue mentioned there except the reading and study of the scriptures (252). In an earlier publication he had affirmed that "it is highly likely that in the period when the temple still stood, a synagogue could have been nothing more than a private house or part of a larger structure set aside for worship."[34] Although in this recent article Meyers treats the Theodotus inscription as a single exception to his observation about *synagōgē* as a meeting, not a building, the description of the synagogue embodied in that inscription is simply passed over in silence, and the conclusion is still offered that the earliest distinct Palestinian synagogue buildings date from the mid-third century C.E.[35] These vary widely in style and

---

32. *The Synagogue: Studies in Origins, Archaeology and Architecture*, ed. Joseph Gutmann (New York: KTAV, 1975), xi. Although the revised edition of Schürer's *History of the Jewish People* (Edinburgh: T. & T. Clark, 1979), 2:463, assumes that there were special synagogue buildings in the post-70 period, there is acknowledgment that the so-called synagogue at Herodium was simply converted from a dining room by the nationalists during the first Jewish revolt.

33. An obvious example of the absence of such a distinction is to be found in the article in *NTS* 39, no. 2, by Richard E. Oster, in which he challenges my interpretation of the evidence about the synagogue in Luke-Acts.

34. Eric M. Meyers and James F. Strange, *Archaeology, the Rabbis, and Early Christianity* (Nashville: Abingdon, 1981), 141.

35. Marilyn J. S. Chiat, in *Handbook of Synagogue Architecture*, BJS, ed. J. Neusner (Chico, Calif.: Scholars Press, 1982), includes the Theodotus inscrip-

interior arrangements, so that it is impossible to trace the architectural evolution of the synagogue (141). For example, although pious Christian pilgrims to the holy land have long been shown the remains of the synagogue in Capernaum, where (it was assumed) Jesus taught, Meyers and Strange agree with V. Corbo, the excavator of the site, that the synagogue dates from the fourth century c.e., and that it was built on top of a house (51),[36] which may have served as a gathering place for pious Jews from the first century c.e. onward.[37]

Archaeological analysis of synagogue sites in the Jewish Diaspora shows this same pattern of architectural adaptation. L. Michael White notes that the meeting place of the Jewish community in Delos was originally a private house, dating from as early as the late second century b.c.e., modified to serve as an assembly hall, just as was the case with a first-century c.e. house in Ostia. Evidence for analogous development of not only Jewish and Christian religious community centers, but also those of the cult of Mithras, was found in the excavation of Dura-Europos sixty years ago, where the synagogue, the church and the Mithraeum were clearly evolved from earlier stages in which they were simply houses.[38]

Other analyses of specific archaeological sites in Galilee in the Roman-Byzantine period come to the conclusions that what are demonstrably synagogues are later adaptations of multipurpose meeting places, originally in homes or public halls. Excavation of the synagogue at Hammath-Tiberias, for example, has shown that beneath the later synagogue structures, which include a third-century c.e. phase featuring a mosaic with representations of Helios and the twelve signs of the zodiac, are the remains of a plain public building — presumably an assembly hall.[39] Others have noted that the synagogue buildings north of Galilee in the Golan are con-

---

tion even though there is no certain link between it and the architectural fragments that were also found in the cistern, and there was no datable archaeological material found with it. She also includes the details of the synagogue reported in the inscription in her statistical analysis of synagogue facilities.

36. In his essay in *Ancient Synagogues Revealed* (Jerusalem, 1981), 52, S. Loffreda suggests a date for this synagogue in the last decade of the fourth to the mid-fifth century c.e.

37. This phenomenon of the replacement of private houses used as gathering places for study of Torah and worship has been demonstrated in several synagogue sites in the Diaspora: L. Michael White, *Building God's House in the Roman World* (see note 28 above).

38. White, *Building God's House,* 7–8, 64–71

39. M. Dothan, "The Synagogue at Hammath Tiberias," in *Ancient Synagogues Revealed,* ed. L. Levine, 52.

structed in the Greco-Roman style of public halls and date from the fifth and sixth centuries C.E.[40]

A survey of "Early Jewish Art and Architecture" by Rachel Hachlili.[41] includes description and analysis of buildings, some of which are allegedly and some obviously synagogues. Commenting on the published finds from Masada, Herodium and Gamla, she notes that "The excavated structures are assumed by scholars to be synagogues because of circumstantial evidence of similarity to each other in architectural plan and, therefore, in function, even though no actual proof has been uncovered" (449). Yet, she continues, "they differ from later synagogues in plan, function, and decoration." There are no characteristic architectural features, but only local "extemporization." The buildings did not last long and were not rebuilt, except when a more formal synagogal structure was built over an earlier house, as in Capernaum. Lacking in all of them is "the most important feature of the later synagogue: the Torah shrine." She concludes that "these local centers of worship probably existed as community assembly halls, where services could be conducted only on sabbaths and feast days." These local centers began to develop as "sites of local worship" and "the distinctive feature of the later synagogues, the Torah shrine, began to emerge" (450) only after the destruction of the temple. Hachlili's description of the architectural development of the synagogue spans the period from the third to the seventh centuries, and includes such characteristic decorative features as the menorah, the ark of the scrolls, and the zodiac panels (450–4). Obviously, none of these is found in the assembly halls that date from the first century C.E.

Important for our purposes is the fact that, apart from Meyers's mention of the Theodotus inscription at the opening of his article, none of the details of the facilities enumerated in the inscription (hostel, dining area, terraces) is referred to in either his or Hachlili's descriptions of the earlier structures that preceded the actual development of the synagogue as a distinctive type of structure. As is evident from the excavations, those features mentioned on the inscription are not in the remotest degree characteristic of the places of assembly in the pre-70 period that preceded the institutional development of the synagogue, which began in the third century, as is evident from these excavations.

---

40. Zvi Uri Ma'oz, "Ancient Synagogues of the Golan," *Biblical Archaeologist* 51, no. 2 (1988): 116–28.

41. In *Anchor Bible Dictionary* (New York: Doubleday, 1992), 1:447–54.

Historical Analysis of Palestinian Judaism
after Hadrian

In spite of extensive excavations in the Jerusalem area from the early part of this century to the present, archaeologists have found no structural evidence of synagogues there. Accordingly, the *Anchor Bible Dictionary* article on Jerusalem simply adopts the tradition from Eusebius that, after Hadrian's decree, Jews were forbidden to live in Jerusalem.[42] One might assume that this lack of evidence confirmed the Deissmann opinion that the synagogue mentioned in the Theodotus inscription must be pre-70. But several eminent scholars have undertaken careful historical analysis of the post-Hadrianic period concerning the presence and activity of Jews in Jerusalem during the post-Hadrianic period. It is a feature in the work of Dan Bahat, in his *Historical Atlas of Jerusalem*,[43] and is treated extensively in Michael Avi-Yonah's *The Jews of Palestine: A Political History from the Bar Kochba War to the Arab Conquest*[44] and by E. Mary Smallwood, in her masterful work, *The Jews under Roman Rule*.[45]

In Bahat's description of Jerusalem in the period of the Second Temple he includes as part of the evidence the Theodotus inscription, which he dates "to the time of Herod" on the basis of "the style of its characters," and which he asserts was associated with a building of "splendor," fragments of which were also found in the cistern.[46] Yet he also undercuts the major assumption on the basis of which Deissmann and others since his time have assigned this find to the pre-70 C.E. period: that there could have been no synagogue building in the city in the post-70 period because for several centuries after that date no Jews could live in Jerusalem. Bahat thinks that during the reign of Septimius Severus (193–211) Hadrian's edict against Jews entering Aelia Capitolina was no longer observed and that they indeed returned to the city. He notes the report of the fourth-century Christian bishop Epiphanius (born in Palestine of Jewish parents; 320–401) that synagogues were standing in Jerusalem down to the time of Constantine. Eusebius and Jerome, on the other hand, claim that Hadrian's prohibition of Jews in Jerusalem

---

42. Philip J. King, in *Anchor Bible Dictionary*, 3:761–62.
43. Jerusalem, 1983.
44. Translated from the Hebrew original; English edition New York: Schocken, 1976.
45. Subtitle, *From Pompey to Diocletian*, Studies in Judaism and Late Antiquity, ed. Jacob Neusner (Leiden: Brill, 1976, 1981).
46. Bahat, *Atlas*, 45.

was still in effect in the fourth century, but the probable motivation for these assertions was the Christians' effort to claim that Jerusalem had lost its identity as a Jewish center and that it was now the central Christian city.

Avi-Yonah notes that as early as the reign of Hadrian's successor, Antoninus Pius (138–61), Hadrian's anti-Jewish edicts were rescinded, so that Jewish rights to religious and communal autonomy were affirmed, and the Jewish patriarchate and religious council (*synedrion*) were granted power. Inscriptions from Galilee attest to the friendly attitude of Septimius Severus and the Jews' grateful response. Although the decree forbidding Jews to enter Jerusalem may have remained on the books, there are reports in the rabbinic sources of Jews going to the city and of permission granted in the early days of the Severan dynasty for Rabbi Meir to settle there with a group of pupils. The claim is made that they founded a "holy community" in Jerusalem.[47]

Mary Smallwood's account of the relations between Jews and the emperors of the Antonine and Severan dynasties provides supporting evidence for growing cordiality toward Jews on the part of the emperors and for substantial recovery of rights and power by the Jewish community and its leadership. The Jewish council (*synedrion*) was permitted to rule on intra-Jewish matters, and a Jewish patriarch was appointed and enabled to function. Land confiscated by Romans gradually returned to Jewish ownership, including vast estates taken over by leading rabbis. Jews were permitted to enter Jerusalem initially on the ninth of Ab (the anniversary of the Fall of the Temple to Titus), but soon other visits became more common, with the apparent quiet acquiescence of the Roman authorities. The Jewish leadership responded to the Roman rule with a mix of inevitability and gratitude for the benefits that came to the regional Jewish ruling class. An inscription found in northern Galilee includes a Jewish prayer for the well-being of Severus and his sons.[48]

Archaeological evidence has been recovered of extensive synagogue building in Galilee beginning in the late second century C.E., much of it conforming to contemporary Syrian architecture. The material in the Mishnah likely also began being reduced to writing at this time as well. The ban on visits of Jews to Aelia had been quietly relaxed since the days of Antoninus, but from the Severan

---

47. Avi-Yonah, *Jews of Palestine*, 77–80.
48. Smallwood, *Jews under Roman Rule*, 469–78.

period on, Jews were allowed not only to visit the city but also to establish residence there. By the late second century rabbis resided in Aelia, in association with the "holy community" and the "people of Jerusalem" mentioned in rabbinic traditions from this period. Caracalla (211–17) published the *Constitutio Antoniniana,* which granted Roman citizenship to all free inhabitants of the empire, including the Jews. The effort of Hadrian to repress the Jews and to exclude them from residence in Aelia Capitolina had utterly failed within decades of the promulgation of his decrees.

Conclusion

What conclusion may be drawn from these three kinds of evidence? From the mid-second century on, the development in Jerusalem of facilities such as those described in the Theodotus inscription, including a place of study and guest accommodations for pilgrims, is completely plausible. A mid- to late third-century date for the inscription, looking back on two previous generations of such an operation, is compatible with the historical, linguistic, and archaeological evidence of the development of the synagogue in the first four centuries we have surveyed. Thus the Theodotus inscription takes it place in the overall scheme of the evolution of the synagogue from voluntary gathering to institutionalized structure and organization, not as proof of the institutional and architectural form of the synagogue in the time of Jesus, but as a process taking place in the pre-Constantinian period.

CHAPTER TWO

Ancient Texts, Archaeology as Text, and the Problem of the First-Century Synagogue

James F. Strange
University of South Florida, Tampa

In this study, I am attempting first to determine to what extent an outline of synagogue liturgy derived from the literature can shed light on excavated buildings some archaeologists identify as first-century synagogues. In the process of pursuing this clarification, I conclude that another element in their structures is more telling and connects with the Second Temple.[1]

The Problem of First-Century Synagogue Liturgy

For some years various scholars have attempted to reconstruct elements of the synagogue liturgy from the Jewish literature of the later centuries, most notably from the Mishnah and Yerushalmi.[2] Many attempts have been made to use the evidence of Josephus, Philo, and

1. This paper was prepared for the Philadelphia Seminar on Christian Origins in the Religious Studies Department of the University of Pennsylvania. I wish to thank Professor Robert Kraft and the other participants of that seminar, especially Professor Howard Clark Kee, for a stimulating and challenging discussion. As a result of those discussions this paper is quite different from that presented and, I hope, clearer and more thickly textured.

2. Ismar Elbogen, *Der Jüdische Gottesdienst in seiner geschichtlichen Entwicklung,* 3d ed. (Frankfurt am Main: J. Kauffman, 1931; reprinted Hildesheim: G. Olms. Verlagsbuchhandlung, 1962); Eng. trans. *Jewish Liturgy: A Comprehensive History,* trans. Raymond P. Scheindlin (Philadelphia: Jewish Publication Society, and New York: Jewish Theological Seminary of America, 1993); L. Hoffman, "Jewish Liturgy

the Gospels and Acts in the same way. I do not intend to rehash that evidence, but I am at pains to point out that a kind of consensus is emerging on the outlines of a first-century synagogue liturgy. For example, Shmuel Safrai has concluded that the literary evidence for pre-70 C.E. synagogue liturgy is unambiguous and clear only about the reading of Torah selections.[3] On the other hand Safrai points out that the evidence is slim for other liturgical matters well known in later texts, such as reading of *haftarah* and the recitation of set prayers, the decalogue, the Shema',[4] and various Psalms, and the delivering of a homily.

Richard Oster has identified in inscriptions, in Philo, and in Josephus three "formal ceremonies" associated with synagogues: manumission of slaves, donations to the Second Temple, and communal meals.[5] Therefore Oster argues that it is no surprise that Luke should present the pericope of Jesus in the synagogue at Nazareth with certain formalities: He stood up to read (4:16), a scroll of Isaiah was at hand (4:17), and an attendant was present (4:20). May I add that, if he stood up, he and the congregation were surely seated. That a scroll of the prophet Isaiah was at hand suggests he was engaged in *haftarah* reading, following Levine.[6] *Haftarah* reading implies Torah reading.

Philo has informed us that in Jewish synagogues in every city on the Sabbath the congregation sat in a seemly fashion while a person knowledgeable in the task stood to read.[7] Josephus also contends that reading and study of scripture was an important part of sabbath observance.[8]

Lee I. Levine attempted to correlate certain elements of the archaeological and literary evidence in *Ancient Synagogues Revealed*

and Jewish Scholarship," chap. 8 in *Judaism in Late Antiquity*, part 1: *The Literary and Archaeological Sources* ed. Jacob Neusner (Leiden: Brill, 1995), 239–66.

3. Shmuel Safrai, *In Times of Temple and Mishnah* (Jerusalem: Y. L. Magnes. [Hebrew], 1994); Cf. Mishnah Shekelim 4.10.

4. Reuven Kimelman, "The Shema and Its Rhetoric..." *Jewish Thought and Philosophy* 2 (1992): 111–56.

5. Richard Oster, "Supposed Anachronism in Luke-Acts' Use of ΣΥΝΑΓΩΓΗ: A Rejoinder to H. C. Kee," *NTS* 36 (1993): 178–208. See the inscription from Panticapaeum of the manumission of a slave named Elpias, discussed in Irina Levinskaia, *The Book of Acts in Its Diaspora Setting* (Grand Rapids: Wm. B. Eerdmans, 1996), 74.

6. Lee I. Levine, ed., *The Synagogue in Late Antiquity*, A Centennial Publication of the Jewish Theological Seminary of America (Philadelphia: American Schools of Oriental Research, 1987).

7. Philo, Spec. Leg. 2.62.

8. Josephus, *Contra Apion* 1.42; *Ant.* 16.43–45. One must note the scriptures found inside the Masada synagogue.

(1981) and in *The Synagogue in Late Antiquity* (1987). Levine has appealed to a "general agreement" and to the evidence of the Theodotus inscription to establish a customary pattern of Torah reading and instruction in the commandments as at least two pillars of synagogue worship in the first century.[9] But, since we only have one piece of evidence to support "instruction in the commandments," the Theodotus inscription, and since that piece of evidence is being reevaluated as later than the first century,[10] then it seems appropriate to use the New Testament, Philo, and Josephus to affirm simply that someone addressed the congregation. The question of the archaeologist, then, following Safrai, Oster, Levine, and others, is whether regular sabbath observance with reading of scripture and with someone addressing the congregation requires architecture.

The answer to that question is undoubtedly "yes," given that human society in the Hellenistic and Roman periods ordinarily endowed recognized institutions with architecture. That is, given that the institution in question fills a perceived need in the society in question, it is not long before the institution comes to expression in architecture as well as in language and in a social structure.

Moreover, to further the argument about the possibility of early Jewish set prayers, Lawrence Schiffman argued that certain liturgical texts from Qumran support reconstruction of a repeating pattern, that is, a set regimen of morning and evening prayers by the Qumran sect.[11] Though research on Qumran liturgy is in its infancy, this provides some hope of finding a precedent for the Tannaitic tra-

---

9. Levine, 17.

10. Howard Kee, "The Transformation of the Synagogue after 70 C.E.: Its Import for Early Christianity," *NTS* 36 (1990): 1–24. On the paleographic dating of the Theodotus inscription see Rainer Riesner, "Synagogues in Jerusalem," in *The Book of Acts in Its Palestinian Setting,* ed. Richard Baukham (Grand Rapids: Wm. B. Eerdmans, 1995), 194–95. Riesner mentions that a discovery of an inscription of Herod the Great dating to the twentieth year of his reign gives us letters which match those of the Theodotus inscription quite closely, p. 195, which tends to confirm a pre-70 C.E. date for the Theodotus inscription. For the text of this inscription see Benjamin Isaac, "A Donation for Herod's Temple in Jerusalem," *IEJ* 33 (1983): 86–92, and P1.9B.

11. Lawrence Schiffman, "The Dead Sea Scrolls and the Early History of Jewish Liturgy," in *The Synagogue in Late Antiquity,* ed. L. I. Levine (Philadelphia: American Schools of Oriental Research, 1987), 33–48. The argument that there is no evidence for sabbath worship for non-priestly Jews before the end of the second century C.E. appears in Heather McKay, *Sabbath and the Synagogue: The Question of Sabbath Worship in Ancient Judaism,* Religions in the Greco-Roman World 122 (Leiden: Brill, 1994), 251. Levine argues that there is no pre-70 organized, communal prayer *within Palestine* in "Synagogues" in *The New Encyclopedia of Archaeology in the Ancient Near East,* ed. Eric M. Meyers (Oxford: Oxford University Press, 1996), 5:118.

ditions about set prayer. Furthermore, Morton Smith has asserted that the *yôsêr* in its two main versions goes back to Qumran in one way or another.[12] Furthermore, we have Palestinian texts that mention prayers of non-priestly Jews both in the temple courts and in synagogues: Matthew 6:5 and Josephus, *Contra Apion* 1.209–11. In other words, the current state of research indicates that it is reasonable to hypothesize that some form of set prayer characterized the first-century liturgy.[13]

In this connection it seems clear, following Levine, that we must not overlook the simple fact that the main word for the first-century synagogue outside the New Testament is *proseuché*. This word appears about thirty times in inscriptions, Josephus, Philo, and the Egyptian papyri. The name itself gives away that the synagogue's primary purpose is congregational prayer.[14]

The question for the archaeologist becomes, then, "Does such a set pattern in prayers demand special space?" That is, is architecture in some sense of a "synagogue" required for set prayers, or even for free prayers? Furthermore, how do we recognize this building? Again, the answer to this question is also a qualified "yes," if institutionalized prayer is as integral a part of the social world of ancient Judaism as we believe it to be. There is ample precedent in Greco-Roman society for setting aside space for prayer. For the question of how to recognize this building, we must respond that this is exactly what is under analysis.

Does ΣΥΝΑΓΩΓΗ Mean Architecture?

Howard Kee has asserted, somewhat in the vein of Tsvi Ma'oz,[15] that it is an anachronism to use the term *synagogê* in pre-70 Palestine in the sense of architecture.[16] If so — that is, if there is no architectural symbol for the activity of worship outside the temple — then there is little reason to allege nontemple worship in the sense of a common liturgy. On the other hand Richard Oster has argued from a Greek inscription in North Africa that the term *synagogê* has to

---

12. Morton Smith, "On the *Yôsêr* and Related Texts," in *The Synagogue in Late Antiquity,* ed. L. I. Levine (Philadelphia: American Schools of Oriental Research, 1987), 87–96.

13. Hoffman, 249f.

14. Levine, 20.

15. Tsvi Ma'oz, "The Synagogue in the Second Temple Period," *Eretz Israel* 23 (Jerusalem: Israel Exploration Society, 1992), 331–34, English summary pp. 157*–158*.

16. Kee, "The Transformation of the Synagogue after 70 C.E.," 1–2.

mean the "congregation" once and the "building" a second time, establishing the possibility that the word *synagogê* can indeed refer to architecture in the first century C.E.[17] The inscription in question, from Berenice of Cyrenaica, today's Benghazi, reads as follows:

> In the second year of the emperor Nero Claudius Caesar Drusus Germanicus [56 C.E.], on the 16th of Chorach, it was resolved by the congregation of the Jews (ΣΥΝΑΓΩΓΗ ΤΩΝ ΙΟΥΔΑΙΩΝ) in Berenice that [the names of] those who donated to the repairs of the synagogue (ΣΥΝΑΓΩΣΗΣ) be inscribed on a stele of Parian marble.[18]

This inscription demonstrates the credibility of a pre-70 C.E. use of the word *synagogê* for architecture used by Jews, and in an inscription outside Palestine. It is also notable that the same word can indeed mean "congregation," as Howard Kee insists, but in no way need *synagogê* mean "congregation" every time it appears in pre-70 texts. This inscription, furthermore, indicates that the door is open to seek an architectural symbol for the activity of worship outside the Second Temple. If so, then there is no necessary barrier to looking for traces of synagogue worship in our literary sources, or for attempting to identify certain enclosed spaces as synagogues.

The Possibility of Identifying
First-Century Synagogues

We do not seem to be resolving the debate about the plausibility of calling the structures of Gamala, Masada, Magdala, Herodium, and possibly P. L. O. Guy's Chorazin structure "synagogues." On the other hand, if we accept the assertion of Shaye Cohen, Lee I. Levine, Richard Oster,[19] and others that the term "synagogue" likely refers to a collection of meanings, even in Jewish contexts, then we may be prepared to test the thesis that worshipers used the space in various first-century buildings currently designated "synagogues." We

---

17. Oster, "Supposed Anachronism in Luke-Acts' Use of ΣΥΝΑΓΩΓΗ," 207.

18. Ibid., 187; same information in J. M. Reynolds, *Excavations at Sidi Khrebish Benghazi (Berenice)*, vol. 1: *Buildings, Coins, Inscriptions, Architectural Decoration,* Supplements to Libya Antiqua 5, ed. J. A. Lloyd (Hertford: Stephen Austin and Sons, 1977), no. 16. See also Shimon Applebaum, *Jews and Greeks in Ancient Cyrene,* ed. Jacob Neusner, Studies in Judaism in Late Antiquity 28 (Leiden: Brill, 1979), 162, n. 149.

19. Shaye Cohen, *From the Maccabees to the Mishnah* (Philadelphia: Westminster Press, 1987); Levine, *The Synagogue in Late Antiquity*; Oster, "Supposed Anachronism in Luke-Acts' Use of ΣΨΝΑΓΩΓΗ."

must analyze the space within each posited "synagogue" to establish the plausibility that these buildings are to be understood as a set of roofed, organized spaces intended at least on occasion for Jewish liturgical purposes. But we must also allow these spaces to be diverse, not requiring them all to be cut from the same template. This analysis, then, will likely not settle the question whether these are synagogues in some narrow sense. Nor will it establish the likelihood that one or the other reconstructions of the synagogue liturgy is correct, but it may advance the discussion by allowing us to recognize the connection between specific architecture and nontemple worship.

First, some general remarks about liturgy and architecture in the ancient world are in order. From the comments above about specific actions that appear to have taken place in a synagogue, we can make a few inferences about how architecture might be an aid to worship rather than a hindrance. To recapitulate, it seems that we can postulate minimally congregational reading and study of scripture, some form of congregational address, and congregational prayers. Furthermore we note that the congregation sat to hear scripture read while the leader stood. An attendant and perhaps other synagogue officers were present,[20] and some provision was made to shelve or stow a copy or copies of the scriptures until such a time as they were needed. Generally, congregants stood *orans* while praying. This posture is depicted in ancient art from remote antiquity.

Second, the surprisingly rich vocabulary for Second Temple synagogues surely reflects activities within them and how their communities, and on occasion outsiders, understood them. This vocabulary may also help us understand the features in the architecture used for these activities. Lists of terms are to be found in Levine and Oster.[21] Twelve Greek words and one Latin word (*templum*) are documented.

That a synagogue is called an "amphitheater" four times in inscriptions in North Africa is instructive, as the name suggests the possibility that the building had at least two uses and that it had seating arranged in a circle or ellipse. Philo calls the synagogue a *didaskaleion* twice, but we do not yet know the architecture of schools or buildings used for instruction. We all know the word *proseuchê*

---

20. Donald D. Binder, "Into the Temple Courts: The Place of the Synagogues in the Second Temple Period," Ph.D. dissertation, Southern Methodist University, 1997, chap. 5, "Synagogue Functionaries" 272–307.

21. Levine, 13f.; Oster, 186.

or "place of prayer." At least once in the papyri it is called a *eucheion,* and at least once in Philo it is called a *proseukterion.* These terms bolster the idea that, if it is architecture, it provides space for congregational prayer, whether set or free.

The other terms to help us deduce the general form the building might take include the term *hieros peribolos,* which appears once in Philo and once in an Egyptian papyrus. Surely this term means "holy space" or "holy enclosure," and it may also be the meaning of *to hieron,* a word that Josephus uses at least five times, and also appears once in 2 Maccabees and three times in Philo. The word *topos,* which appears five times in Josephus, once in Philo, and twice in 3 Maccabees, may be shorthand for *to hagios topos.* The terms *hieros peribolos, to hagios topos* (which appears twice in inscriptions), *hieros topos,* and Josephus's word *to hieron* suggest that the space is "fenced" or "erased" — a valuable clue for recognizing this cultic space.[22] In archaeological terms, this suggestion implies that the space is enclosed so that outsiders may not enter at awkward moments.

The term *sabbateion,* occurring once in Josephus, indicates when the gathering took place, not the activity. On the other hand, this term surely indicates that the social institution is built around sabbath observance, as Luke 4 indicates.

Oikema, another term that occurs twice in Josephus, may support the general theory that some synagogues were converted houses.[23] The Latin word *templum* occurs once, which reflects the cultural perception of a place of worship.

Since the congregation sits, we expect some form of mass seating, which in the Greco-Roman world is usually on concentric benches. We expect a leader, a reader or one who addresses or instructs the congregation, to stand either in one special area at one end or at the center. The "attendant" and other leaders, whom we do not expect to see separated from the leader, also require special space. There may be something to house the scriptures when they are not in use, but this need not be architecturally defined. It may be a piece of furniture. In addition to seating, we require space for the

---

22. Colin Renfrew, *The Archaeology of Cult: The Sanctuary at Phylakopi,* British School of Archaeology at Athens (London: Thames & Hudson, 1985), 179-80.

23. L. Michael White, *Building God's House in the Roman World: Architectural Adaptation among Pagans, Jews, and Christians* (Baltimore: Johns Hopkins University Press, 1990), 102–39. On the other hand Josephus says that the *proseuchē* in Tiberias is a *megiston oikēma,* or a "huge building," which suggests it was *not* a converted house.

congregation to stand *orans,* if set or even free prayers are part of the worship. We expect this space to be immediately adjacent to the seating space or integrated into the seating space.

The missing item in this case is taken for granted in much later synagogues. No requirement necessitates that the building be decorated in any specific fashion. As long as the Temple is standing with its ritual equipment, there is no social need to draw or carve representations of this equipment on the architectural members of the synagogue. Even the menorah, which can be shown to be the quintessential Jewish symbol after the destruction of the Second Temple, only appears on the wall of a private house in Jerusalem while the Second Temple still stands. In other words, there is no necessary iconographic vocabulary for the synagogue.

There is also no provision for gendered space — no gallery for women, no separate entrance, and no "erased space" to house women. Although one may wish to argue from silence, from our outline of synagogue worship we need not posit gendered space in the architecture.

There is no *bema,* no seat of Moses, and no specific orientation. Furthermore there is no necessary connection with a ritual bath, although it may be presupposed.

Generally speaking, social architects and those working in the semiotics of architecture distinguish two major types of gatherings that might match the above set of formal ceremonies. One is with the congregants standing or sitting, all facing in the direction where their leader stands facing them. The other is with all congregants standing or sitting, facing toward the center where their leader is standing. In this second arrangement, we do not always encounter a complete circle around the leader. He or she may stand, but those standing or seated behind the leader are often other leaders. Typically the leader's position is marked by the architecture itself in some way. Typically the position of the congregants is also marked by the architecture.

Of course we already have such architecture in the Greco-Roman world. On a small scale we have an *odeion,* which resembles a small theater, for declamation, recitation of poetry, singing competitions, and other such formal ceremonies. In this piece of architecture the seating is in a nested semicircle, as in a theater, with a small raised platform close to the center of the semicircles of seats. The congregation is expected to sit, but nothing prevents them from standing in front of their seats, and in fact they have room to do so. We also find a *bouleuterion* in major cities, and at least one scholar has suggested that the origins of the synagogue are to be found in the *bouleuterion* and *ecclesiasterion*.[24] The bouleuterion is a much smaller building, as the βουλή or council of a city is not necessarily a large body. It is often arranged in a semicircle as well, though we also have examples in which the seating is arranged in concentric squares open on one side around a central raised platform, also square. The seating surrounds three sides of the nested squares.

The public basilica in the Roman world often provided for the seating of a council or other official body. These seats are apsidal structures at either end of the long axis of the basilica. In these apses semicircular benches are raised in tiers, as in the *odeion*, or theater. No raised platform is present at the focal point of the semicircles, but the apse itself can be designed to focus the sound of the speaker's voice without such a feature.[25]

Spatial Analysis of Four First-Century "Synagogues"

As mentioned above, structures at Gamala, Masada, Herodium, Magdala, and perhaps the building at Chorazin described by P. L. O. Guy have been identified by their excavators or by others as first-century synagogues. However, since I cannot personally find P. L. O. Guy's structure, I will not use it.

All these halls were identified as synagogues because of their general resemblance to later synagogues in the land of Israel, because of their orientation toward Jerusalem, or because they were found at Jewish sites and were clearly designed for gatherings, ergo a synagogue.

Gamala

Gamala has been touted as a synagogue or possible synagogue since its first publication in 1976 (or 1968?). The topography of the site matches the description in Josephus.[26] It is also a walled site, a requirement if the city was truly the casualty of siege warfare as

---

24. Gideon Foerster, "The Synagogues at Masada and Herodion," in *Eretz-Israel* 11, ed. Joseph Aviram (Jerusalem: Israel Exploration Society, 1973), 224–28, idem., "The Synagogues at Masada and Herodium," *Journal of Jewish Art* 3, no. 4 (1977): 6–11; idem., "The Synagogues at Masada and Herodion," in *Ancient Synagogues Revealed,* ed. Lee I. Levine (Jerusalem: Israel Exploration Society, 1982), 24–29.

25. D. S. Robertson, *Greek and Roman Architecture,* 2d ed. (Cambridge, 1969), 177-79. William L. MacDonald, *The Architecture of the Roman Empire,* vol. 2: *An Urban Appraisal,* Yale Publications in the History of Art 35, rev. ed. (New Haven and London: Yale University Press, 1982), 122.

26. *BJ* 4.1ff.

depicted in Josephus. There are no other finds except for the putative *mikveh* west of the synagogue to confirm or disconfirm the
otherwise entirely reasonable thesis that this is a Jewish city.

Gutman was the first to claim that the building in question was
a synagogue.[27] His argument was analogical, comparing this structure to the putative synagogues at Masada and Herodium. He also
cited the absence of pagan motifs, separate entrances as though
for the separation of the sexes, its orientation toward Jerusalem,
the presence of heart-shaped or corner columns, the carvings on the
lintel, which resemble art in later synagogues, and the large niche in
the western corner. This thesis was taken up by Gideon Foerster in
1977 and repeated again by Gutman in 1982. Foerster even argued
that the probable synagogues of Gamala, Herodium, Masada, and
Magdala form a single Second Temple type of synagogue. Recently
Lee Levine has argued that the building is a synagogue because of
its orientation toward Jerusalem (it faces southwest), because of the
nearby ritual bath, and because Gamala, according to Josephus, was
such a hotbed of Jewish nationalism.[28] Others have noticed that
the facade points toward Jerusalem because it is built up against
the city wall, which at that point would require any structure built
against it to face Jerusalem.[29] We observe that the locals may have
built it in this precise point against the city wall with its orientation
northwest to southeast so that the resulting building would face
Jerusalem. The immediate reason for its orientation on Jerusalem
is topography and opportunity. We do not know the more remote
reasons for its orientation.

Marilyn Chiat has cautioned that neither a plan nor a location
within a Jewish town qualifies any building to be a synagogue.[30]
She also points out that the sites used to confirm that Gamala is a
synagogue have not themselves been proven to be synagogues.[31] On
the other hand Tsvi Ma'oz has argued forcefully that the elements
of Jewish art found on the lintel of the building confirm that this
is a synagogue.[32] Richard Oster has combined this argument with
the arguments of Levine to contend that the structure at Gamala is

---

27. S. Gutman, "Gamala," *Hadashot Arkheologiyot,* 6 (Hebrew; Oct. 1976).

28. Levine, 11.

29. Oster, 195.

30. M. Chiat, *Handbook of Synagogue Architecture,* Brown University Judaic
Studies (Chico, Calif.: Scholars Press, 1982), 2–3.

31. Ibid., 283.

32. Tsvi Ma'oz, "The Synagogue of Gamala and the Typology of Second-Temple
Synagogues," *Ancient Synagogues Revealed,* ed. L. I. Levine (Jerusalem: Israel
Exploration Society, 1981).

most likely a synagogue because of the proximity of the ritual bath, the Jewishness of the city, and the Jewish iconography on its lintel.[33]

Tsvi Ma'oz has recently published a very complete though somewhat conjectural plan that makes it plain that the Gamala synagogue is part of a complex of rooms.[34] Here we will follow his architectural analysis with some additional comments.

The rectangular complex of rooms is bounded on three sides by the streets of the city of Gamala. The possible mikveh is across the street from the entrance to the complex, which measures 33 x 27 m in toto. One enters the complex in a small (2 x 3 m) anteroom, which itself lets into a long, narrow courtyard about 2.2 x 7.5 m. One enters into the long hall at the center of its narrow end through double leaf doors. At that point one is standing at the lowest level of the interior space, but facing and separated from the innermost space by a surround of four rows of Doric columns forming a peristyle. Corner columns stand at the four corners of the peristyle. Around the peristyle one steps up four times on benches on all sides to reach the highest landing, which is more than two meters broad at its top all the way around the hall. The top area around the peristyle or upper landing is paved on three sides, the steps or benches down to the columns are paved, and the lowest space up to and including the columns is paved. The central rectangle or nave is not paved, but a stylobate with two columns divides this space into two unequal rectangles, one about 6 x 6 m and the other 6 x 3.6 m. Ma'oz suggests that the roof is raised and pierced above this innermost, unpaved space to let in light. Architecturally, it makes sense to have a stylobate with two columns across innermost space if the intent is to roof the space.

Ma'oz further notes that the city wall is a casemate wall and that three casemate cells or rooms within the wall form part of the complex in question. He suggests that the room to the east on the central axis of the central hall or nave is gendered space, that is, designated for women, though he had previously denied this possibility.[35] His basis for the suggestion is that this room is entered from the street and that its only access to the main hall otherwise is from a broad window overlooking the interior.

My own analysis is rather different. First may I point out that we do not yet know that the 4 x 5 m pool hardly 4 meters from the front

---

33. Oster, 195.
34. Ma'oz, "The Synagogue in the Second Temple Period," 332.
35. Ma'oz, "The Synagogue of Gamala," 39.

entrance of the putative synagogue is a ritual bath. It may be, but it may also simply be a bath in its own, separate, and perhaps even domestic complex. We had best lay aside any definitive argument based on its presence. The same is true of the orientation of the building. We cannot yet say that the builders deliberately oriented it on Jerusalem.

We notice that the Gamala building makes provision for mass seating, in this case on concentric, square benches. (A single bench is also located against the wall built against the city wall.) There is ample room for standing on the same benches. The seated or standing assembly would be focused on the central, unpaved space. Therefore reading of Torah and *haftarah* and addressing the congregation would have to occur from this central space, which Ma'oz believes was covered with carpets.[36] Since there are really two rectangular central spaces, it is tempting to assign one to a reader or to the one who addresses or instructs the congregation, and then to assign the other to the remaining leaders not functioning in the liturgy. There is no *bēma*, platform, or tribunal, to use the Latin term, to address those gathered, unless that stylobate across the central space housed one of wood. Since we cannot know that now, we leave it out of the reckoning.

Is there something to house the scriptures when they are not in use? One can no longer say. Were there collections of nails here and there to indicate the location of furniture? Gutman reported that many nails were found in the interior space of the hall, probably from the roof. One very large group of nails came from the northeastern corner of the hall in a burn layer where the second entrance stood.[37] It is noteworthy that no nails were found in the niche in the southwest. Gutman proposed that the niche was a clue to the building's use as a synagogue.[38]

Notice that the argument from ancient art has been dropped. The Gamala building was decorated with geometric rosettes, but also with meanders and vine wreaths, and the lintel possibly bore a date palm.[39] These same motifs decorate ornamental elements from the Second Temple in Benjamin Mazar's excavations. Yet, except

---

36. Ibid., 38.

37. S. Gutman, *Gamala: The First Eight Seasons of Excavations* (Tel-Aviv: Ha-Kibbutz Ha-Meuchad [Hebrew] 1981), 33.

38. S. Gutman, "The Synagogue at Gamala," *Ancient Synagogues Revealed,* ed. L. I. Levine (Detroit: Wayne State University, 1982), 30–34; Gutman, *Gamala: The First Eight Seasons of Excavations,* 34.

39. Ma'oz, "The Synagogue of Gamala," 39.

perhaps for the palm tree, they are not unambiguously Jewish in the first century. The palm tree appears on coins of Herod Antipas, on coins of the First Revolt, on Latin issues of Herod Agrippa, and on coins of Sepphoris under Trajan. Palm trees also appear on Roman issues of the Iudea Capta series, which tends to suggest that the Roman rulers would understand the palm tree and the weeping captive, but only with the help of the Latin legend.

So what is our initial conclusion about Gamala? This building could indeed serve the interests of the Jewish synagogue liturgy as outlined above. This is a necessary but not a sufficient conclusion to show that the Gamala building served the community solely for liturgical purposes. We must consider that the interior of the building is completely isolated and concealed from the streets around it. From outside observation it would be impossible to deduce the use of the interior space.

Second, the building is assembled of very finely cut members, generally much more finely cut than those in the remainder of the site. This is also true of the relief decoration on the capitals of the building. As the social archaeologists have noticed, isolation and exceptional workmanship are often markers of cult.[40]

Thus the general design of the building, its fine workmanship, its isolation, and the presence of the palm tree motif argue for a building of Jewish cultic identity, though the argument is not conclusive. On the other hand, as Ma'oz points out, the building is a sophisticated, unique design, fusing elements of the bouleuterion and of the basilica. That is, it has as many elements in common with the Greco-Roman world as its final design is unique.

Masada

We are less hesitant to identify the finds at Masada as those of a synagogue, probably because of something like a Geniza next door. As early as 1966 in his popular book *Masada,* Yigael Yadin identified the remains as those of a synagogue because of its orientation on Jerusalem, its provision for mass seating on benches, its erection at a Jewish fortress by Zealots, and the presence of the Geniza.[41] Yadin also mentioned that an ostracon from the floor read "priestly tithe" and a second inscribed sherd bore the name

---

40. C. Renfrew, C. and P. Bahn, *Archaeology: Theories, Methods, and Practice* (New York: Thames and Hudson, 1991), 359f.

41. Yigael Yadin, *Masada: Herod's Fortress and the Zealots' Last Stand* (New York: Random House, 1966), 181–91.

"Hezekiah," which he thought might be the name of a priest. Critics have pointed out that the structure was built in a cell of the casemate wall, so its orientation on Jerusalem could be an accident. The presence of mass seating only proved that some kind of assembly hall was necessary. Finally, critics comment that, although fragments of Deuteronomy and Ezekiel were found in the putative Geniza, many other fragments were of noncanonical books. Finally, critics said that the ostraca on the floor could be accidental finds.

Instead of reviewing Yadin's arguments and the counter-arguments of his critics, let us accept the archaeological phasing of the building and turn to our own analysis of space. We notice that the building in Phase 2 at Masada makes provision for mass seating, in this case also on concentric squares of benches. There is also ample room for standing on the same benches. The seated or standing assembly would be focused on the central, unpaved space. Therefore reading of Torah and *haftarah* and addressing the congregation would have to occur from this central space, exactly as at Gamala. The central, unpaved space is large (about 7 x 8 m), but also rather like two bouleuteria conjoined. There is room for a leader, but no second space for any remaining leaders not functioning in the liturgy, though there is room for several people in the central space. There is no *bēma,* platform, or tribunal to address those gathered. There is no courtyard or entryway to receive visitors. Does something house the scriptures when they are not in use? It is possible that the corner room housed such a piece of furniture, but we cannot confirm it.

What is our conclusion about Masada? This building could indeed serve the interests of the Jewish synagogue liturgy as outlined above. This is also a necessary but not a sufficient conclusion to show that the Masada building served the community for liturgical purposes. On the other hand the find of both Deuteronomy and Ezekiel supports the hypothesis that Torah and *haftarah* were read. The interior of the building is more or less isolated from the street, but not as elaborately as at Gamala. From outside observation it would be impossible to deduce the use of the interior space unless one could hear familiar clues.

Second, the building is designed like two bouleuteria placed together, though with the intrusion of a corner room. Furthermore, one actually crosses over two of the interior benches to get *down* into the inmost, unpaved space. That is, the interior benches at Masada seem to be another instance of the interior design of the Gamala edifice, complete with columns interior to the ranges of

benches on four sides, but without the finely cut members and putative Jewish art. The builders relied upon plaster to emulate careful
stone masonry. On the other hand almost the whole of Masada
relies on plaster to emulate finely cut stones and architectural members. Therefore, this feature is a function of the site, not of the
building. Thus the general design of the building, its generally careful workmanship, and the presence of scrolls of Deuteronomy and
Ezekiel in its floor argue for a building of Jewish cultic identity.
On the other hand nothing could prevent the use of the building
for other gatherings. The building most strongly resembles that at
Gamala in terms of the interior organization of space. The Masada
building is also a sophisticated, unique design, fusing elements of
the bouleuterion and of the basilica.

Magdala

The excavators Loffreda and Corbo first presented the Magdala
building as a synagogue in 1976.[42] It later figured in Gideon
Foerster's attempts to interpret Masada and Herodium.[43]

The small building in question stood at the intersection of two
streets in Magdala. In its first stage, it was built of very finely cut
stone members so that its inner space measured about 8 x 7 m, or
almost exactly the size of the inner space of the building at Masada.

A rank of five benches was built into the north wall, and one must
assume that entrance was made into the inner space down and over
these benches, rather like at Masada. It is striking that there is no
courtyard to receive visitors. The space that one entered into was
defined as a nave and three side aisles by interior columniation. The
columns and the one surviving capital are quite simply, but carefully
cut. Corner or heart-shaped columns stand at the back corners of
the columniation. There is no decoration of any kind. Interpretation
of the space has been rendered difficult by its use as a pond in the
second century.[44]

What is our conclusion about Magdala? This building could also
serve the interests of the Jewish synagogue liturgy as outlined above.

---

42. S. Loffreda and V. Corbo, "La Città Roma di Magdala," *Studi Archeologici I:
Studii Biblici Franciscani,* Collection Major 22 (Jerusalem: Franciscan, 1976), 355ff.
43. See Foerster's attempts to interpret Masada and Herodium: "The Synagogues
at Masada and Herodium," *Journal of Jewish Art* 3, no. 4 (1977): 6–11.
44. Ehud Netzer has argued that the structure at Magdala was a springhouse in
the second century C.E. See Ehud Netzer, "Did the Magdala Springhouse Serve as a
Synagogue?" in *Synagogues in Antiquity,* ed. Aryeh Kasher, Aharon Oppenheimer,
and Uriel Rappaport (Jerusalem: Yad Izhak Ben Zvi, 1987), 165–72. He argues that
there is no Jewish art at present. This is not a decisive argument.

This is also a necessary but not a sufficient conclusion to show that the Magdala building may have served the community for liturgical purposes. The interior of the building is isolated and concealed from the street, as in the case of Gamala and Masada. Second, one observes that the building is designed rather like a fragment of a bouleu-terion. That is, the interior benches at Magdala seem to be another instance of the interior design of the Gamala edifice, complete with columns interior to the range of benches. We also find very finely cut members, but no putative Jewish art. Thus the general design of the building and its very careful workmanship, argue for its occasional use as a building of cultic identity. On the other hand the building most strongly resembles that at Gamla and Masada in terms of the interior organization of space. The Magdala building is the third instance of a unique design, fusing elements of the bouleuterion and of the basilica, again with no clearly Jewish elements.

Herodium

The four-columned structure at the Herodium was first identified as a synagogue by V. Corbo in 1967, the first excavator of Herodium. G. Foerster also argued for its identification as a synagogue in 1973, and Foerster advanced the excavations. It remains to be seen whether Ehud Netzer, the current excavator, will continue to maintain the identification.[45] The building in question is usually understood to be a triclinium for Herod the Great, later converted into a synagogue by Zealots of the First Revolt. The later renovators added the four columns seen in the innermost space today. They also added ranges of benches around three of its four sides, leaving the fourth side, the east, open for the entrance. If one were standing in the interior space of the building and walked toward the wall, one would step up on two benches to a landing less than two meters wide. Then one could approach the third bench built against the wall on three sides. The interior space measures about 15 x 10 m. The interior walls were plastered, but not decorated in any fashion.

Those who converted the triclinium added a ritual bath just out-side the major entrance and to the right. It is fascinating that this small bath and its steps are not in an enclosed building, but simply built up against the wall of the proposed synagogue. Any activity there was public activity, especially since no courtyard was built

---

45. Ehud Netzer, *Masada: The Buildings, Stratigraphy and Architecture*, The Yigael Yadin Excavations, vol. 3: 1963–65, Final Reports (Jerusalem: Hebrew University, 1993).

around it. This addition argues for a Jewish use of the building, and indeed for a cultic use.

The interior space of the Herodium building seems to be a simpler version of that at Gamala. An uppermost bench at Gamala is only on the wall opposite the main entrance. But otherwise the use of a wide landing above benches is a device used at Gamala as well as at Herodium. One room is accessible from the Herodium, but no one knows its use.

What is our conclusion about Herodium? It is the same, namely, that this building could also serve the interests of the Jewish synagogue liturgy as outlined above. This is also a necessary but not a sufficient conclusion to show that the Herodium building served the community for liturgical purposes.

Yet observe that this building is also designed like a fragment of a bouleuterion. That is, the interior benches at Herodium seem to be a simpler instance of the interior design of the Gamala edifice, complete with columns interior to the range of benches. We also have very finely cut members, but again no putative Jewish art. Thus the general design of the building and its careful workmanship, as well as its direct association with a public ritual bath, argue for its sometime use as a building of Jewish cultic identity. On the other hand, the building most strongly resembles that at Gamla and Masada in terms of the interior organization of space. The Herodium building is the fourth instance of a unique design, fusing elements of the bouleuterion and of the basilica.

Conclusions

We are coming to a testable hypothesis developed from the literature and from the remains of the four buildings that have been tentatively identified as synagogues by the excavators. Several observations are in order.

First, it seems clear that these buildings organize innermost space in a similar manner, namely, that it is always a rectangle provided with columns. Ranges of benches surround the columns on one, three, or four sides, and one must step down the benches as steps from the top bench. More important are the rows of columns. It is striking that those who sat or stood on the benches had to look between the columns to see the activity transpiring in the central space. This peculiar arrangement of the columns between the benches and the central space is especially arresting when one realizes that it is more or less the norm in the excavated synagogues of ancient Palestine from Galilee to Gaza. When synagogues are without interior columniation, as at Eshtemoa or Susiya in Judea, it is all the more noticeable.

Second, the elements that resemble a bouleuterion are concentric, square ranges of benches for mass seating and a central, rectangular space for the leader or leaders. On the other hand the elements that resemble a basilica are space divided on the interior into a nave and aisles by columniation and principal entrances on the narrow end of the building. The columns standing in front of the congregants are unique to these putative synagogues and to those later structures that are unambiguously synagogues.

Third, the Jewishness of these four structures is given by their context, not by their building elements, though the palm tree decoration at Gamala is a candidate for a Jewish decoration. The simple explanation is that builders and designers would have seen no need to identify a structure as uniquely Jewish if the entire population is Jewish.

Fourth, these structures can be arranged on a straight line continuum from most to least complex architecturally. Gamala seems to be the most complex, followed by Masada, then Magdala, and finally by Herodium.

Fifth, it seems clear, since these buildings resemble hybrid Hellenistic buildings, that the Jews of ancient Palestine adopted what architecture they needed from Hellenistic culture. Since the buildings exhibit so few markers that archaeologists recognize as indicators of cult, we need not view them as unique, cultic structures. Part of their use could indeed be for Jewish liturgy, but they could also be used for any other local needs for assembly.

Since these four buildings are more like one another than not, then it may well be that these represent a type. This commonality also suggests strongly that their builders were seeing some structure or structures that gave them the idea. It is surely no accident that two of these structures were built by Zealots in the First Revolt. They even founded the four columns at the Herodium poorly, which suggests that function took precedence over form. That is, in the minds of the builders it was necessary to have the columns between the central space and the benches for some functional reason.

Surely we must look to Jerusalem as the source of this idea, and specifically to the Second Temple. There is no need to move to Alexandria to find the source of the origin of the synagogue (contra Ma'oz 1992). In reconstructions of the Second Temple on paper, one architectural detail found in Josephus is not normally represented. This detail is that porches or cloisters with a single row of columns surrounded the inner courts of the Temple. Thus those in the Court of Women, for example, were surrounded visually by a row of columns. Those who stood in the cloisters had to look through a balustrade of columns to see activity in the central courtyard.[46]

In fact, porticoes or porches surrounded all the open courtyards of the Second Temple. Courts with two or three rows of columns, and an additional row worked into the wall as pilasters surrounded the largest courts, those everyone entered from the south.[47] Therefore visitors to the temple were left with the dominant visual experience of looking between columns to see the activity in any court. This visual element of a visit to the temple, together with the virtual architectural signature of the synagogue as columns between benches and central space, formed a kind of template, signature, or symbol for the Second Temple in the minds of the visitors. The regularity with which this architectural signature appears in excavated synagogues — except in certain broadhouses and in Samaritan synagogues[48] — suggests that these four buildings of the first century are indeed synagogues, a Palestinian Jewish invention of space for cultic and other purposes in the first century.[49]

---

46. *BJ* 5.199.

47. *BJ* 5.2–3 or 190–206. The author of Nehemiah thought Ezra read the Torah to Israel in the Water Gate of Jerusalem (Nehemiah 8:1–7). But the author of 1 Esdras placed this event in the outer courts of the temple (1 Esdras 9:38): "And the whole populace came together with one accord into the open space of the holy porch toward the east." This placement in 1 Esdras suggests that the Hasmonean author regarded the temple courts as appropriate venues for this type of event, which in turn suggests that the temple porches and courts can form a kind of architectural template for such activities in the synagogue.

48. Y. Magen, "Samaritan Synagogues," in *Early Christianity in Context: Monuments and Documents,* ed. F. Manns and E. Alliata (Jerusalem: Studium Biblicum Franciscanum, 1993), 193–230.

49. J. F. Strange, "The Art and Archaeology of Early Judaism," chap. 4 in Jacob Neusner, ed., *Judaism in Late Antiquity, Part One: The Literary and Archaeological Sources* (Leiden: Brill, 1995), 75. For a similar idea of Temple space in later synagogues, see Joan R. Branham, "Vicarious Sacrality: Temple Space in Ancient Synagogues," in *Ancient Synagogues: Historical Analysis and Archaeological Discovery,* ed. Dan Urman and Paul V. M. Flesher (Leiden: Brill, 1995), 319–45.

CHAPTER THREE

Synagogues in Galilee and the Gospels

Richard A. Horsley
University of Massachusetts Boston

The synagogue has been the central institution in Jewish life for nearly two millennia. Thus the question of its origin is of considerable importance, both for the origin of Judaism and for that of Christianity, which is understood as emerging from Judaism. The extreme paucity of evidence for synagogue buildings in the land of Israel until late antiquity, however, has made the issue a poignant one in research and interpretation of Jewish and Christian origins. Expanded archaeological explorations have produced exciting new evidence for synagogue buildings in late antiquity.[1] Such evidence, however, has also led to some critical "second thoughts," particularly about when and where synagogues came into prominence. Recent critical studies have pushed the date of what constitutes reliable evidence for the wider presence of synagogue buildings in the land of Israel gradually forward from early Second Temple period to late antiquity.[2]

---

1. Several collections of essays offer valuable updating of evidence and interpretive debate: Joseph Gutmann, ed., *The Synagogue: Studies in Origins, Archaeology, and Architecture* (New York: KTAV, 1975); Joseph Gutmann, ed., *Ancient Synagogues: The State of Research,* BJS 22 (Chico, Calif.: Scholars Press, 1981); Lee I. Levine, ed., *Ancient Synagogues Revealed* (Jerusalem: Israel Exploration Society, 1981); Lee I. Levine, ed., *The Synagogue in Late Antiquity* (Philadelphia: American Schools of Oriental Research, 1987); Den Urman and Paul V. M. Flesher, eds., *Ancient Synagogues: Historical Analysis and Archaeological Discovery* (Leiden: Brill, 1995).

2. Lester L. Grabbe, "Synagogues in Pre-70 Palestine: A Re-Assessment," *JTS* 39 (1988): 401–10; Paul V. M. Flesher, "Palestinian Synagogues before 70 C.E.: A Review of the Evidence," in *Approaches to Ancient Judaism,* ed. J. Neusner and E. Frerichs (Atlanta: Scholars Press, 1989), 6:67–81; Howard C. Kee, "The Trans-

The conceptual apparatus with which we moderns approach the issue, however, may be as problematic as the lack of evidence for synagogue buildings in the late Second Temple and early rabbinic period. Most treatments are couched in abstract general terms of the synagogue, as if there must have been a standard institution for which evidence from wide-ranging places and sources can be adduced. Most treatments assume that the synagogue is basically a religious building. Indeed, such terms and assumptions are simply parts of a standard conceptual apparatus enshrined in handbooks and embedded in scholarly habits. Judaism is conceived of primarily as a religion over against which Christianity emerged as another religion. Judaism is understood as having been institutionalized locally in the synagogue, particularly after the destruction of the Temple. The synagogue, moreover, is viewed as having been defined and led by the rabbis understood as the successors of the Pharisees.

Now it may well be that in late antiquity there was a synagogue "down the street," as it were, from the church in many Hellenistic and Roman cities. In recent decades, however, we have come to recognize the considerable diversity in ancient Jewish as well as Christian literature and ideas.[3] The diversity of writings and worldviews, moreover, was rooted in different geographical-political circumstances and social situations. Not only were there differences between Jewish communities in the diaspora and Jewish society in Palestine, but there were also regional and class differences within Palestine itself. Moreover, in contrast with structurally differentiated modern Western society, in ancient agrarian societies such as Jewish Palestine, religion was inseparable from, indeed embedded with, other dimensions of life such as the political and economic and ethnic. Finally, the very meaning of the Greek term *synagōgē* at the root of our term "synagogue" should suggest that perhaps something more than and/or distinguishable from a build-

---

formation of the Synagogue after 70 C.E.: Its Import for Early Christianity," *NTS* 36 (1990): 1–24; and similarly in "Early Christianity in the Galilee: Reassessing the Evidence from the Gospels," in *The Galilee in Late Antiquity*, ed. Lee I. Levine (New York: Jewish Theological Seminary of America, 1992), 3–10, and "Defining the First-Century CE Synagogue: Problems and Progress," *NTS* 41 (1995): 481–500, including a critical review of the dating of the Theodotus inscription.

3. Recognizing the diversity of ancient Jewish literature even in Palestine, some scholars refer in the plural to "Judaisms." Recognizing that what has been referred to as Judaism in late Second Temple times involved much projection backwards of late rabbinic materials and did not in fact emerge until the third or fourth century C.E., Neusner and others refer to "formative Judaism."

ing may have been involved in the development of what, perhaps later, became *the synagogue.*

Such observations suggest that our approach to ancient Jewish life and institutions and how they may bear on the emergence of early Christian communities should be more historically sociological. Inquiry into concrete social forms can open up contexts for interpretation of texts and artifacts. Because of the importance of Galilee as the context of Jesus' ministry, the development of the synoptic Gospel traditions, and the subsequent emergence of rabbinic Judaism, this investigation will focus on the social form that the synoptic Gospels refer to as the *synagōgai.*

Synagogues: Local Community Assemblies

A great deal of interest has focused on the excavation of many buildings in Galilee interpreted as Jewish synagogues.[4] Ironically, closer attention to the dating of these buildings has led to a certain confusion regarding the origins and nature of "the synagogue." Levine, who is eager to demonstrate that synagogues-as-buildings were ubiquitous by the first century, and Flesher, who is sceptical, agree that there are only three structures where sufficient evidence exists even to consider that they may have been "synagogues."[5] However, Levine admits that the evidence at Gamla remains inconclusive, while Flesher, along with other recent critics, decisively refutes the case for the rooms in the royal fortresses / palaces of Masada or Herodium. "None of these structures have any features that would identify them as specifically Jewish, let alone as synagogues."[6] Nor could one justifiably extrapolate from the use of rooms in Herodian royal fortresses to social-religious practices in

---

4. Recent survey, including bibliography by site, in Gideon Foerster, "The Ancient Synagogues of the Galilee," in *The Galilee in Late Antiquity,* ed. Lee I. Levine (New York: Jewish Theological Seminary, 1992), 289–319.

5. Lee I. Levine, "The Second Temple Synagogue: The Formative Years," in *The Synagogue in Late Antiquity,* 10–12; Flesher, "Palestinian Synagogues before 70 C.E.," 75–80. Gideon Foerster ("The Synagogues at Masada and Herodium," *Journal of Jewish Art* 3, no. 4 [1977]: 6–11) argued for "a well-defined group of synagogues dated to the Second Temple Period." His argument is refuted by Marilyn J. Chiat, "First-Century Synagogue Architecture: Methodological Problems," in *Ancient Synagogues: The State of Research,* ed. J. Gutmann, 50–58.

6. Flesher, "Palestinian Synagogues before 70 C.E.," 76. For the supposed "synagogues" at Masada and Herodium, "there is no proof of piety or of a definite place of worship...," according to S. B. Hoenig, quoting his own review of Y. Yadin, Bar Kokhba, in "The Ancient City-Square: The Forerunner of the Synagogue," *ANRW* 2.19.1, 453 n. 32.

Judean or Galilean villages. It is unclear what was found at the "private houses" in Magdala and Gamla that would suggest that "the pious gathered [there] for prayer."[7] Gutmann believes that we can declare confidently that "no building dating from the first century has so far been positively identified as a synagogue."[8] Thus, because virtually all of the "synagogue" buildings that have been excavated in Galilee date from the third century C.E. or later,[9] critical investigation of synagogues as religious buildings has apparently returned to the view dominant early in the twentieth century, that even the earliest synagogue buildings in the land of Israel cannot be dated prior to 200 C.E.[10] It is interesting to note, although not as significant with regard to the situation in Galilee and Judea, that of the six buildings identified as Jewish "synagogues" in the diaspora, only the converted house at Delos (first B.C.E. to second C.E.) is dated prior to the second century C.E.[11] Thus the discovery of so many synagogue buildings, virtually all of which date from late antiquity, leads us to wonder why we are not finding such buildings from earlier times. Were synagogue buildings not constructed in late Second Temple Galilee?

Earlier generations simply assumed that literary references to *synagōge* referred to a building used for primarily religious purposes, and even recent studies aware of the lack of archaeological evidence in late Second Temple Palestine still operate on that assumption. The basic evidence of language usage should have been the clue. *Synagōgē* indicates an assembly or gathering, without any special religious connotations or indications of a building or place. In the LXX it renders mainly *edah,* and sometimes *qahal* (which is more frequently rendered by *ekklēsia*), referring to the local or tribal

---

7. So H. C. Kee, "The Transformation of the Synagogue," 8, following Eric M. Meyers and James F. Strange, *Archaeology, the Rabbis and Early Christianity* (Nashville: Abingdon, 1981), 141.

8. Joseph Gutmann, "The Origins of the Synagogue: The Current State of Research," in *The Synagogue: Studies in Origins, Archaeology and Architecture,* ed. J. Gutmann (New York: KTAV, 1975), 76.

9. See, e.g., Eric M. Meyers, "Galilean Regionalism as a Factor in Historical Reconstruction," *BASOR* 221 (1976): 99; and, for the building at Capernaum previously dated in the first century but now dated in the fourth century, see the review essays of the archaeological reports, Gideon Foerster, "Notes on Recent Excavations at Capernaum," *IEJ* 21 (1971): 207–11; and James F. Strange, "The Capernaum and Herodium Publications," *BASOR* 226 (1977): esp. 69–70.

10. Heinrich Kohl and Carl Watzinger, *Antike Synagogen in Galilaea* (Leipzig: J. C. Hinrichs'sche Buchhandlung, 1916).

11. A. T. Kraabel, "Social Systems of Six Diaspora Synagogues," in *Ancient Synagogues: The State of Research,* ed. J. Gutmann (Chico, Calif.: Scholars Press, 1981), 79–81.

assembly or the congregation of all Israel. The Mishnaic Hebrew term *knesset*, like the Aramaic equivalent, also means an assembly, whether local or peoplewide (cf. Neh 8–9).[12]

A survey of literary and inscriptional evidence, moreover, indicates that in the first-century diaspora, *synagōgē* usually referred to a local assembly with sociopolitical as well as religious functions, connotations of a building in which the assembly met being rare.[13] Inscriptions, papyri, and certain literary references give evidence for the existence of Jewish meeting places at various locations around the Mediterranean, from as early as Ptolemaic times in Egypt. But the usual term for such places or buildings is *proseuchē*, "prayer(-house)." Whether in Philo's writings, catacomb inscriptions in Rome, or inscriptions in Asia Minor near the Bosporus *proseuchē* is the dominant term used to indicate a building in which Jewish communities gathered.[14] The gathering itself, the congregation or assembly, was often referred to as the *synagōgē*, although

---

12. It is thus misleading to say that the equivalent of a synagogue building was *bet knesset;* vs. M. Hengel, "Proseuche und Synagoge: Jüdische Gemeinde, Gotteshaus, und Gottesdienst in der Diaspora und in Palästina," in *Tradition und Glaube: Das frühe Christentum in seiner Umwelt*, Festschrift für K. G. Kühn, ed. G. Jeremias, H. Kühn, and H. Stegemann (Göttingen: Vandenhoeck & Ruprecht, 1971); now in *The Synagogue: Studies in Origins, Archaeology, and Architecture*, ed. J. Gutmann (New York: KTAV, 1975), 179; and E. M. Meyers and J. Strange, *Archaeology, the Rabbis, and Early Christianity* (Nashville: Abingdon, 1981), 141. In fact, *bet haknesset* should probably be rendered as simply "assembly" (without necessarily implying a building, as in *bet din*, "court") unless the literary context clearly requires a place or building. Schürer-Vermes, *The History of the Jewish People* (Edinburgh: T. & T. Clark, 1979), 2:429–30, make the inappropriate qualification that *knesset* refers to a community "in so far as the community is regarded as religious," but do observe that *bet knesset* refers to the members and that *synagōgē* refers primarily to the empirical reality of a community established in some location, while *ekklēsia* refers to the ideal community of Israel. The recent study by Stuart S. Miller, "On the Number of Synagogues in the cities of 'Erez Israel," *JJS* 49 (1998): 51–66, esp. 59–63, provides revealing discussions of rabbinic texts that were previously understood to refer to synagogue buildings but when examined more carefully are understood to refer to assemblies or gatherings of people.

13. The Schürer-Vermes treatment (*The History of the Jewish People* [Edinburgh: T. & T. Clark, 1979], 2:423–54) notes that *synagōgē* usually refers to the assembled people, but reverts to an overall synthetic synchronic presentation and still reduces the synagogue to its religious dimension, despite noting evidence to the contrary.

14. See, e.g., H. J. Leon, *The Jews of Ancient Rome* (Philadelphia: Jewish Publication Society of America, 1960), 139; W. Schrage, *"synagōgē,"* TDNT 7:806ff; M. Hengel, "Proseuche und Synagoge," 169, 172, 181; and A. T. Kraabel, "The Diaspora Synagogue: Archaeological and Epigraphic Evidence since Sukenik," in *ANRW* 2.19.1, 477–510. Ironically, this point is demonstrated by the chart provided by Richard E. Oster ("Supposed Anachronism in Luke-Acts' Use of Synagoge," *NTS* 39 [1993]: 185): thirty instances of *proseuchē*, compared with four of *amphitheatron*, four of *hieron* (Josephus), four of *topos* (three in Josephus), and nine of *synagōgē* (six in Josephus's accounts of three different buildings, on which see below).

Philo's usage and other Egyptian evidence suggests that Egyptian Jewish communities did not yet use "synagogue" even for the congregation.[15]

These congregations of Jews, including those referred to with the term *synagōgē*, were clearly more than a worshiping group. They were socioethnic, even quasi-political, communities of Jews resident in a particular city attempting to run their own affairs insofar as the imperial and civic authorities would allow. The decree cited by Josephus of the *boulē* and *dēmos* of Sardis, where a Jewish community thrived for centuries, including meeting houses, may be the best available indication of the full sociopolitical dimensions of such Jewish "congregations:"

> that as their laws and freedom have been restored to them by the Roman Senate and people, they may, in accordance with their accepted customs, come together and have a community life (*synagōntai kai politeuontai,* where the connotation is almost "civil life") and adjudicate suits among themselves, and that a place be given them in which they may gather together with their wives and children and offer their ancestral prayers and sacrifices to God.... (*Ant.* 14.260)

While appreciating the special significance of the "ancestral prayers and sacrifices to God" here, we can discern also the sociopolitical dimensions of such Jewish congregations which (again in Sardis)

> from earliest times... had an association of their own (*synodos idia*) in accordance with their native laws and their own place, in which they decide their affairs and controversies with one another. (*Ant.* 14.235)

They also clearly had a significant economic dimension in that they were gathering funds and/or sending funds to Jerusalem.[16]

The reports of Josephus provide the principal evidence for the use of *synagōgē* for an assembly building and the only literary evidence of Jewish meeting houses (other than the Temple) in or around Palestine prior to 70 C.E., in Syrian Antioch, in the coastal cities of Caesarea and Dora, and in the royal city of Tiberias,

---

15. Hengel, "Proseuche und Synagoge," 169–70.

16. See A. T. Kraabel, "Unity and Diversity among Diaspora Synagogues," in *The Synagogue in Late Antiquity,* ed. Lee I. Levine (Philadelphia: American Schools of Oriental Research, 1987), 51–55, points out that these Jewish communities were far more than a "voluntary association" and that the associations which the Jewish *synagōgai* resemble socially were not particularly "of a religious nature."

founded around 20 C.E. by Antipas. Because of their importance, these references merit some scrutiny.

In Tiberias at one point during the political turmoil in 66–67, says Josephus, "all assembled in the prayer-house, a huge hall (*proseuchē, megiston oikēma*), capable of accommodating a large crowd" (Life 277–80).[17] They were gathered for discussion of political affairs, however, not for prayer, the recitation of Torah, or a religious meal. This "prayer-house" was thus certainly not one of several "synagogues" in the city (which appeared only in late antiquity), but a large hall where a substantial portion of the populace could assemble.

In three passages in particular, Josephus uses the term *synagōgē* apparently in reference to buildings in which Jews met in Dora, Caesarea, and Antioch. One of the three occurrences of the term in the passage concerning Dora, *en tǭtēs synagōgēs topǭ* (literally, "in the place of the assembly"), suggests that the usage of the term is extended from the "congregation" to the place / building of congregation (*Ant.* 19.305, cf. 300). Although the synagogue building is associated with religious rites in two of these accounts (*Ant.* 19.305; *J. W.* 7.44–45), in all three places it is a center for a community that clearly has a political and socioreligious dimension.[18] No conclusion can be drawn for the situation in Judean or Galilean villages and towns, however, since all of these cases are from diaspora Jewish communities in Hellenistic cities on the nearer or farther fringes of Jewish Palestine.

It is ironic that, after noting how *synagōgē* in diaspora sources referred to the congregation and not to its meeting place, scholars take New Testament references to *synagōgai* as evidence for a widespread presence of religious buildings in Jewish Palestine, above all in Galilee.[19] A brief critical survey indicates in fact that, with two or three exceptions, New Testament texts use *synagōgē* to

---

17. The term *oikema* can be used in the sense of a (room in a) temple, but it can also refer to a workshop, a prison, a horse stable, or a brothel (Liddell-Scott-Jones).

18. Note "the twelve leading officers (*dynatoi*) headed by John the tax-collector in Caesarea (*J. W.* 2.287, 292); their long recognized political rights and their own "magistrate" (*archon*) in Antioch (*J. W.* 7.44, 47; cf. *Ag. Ap.* 2.39); and the references to their having been allowed heretofore to conduct their community life according to "the (ancestral / traditional) laws" in Dora (*J. W.* 2.289; *Ant.* 19.301, 304).

19. E.g., Hengel, "Proseuche und Synagoge," 181; Martin Goodman, *State and Society in Roman Galilee* (Totowa, N.J.: Rowan and Allanheld, 1983), 84; L. Grabbe, "Synagogues...," 405; Flesher, "Palestinian Synagogues before 70 C.E.," 72–73.

refer to assemblies or congregations, usually local, sometimes the whole people.[20]

In the few occurrences outside the synoptic Gospels and Acts, συναγωγή *synagōgē* always refers to an "assembly" (Jas 2:2; Rev 2:9; 3:9; John 6:59; 18:20). In the synoptic Gospels and Acts, only in Luke 7:5 (a Lucan addition to Q) and (apparently) Acts 18:7 does *synagōgē* clearly refer to a building. Most frequently in Acts, *synagōgē* clearly refers to an assembly and not a place in which it gathered. We find such references in 6:9; 9:2; 13:43 ("when the synagogue broke up"!); 18:26; 22:19; 26:11. Otherwise the term refers primarily to assemblies, with possible connotations of a meeting place in only a few instances, such as 13:14.

Most significant for reconstructing the Galilean context of the "Jesus movement(s)" and the developing synoptic Gospel traditions are the synoptic Gospel passages, particularly Mark and Q. Clearest are Mark 13:9 and Q/Luke 12:11, where the parallelism with councils, or with rulers and authorities, indicates unambiguously that "synagogues" refers not to buildings but to assemblies with political jurisdiction and authority to suppress agitators. *Synagōgai*, along with *agorai* and *deipna*, in Mark 12:38–39 (cp. Matt 23:6–7; Luke 20:45–46) and the Q parallel, Luke 11:43, point not to buildings, but to public scenes and occasions, in which the scribes/Pharisees love "the best seats and salutations." In all other Markan references (1:21, 23, 29, 39; 3:1; 6:2) and in their Matthean or Lucan parallels, the *synagōgai* are local assemblies in which Jesus teaches and heals, with nothing to suggest that buildings were involved.[21]

If, given the lack of archaeological evidence for buildings, the synoptic Gospels provide our primary evidence for the existence of synagogues in Galilee/Palestine, then it is clear that those *synagōgai* were not buildings but assemblies or congregations. Particular meaning, of course, would have been contextual. One can imagine a *synagōgē* or *knesset* used for the assembly of the whole people or an assembly that represented the whole people. The usage before us in the synoptic tradition, however, is for local assemblies. It is conceivable that in a few passages in Luke-Acts as in Josephus's reports we

---

20. Comparable assemblies in the Psalms of Solomon, where local assemblies are clearly particular manifestations or extensions of the overall congregation of Israel: *Psalms of Solomon* 10:6–7; 17:16, 43–44.

21. The synagogue buildings in certain Galilean towns 200 years later were constructed apparently in those towns with sufficient population and/or productivity (or patrons) that they could afford to build such a structure. See Meyers and Strange, *Archaeology*, 141.

are seeing the beginnings of a transition phase in which buildings where the assemblies met are beginning to be referred to as *synagōgai* by association. Except for the Hellenistic cities of Caesarea, Dora, and Tiberias, however, there is neither literary nor archaeological evidence for "synagogues" as buildings in first-century Galilee.

Although he is still pursuing the origins of a religious building, Hoenig has gathered evidence that clarifies the relation between the local assembly and its meeting place.[22] He is clear, for example, that *knesset* in early rabbinic literature "applied to 'assembly' and designated all communal activities." He then lays out numerous tannaitic sources indicating that the "city-square" (*r'hova shel 'ir*) was the location of the *maamadot,* prayers for fasting, trials, general assemblies, the bringing of first fruits, and prayers for rain. This evidence for the village or town square as the place in which local assemblies and courts met during late Second Temple times and up to the Bar Kokhba revolt suggests a simple continuity with earlier times in ancient Judah when communal matters such as administration of justice, proclamations, assemblies, and social life generally took place in the open space or plaza inside the gate of a town or city (e.g., Jer 5:1; Ezra 10:9; Neh 8:1; Job 29:7; 2 Chr 32:6). The village elders met at "the gate" and, more ominously, executions took place there (Deut 17:5; 21:19; 22:24). Prophets insisted that justice be established at the gate (Amos 5:10, 15). In the capital cities of Samaria and Jerusalem as well as in the villages, the gate was the location of public assemblies for proclamations, judicial decisions, or prophetic appearances (e.g., 1 Kgs 22:10; Jer 38:7). In Levine's recent survey of such functions of "the gate" in the Hebrew Bible, he reports that "most of the activities that found expression in the synagogue at the end of the Second Temple period are already documented for the city-gate area in biblical times."[23] The "town-square" or "gate" can thus be understood as the forerunner of the synagogue building as the location of "the civic and local social activities in the Second Century." The implication of the evidence that Hoenig has adduced for the "town square" and that Levine surveys for "the gate" is that in late Second Temple and earliest rabbinic times the *synagōgē* or *knesset* was the local assembly — as well as

22. Sidney B. Hoenig, "Historical Inquiries: I. Heber Ir. II. City Square," *JQR* 48 (1957–58) 132–39; "The Ancient City-Square: Forerunner of the Synagogue," *ANRW* 2.19.1, 448–76, esp. 448–54. See now the critique of Hoenig's argument by Lee I. Levine, "The Nature and Origin of the Palestinian Synagogue Reconsidered," *JBL* 115 (1996): 432, n. 27.

23. Levine, "The Palestinian Synagogue Reconsidered," 436.

that the local town square or gate was the place where it met prior to the erection of communal buildings as meeting houses.

The Synagogue as the Principal Social Form of Local Community

While most scholarly discussions of the origins and features of the synagogue in ancient times have simply assumed that it was primarily or distinctively a "religious" institution as well as a building, a few critical voices have been arguing alternative explanations. Over sixty years ago Zeitlin, pointing out that historically "many institutions of a purely religious character came into existence as a result of social and economic forces," insisted that in origins synagogues were not only not buildings but also secular in character.[24] He appeals particularly to linguistic usage in tannaitic literature, in which "house of assembly," like "house of judgment," does not necessarily (or even probably) refer to a building, and the leader is referred to as "head of the assembly," not "head of the house of assembly," and the members are "sons of the assembly," not "sons of the house of assembly." In origins, the "synagogues" should be understood as the local assemblies of the inhabitants of villages and towns to deal with typical social and economic problems of their common life.

Yet it would be misleading to claim with Zeitlin that the synagogue was originally "not religious but secular," for we now realize that in such a traditional agrarian society our modern distinctions of "religious" and "political" and "economic" dimensions of life were not yet specified, let alone "institutionally differentiated." Thus, as Safrai states, the synagogue was "the people, the community, the congregation and the place where they assembled" to conduct community affairs such as fund-raising, public projects, or reading of the Torah.[25] The Torah, of course, was more a guide to communal life than devotional literature for individual salvation ("If fewer than

---

24. Solomon Zeitlin, "The Origins of the Synagogue," *Proceedings of the American Academy for Jewish Research* 2 (1930–31) 69–81; 70, 75.

25. S. Safrai, "The Synagogue," in *The Jewish People in the First Century* (Assert: Van Gorcum, 1974–76) 2.908–9. That synagogues were places where community concerns in general were handled was seen already by Samuel Krauss, *Synagogale Altertumer* (Berlin-Vienna: Harz, 1922). Zeitlin (previous note), of course, still has a valid point to the extent that certain distinctively "religious" matters such as prayer are not mentioned by tannaitic sources as taking place in the "house of assembly." "Only in the Amoraic sources does prayer gradually 'begin to occupy an honoured place in the houses of assembly' in the Land of Israel" (Dan Urman, "The House of Assembly and the House of Study: Are They One and the Same?" *JJS* 44 [1993]: 239).

ten are present... neither the Torah may be read, nor a passage
from the Prophets in conclusion." [m. Meg. 4:3]). The assembly
was also the local court, as is clearly assumed in the Mishnah (e.g.,
m. Sebu. 4:10) and in the synoptic tradition (Mark 13:11; Luke
12:11 = Q), there being no difference other than that the assembly
or certain members thereof at points constituted themselves as a
"house of judgment" (*bet din*).

It seems almost unavoidable to draw the conclusion that, beyond
the family or household, "the assembly" was the principal social
form of the local (village or town) community in Jewish Palestine /
Galilee providing for the governance and cohesion of the community. On the basis of the fragmentary literary and inscriptional
evidence, both Jewish and comparative, particularly regarding leaders of the assemblies, we can construct a sketch of this social form
within the local community.

Important aspects of ancient political-economic-religious relations were very different from modern societies. Local communities
in the ancient Mediterranean and other traditional agrarian societies were not "administered" by central or regional governments.[26]
Villages and towns remained semiautonomous local communities
with relatively continuous membership over the generations, communal relations and responsibilities, traditional social forms, and
traditional ways and customs. Rulers such as the Herodians in-
terfered very little in village affairs except to collect taxes. "It
should not, then, be surprising that the tannaitic sources *assume*
a well-regulated administration for the Jewish villages of Galilee.
The Tosefta asserts that the people of an '*ir* (village / town) were
competent to control their own assembly, their market prices, and
the wages of their workers."[27] Religious affairs were not separate
from political-economic matters. Village communities, structured
by lineage and kinship relations, had not evolved a distinctively religious social form(s) separate from the "civil" form(s). Rabbinic
texts do not mention the synagogue officers as having specifically
religious functions.[28] The obvious conclusion: "local government is
constantly identified in our sources with synagogue government."[29]
In the homogeneous Galilean villages and towns, one local assem-

---

26. Anthony Giddens, *The Nation-State and Violence* (Berkeley and Los Angeles:
University of California Press, 1987), chap. 2.

27. Martin Goodman, *State and Society in Roman Galilee, A.D. 132–212*
(Totowa, N.J.: Rowan and Allanheld, 1983), 120.

28. E.g., Schürer-Vermes, *History,* 2:433–34, 437.

29. Safrai, "The Synagogue," 933.

bly with its officers apparently dealt with the various aspects and contingencies of intracommunity life and with certain relations with higher jurisdictions beyond the local community. Town and village assemblies and local courts, moreover, would have had traditional forms well before the first century C.E. In dealing with the basic social patterns of village life, generally characterized by a high degree of continuity from century to century, therefore, the dangers of "reading back" later evidence is appreciably less than in dealing with the later rabbis and the earlier Pharisees, where the respective historical situations changed so dramatically from Second Temple Judea to second- and third-century Galilee. The procedure here is first to discern social patterns and practices of second-century Galilee and of fourth-century Hauran, and only then to extrapolate critically back to first-century Galilee.

Villages and towns apparently held assemblies twice a week, Mondays and Thursdays, the same days on which courts were held if necessary and the same as "market" days for selling and bartering. These also appear to have been the days on which the Torah was read or recited, although the latter may also have been done on special occasions (m. Ta'an. 4:2–3).[30] As in biblical times, fasts were also connected with public assemblies.[31] Local leadership entailed more than a single "ruler of the synagogue," the mistranslation in a few New Testament texts of *archisynagōgos* = "head of the assembly" (see esp. Mark 5:22, 35–38; Acts 13:15). The bewildering variety of terms in the sources for local officers or magistrates reflects local and regional differences. Yet it seems possible to discern common patterns in community leadership.

Rabbinic texts refer to *parnasim* (the root means "assign") and/or *gabbaim* (the root means "collect"). Both collected goods for distribution to the local poor (e.g., m. Pe'a 8:7; m. Dem. 3:1).[32] In such matters they often acted in twos and threes. *Parnasim* also appear in Judean desert documents from Bar Kokhba times, certifying a man's ownership of an ox to prevent its confiscation, or leasing out land (for the village?).[33] What is the relation of these *parnasim*

---

30. This is an example of a rabbinic text referring (with a verbal form) to the people "assembling in their towns" to recite the creation story, read by scholars as a reference to synagogue buildings. E.g., L. I. Levine, "Ancient Synagogues — A Historical Introduction," in *Ancient Synagogues Revealed*, 3.

31. Safrai, "The Synagogue," 919.

32. Goodman (*State and Society*, 121–22) reads "money" into texts where agricultural produce is subject to tithes. The village economy was not "monetarized," although money may have been involved in certain connections.

33. *Parnasim* appear in Judean desert documents from Bar Kokhba times, ap-

and *gabbaim* to local officials referred to by other terms, such as *archontes, presbuteroi, archisynagōgos / rosh haknesset,* or *hazzanim?* On the basis of "normal practice elsewhere in the Roman Empire," Goodman believes that "these magistrates ... were in some way related to the members of the local village court ... likely (acting) as the leading members and the executive officers of the *beth din*."[34] His presentation then becomes uncertain and confusing. He first declares his uncertainty about what connection the *hazzan* "appointed by the court to carry out its executions" had with "the identically named official who apportioned tasks in the synagogues or the hazzan on an Apamean inscription." He then asserts that, since "outside Palestine, synagogue officials appear to have been the leaders of the community ... one would expect the same to be true in Galilee." Then apparently reversing his argument, he writes that "it would seem that community control over the synagogue was exercised by officials selected for that purpose, but that there is no reason to assume that they had any considerable secular power."[35]

Goodman's reading of, and confusion about, the sources appear to be determined by two of the inapplicable assumptions discussed above: that is, that the sacred and secular were separate, and that the synagogue was a religious building. Such modern scholarly assumptions create problems where they do not exist in the sources. As Goodman himself points out, "the only evidence of his (the hazzan's) precise synagogue function comes from outside Palestine — he is said to have conducted the public liturgy in the huge synagogue of Alexandria by waving a scarf so the congregation would know when to say Amen."[36] In tannaitic texts, on the other hand, the *hazzan* executed the decisions of the assembly or court (e.g., *t. Mak.* 5:12). The *hazzan* may have acted as master of ceremonies during assembly services, taking charge of scrolls (cf. the *hyperētēs* in Luke 4:20) and giving signals for certain speakers or responses.

---

parently as local magistrates, DJD 2.155–59 #42; and 124 #24B. Goodman, *State and Society,* 131, points out that the local "treasurers" responsible for local "tax-collection" were clearly different from the "tax-collectors" (*mokhsin*) sent out by the ruling cities in Galilee or Rome. James Burtchaell, *From Synagogue to Church* (Cambridge: Cambridge University Press, 1992), 228–71, provides a survey of synagogue leaders or officers. Tessa Rajak and Dov Noy, "*Archisynagōgos:* Office, Title, and Social Status in the Greco-Jewish Synagogue," *JRS* 83 (1993): 75–93, in particular discusses one leader of the assemblies.

34. Goodman, *State and Society,* 122–23.
35. Ibid., 123–24.
36. Ibid., 123–24.

But he apparently also carried out certain judicial, instructional, or financial duties. According to the Mishnah, a *hazzan* administered the beating when such a penalty was ordered by the "house of judgment" (*m. Mak.* 3:12). The *hyperētēs* in Greek texts is often responsible for tax collection and enforcement of court rulings against debtors, which would fit the context in Matthew 5:25–26, except that the municipality concerned would have to be fairly large to have a prison (hence the reference may be to a royal or city court, i.e., a level of jurisdiction above the village level).

Variation in terminology seems likely to reflect parallel terms for similar functions or officers rather than separate religious and secular structures within the local community, and that the same people could be referred to with different terms depending on their function or role. Such variation in terms for local officers can be illustrated from the earlier (late second century B.C.E.) book of Judith. The three *archontes* of the town, Uzziah, Chabris, and Charmis, call together "all the elders of the town," whereupon all the young men and women run to the assembly (*ekklesia,* 6:14–16). Subsequently, however, Chabris and Charnis are referred to as "the elders of the city" (8:10) and Uzziah takes a leading role, presented as "Uzziah and the *archontes*" (8:35) and "Uzziah with the elders of the town, Chabris and Charmis" (10:6). Yet the phrase "the elders of the town" elsewhere seems to refer to a larger group than the two or three (13:12, as in 6:14–16). Thus "the elders" seem to function as a special, distinguished number (more than three) within the whole assembly, and the *archontes,* three leaders or officers from among the elders, with Uzziah apparently being the head of the assembly.

With this portrayal in Judith in mind, it seems likely that the *parnasim* and/or *gabbaim* and/or *hassanim* of tannaitic texts refer to certain functions or roles that could have been termed generally *archontes* in Greek, and that such officers or administrators would have emerged from among the elders of a local community assembly, and that one or more of those officers would have played the role of "head," *rosh haknesset* or *archisynagōgos?* Passing references in tannaitic texts indicate that the officers of local assemblies often acted in groups of two, three, or even seven. In Susanna two "elders" are appointed as "judges" and then overruled and executed by "the whole synagogue" (Sus 5, 41, 60). Josephus's claim that in 66 C.E. he structured the government of Galilee with "seven men in each town to adjudicate upon petty disputes" (*J.W.* 2.570–71) surely reflects the traditional indigenous local government.

Inscriptional evidence from villages and towns of Syria in late antiquity suggests a similar pattern.[37] The principal village officers appear sometimes as *protokōmētai*, sometimes as *kōmarchoi*, and sometimes as *stratēgoi*. That there was no *kōmarchos* where there was a *stratēgos* suggests that such terms designated the most important official in a village. Most telling for comparison with early rabbinic evidence are the inscriptions concerning multiple officials with various names, all of whom have similar functions, usually concerning finances and public works and often involving religious matters. Six different Syrian inscriptions present between two and seven *pistoi* supervising the building of a temple or a house at common village expense.[38] In inscriptions from other villages, groups of from two to four *pronoetai* had similar duties, and in another, two *pronoetai* worked together with two *pistoi* on the construction of a "common house."[39] In six other inscriptions, three, four, or even thirteen *dioiketai*, explicitly designated as elected by the people of the village in one case, supervised the erection of a gate or a building.[40] These inscriptions frequently indicate other officials (as many as six in one place) called *epimelētai*, supervising funds of the god or of the village or tending to the village water supply. The *epimelētai* were apparently not the highest officials of their villages, since an inscription from one of those same sites also mentions a *protokometes* (cf. the distinction between a *rosh haknesset* and a *hazzan* or several *gabbaim*). Other inscriptions mention *episkopoi* charged with building projects or supervision of the local market (i.e., analogous to *agoranomoi* elsewhere).[41] A similar picture has been sketched by more recent work on such inscriptions from the villages of southern Syria.[42]

The village administration reconstructed from these Syrian inscriptions is remarkably similar to that described in early rabbinic

---

37. Ironically, historians of antiquity and classics scholars have discerned what religious historians often have not seen, that "the religious cult of an ancient community played so important a part in the life of that community that there can have existed no sharp line of division between an official of the cult and an officer charged with ordinary municipal matters." G. McL. Harper, *Village Administration in the Roman Province of Syria* (Princeton: Princeton University Press, 1928), 38.

38. Harper, *Village Administration*, 27–31. Except for the famous story about the younger sons of Herod threatening to make *komogrammateis* out of his older sons (Josephus, *Ant.* 16.203), evidence for such officials comes only from Egypt.

39. Ibid., 31–33, 29.

40. Ibid., 33–34.

41. Ibid., 34–36, 36–38.

42. Henry I. MacAdam, "Epigraphy and Village Life in Southern Syria during the Roman and Early Byzantine Periods," *Berytus* 31 (1983): 103–15.

texts.[43] Villages, apparently operating as semiautonomous communities, preserved native (tribal) structures and customs inside a
democratic framework in which local officials were charged with
supervising communal finances, public works such as common
buildings, gates, or water supply, and religious matters. The *parnasim* in rabbinic texts correspond, for example, to the *proonoetai*
and *pistoi,* similar officials in Syrian villages. Goodman even found
one Tosepta passage (*t. B.Bat.* 10:5) "that introduces the *apa-
malatos* as an official similar to the *gabbai*" — obviously a loan
word corresponding to the *epimeletes* of Syrian inscriptions.

As evident from many cross-cultural studies of agrarian societies,
local social forms are remarkably persistent. It seems reasonable,
therefore, to extrapolate from the representation of local assembly
officers and their responsibilities attested in both rabbinic texts and
Syrian village inscriptions in late antiquity — with full allowance
for changes in terminology and functions — in reconstructing a picture of local assemblies and their operations in first-century Galilee.
Local assemblies operating more or less democratically provided
the governance and cohesion of village communities. Officials such
as the *archisynagōgos* and the *hyperētēs* mentioned in the synoptic Gospel tradition were presumably responsible for supervising
communal finances, aid to the poor, public works, and religious
matters.

The Pharisees: Not Leaders of Local Synagogues

People often suggest that synagogues were connected with scribes
and Pharisees, even that the Pharisees were responsible for the origin
or at least provided the leadership of the synagogues.[44] Yet there
is no evidence that the scribes and Pharisees were leaders or even
members of local assemblies.

Early rabbinic literature does not represent the rabbis as leaders of the assemblies, as *parnasim, gabbaim,* or *hazzanim,* or as
judges in the village courts.[45] If we simply attend to concrete social relations, the reason is obvious: insofar as the assembly and

---

43. Goodman, *State and Society,* 124.
44. E.g., Ellis Rivkin, *A Hidden Revolution* (Nashville: Abingdon, 1978); Kee,
"Transformation of the Synagogue," 12–14; S. Freyne, *Galilee, Jesus, and the
Gospels: Literary Approaches and Historical Investigations* (Philadelphia: Fortress,
1988), esp. 202–10.
45. Goodman, *State and Society,* 101, 119, 128–29; Safrai, "The Synagogue,"
935–36.

court were the forms of local community governance, the leaders were drawn from the local community membership. The rabbis had come to Galilee from Judea after the Bar Kokhba Revolt in mid-second century. Since they established tiny "academies" consisting of only a teacher and a few pupils, they would hardly have become members of very many village communities before locating more permanently in the cities of Galilee in the third century.[46] Indeed, the rabbis viewed association with the villagers, the *am haaretz,* as highly problematic: "Morning sleep and midday wine and children's talk and sitting in the assemblies of the peasants put a man out of the world" (m. 'Abot 3:11). They appear not to have reached out to the peasantry.[47] They focused instead on issues important to wealthy landowners, whose ranks many of them joined (t. Shab 2:5; 13:2; t. Erub. 1:2; 6:2; t. Pes. 10:12; t. Suk. 1:9; t. Ter. 2:13).[48] The rabbis did not come to control the synagogues until much later, perhaps the seventh century C.E.[49]

The notion that the Pharisees, supposedly the predecessors of the rabbis, were leaders of local synagogues is also without any solid evidence. That "Pharisees and law-teachers ... had come from every village of Galilee and Judea and from Jerusalem" (Luke 5:17, author's translation) is Luke's own generalizing statement and can hardly be taken at face value as an accurate sociological representation.[50] Only when read according to the standard old construction of "Judaism" as institutionalized in "synagogues" can synoptic Gospel passages such as Mark 12:38–39 and Luke 11:43 be taken as implying that the Pharisees were leaders of the synagogues. The article by Shaye Cohen in this volume critically examines and dismisses as without basis the old assumptions about certain Gospel

---

46. E.g., Lee I. Levine, "The Sages and the Synagogue in Late Antiquity: The Evidence of the Galilee," in *The Galilee in Late Antiquity* (New York: Jewish Theological Seminary of America, 1992), 220.

47. Shaye J. D. Cohen, "The Place of the Rabbi in Jewish Society of the Second Century," in *The Galilee in Late Antiquity,* ed. Lee I. Levine (New York: Jewish Theological Society of America, 1992), 167. Similarly Dan Urman, "The House of Assembly and the House of Study: Were They One and the Same?" *JJS* 44 (1993): 242–43.

48. Cohen, "The Place of the Rabbi in Jewish Society," 169. This is also one of the main conclusions of the extensive study of the Mishnah by Jacob Neusner. See, e.g., *Judaism: The Evidence of the Mishnah* (Chicago: Chicago University Press, 1981).

49. Cohen, "The Place of the Rabbi in Jewish Society," 173; and *From the Maccabees to the Mishnah* (Philadelphia: Westminster, 1987), 221; and Lee I. Levine, "The Sages and the Synagogue in Late Antiquity: The Evidence of the Galilee," in *The Galilee in Late Antiquity* (New York: Jewish Theological Seminary, 1992), 212.

50. Vs. Halvor Moxnes, *The Economy of the Kingdom: Social Conflict and Economic Relations in Luke's Gospel* (Philadelphia: Fortress, 1988).

passages as providing evidence for the Pharisees as leaders of prayer and Torah reading in the synagogues. That critical examination can be supplemented by other observations about Gospel representations of the Pharisees and of the village assemblies indicates that the former had little to do with the latter.

Mark does not associate the scribes and Pharisees with local assemblies. Only in one of the ten "pronouncement stories" in which they challenge Jesus do the scribes and/or Pharisees appear at a local assembly.[51] Otherwise when Jesus heals or teaches in village assemblies (Mark 1:23–29, 39; 6:1–6), they are not present. Mark 1:21–22 implies only that the people were familiar with the scribes' functions, not that they taught locally. Nor are scribes or Pharisees present as the leaders of the local assemblies or courts in 13:9–10, where Jesus' followers are called, accused, and tried. Far from portraying them as based in local assemblies, Mark represents the scribes and Pharisees as "coming down from Jerusalem" (Mark 3:22; 7:1), which is the location of the scribes when Mark has Jesus criticize them for desiring greetings in the *agorai* and seats of honor at assemblies and banquets (12:38–39; cf. Luke/Q 11:43). These portrayals of the Pharisees, along with Mark's indication that they were based in Jerusalem, fit the recently articulated picture of the Pharisees as "retainers" of the Judean temple-state.[52]

The other canonical Gospels also represent the scribes and Pharisees as based in Jerusalem, where they are apparently representatives of the Temple and high priesthood. In recent treatment, Matthew's discourse against the Pharisees (Matt 23) has figured prominently in the claim that the Pharisees were the leaders of "the synagogue." "The chapter is filled with detailed references to what by the end of the first century C.E. were in process of becoming normative practices in the emergent institutional synagogue."[53] "Moses' seat" (Matt 23:2), however, is surely symbolic of the Pharisees' claim to being the authoritative interpreters of Mosaic

---

51. Cf. Burton L. Mack, *A Myth of Innocence: Mark and Christian Origins* (Philadelphia: Fortress, 1988), 43, 192–98.

52. Fuller exploration of "the social role" of the scribes and Pharisees in the synoptic Gospel tradition will require a separate paper. For a sociological analysis of the scribes and Pharisees as "retainers," see A. J. Saldarini, *Pharisees, Scribes, and Sadducees in Palestinian Society: A Sociological Approach* (Wilmington, Del.: Glazier, 1988), esp. chaps. 3, 5, 11, and 12.

53. Kee, "Transformation of the Synagogue," 14–16. In the parallel subsequent article ("Early Christianity in the Galilee," 11–13) Kee pushes the opposition to this emergent "rabbinic Judaism" discerned in the references to "their synagogues" back to the Gospel of Mark.

Torah.[54] Like Mark, moreover, Matthew represents the Pharisees as based centrally in Jerusalem, not distributed among the villages and towns. Matthew makes this explicit in this very discourse by ending it with the prophetic lament of 23:37–39 so that all of the scribes' and Pharisees' objectionable activities are understood as emanating from Jerusalem, where they are associated with the chief priests as the rulers (Matt 15:1; 21:45; 27:62). The Gospel of John not only has the Pharisees firmly based in Jerusalem (1:19–24), but associates them with the high priests as the temple-based Judean rulers as well (7:32, 45–48; 11:46–57; 18:3). The Johannine Pharisees are thus clearly positioned as high-ranking officials of the Jerusalem temple-state, with power to dispatch armed police as well as to delegate investigative priests and Levites. Far from being associated with village assemblies, the Pharisees never appear outside of Jerusalem in John.

Is There a Conflict between Jesus and the Synagogues in the Gospels?

There is simply no basis, finally, for the frequent assumption that synoptic Gospel traditions reflect conflict between Jesus, his followers, or the church(es), on the one hand, and the synagogue(s), on the other.[55] The only indication of such a conflict in Mark comes in the "synoptic apocalypse" where Jesus' followers are beaten in assemblies and brought before councils (*synhedria*), rulers, and kings (Mark 13:9). The linking of "assemblies" with "councils, rulers, and kings" suggests these are not local village congregations but official assemblies of governing authorities. Otherwise Mark portrays the local village and town assemblies of Galilee as one of the principle contexts of Jesus' preaching and healing activity. Contrary to recent claims, there is no structural opposition between "synagogue" and "house," as if the one were somehow "sacred" and the other "profane," once we recognize that the *synagōgai* in Mark are village assemblies. Mark's portrayal of Jesus' activities in the village assemblies of Galilee parallels the pre-Markan and pre-Q "mission" tradition in which envoys are sent to preach and heal

---

54. On the seat of Moses as a symbol of authority, see I. Renov, "The Seat of Moses," *IEJ* 5 (1955), 262–67. See also L. Y. Rahmani, "Stone Synagogue Chairs: Their Identification, Use and Significance," *IEJ* 40 (1990): 192–214.

55. See, e.g., Kee, "The Transformation of the Synagogue after 70 c.e.," 15–24; and Elizabeth Struthers Malbon, *Narrative Space and Mythic Meaning in Mark* (San Francisco: Harper & Row, 1986), 131–36.

while temporarily living in the village or town communities (Mark 6:10; Luke/Q 10:5)

Luke expands and dramatically sharpens the Markan story of rejection in Nazareth so that Jesus opens his ministry by antagonizing, and nearly being lynched by, his hometown assembly. But Luke in no way pursues a general theme of conflict with the synagogue(s) in his Gospel. Whether in editing his sources or in his own material, Luke presents Jesus as preaching in local assemblies (e.g., Luke 4:15, 44; 6:6; 13:10). Even in Acts the highly positive response to the preaching of Paul and others in most "assemblies of the Jews" (Acts 13:5, 14, 43; 14:1; 17:1–4; 17:10–11; 18:7–8; 18:19–20) far outweighs the few incidents of rejection (Acts 17:5; 18:4–6; 19:9).

It is primarily in Matthew that certain scholars have discerned a general conflict between Jesus' followers or "the church" and the Jewish "synagogue."[56] But that also appears to be the result of the standard synthetic conceptual apparatus that links the Pharisees and the synagogue as interrelated components of "Judaism." If the scribes and Pharisees, on the one hand, and the synagogues, on the other hand, are each recognized for what they are — including their separate identities — in the synoptic Gospel traditions, then it should be clear that Matthew's (or Mark's or Luke's or Q's) sharp condemnation of scribes and Pharisees (Matt 23; Mark 12:38–40; Luke 11:37–52) does not implicate the synagogues. Matthew, of course, contains both a scheme by which Jesus sends the disciples on mission only to Israel until after the Resurrection, at which point they are sent to other peoples (10:5–6; 28:19–20), and also a related theme of the Jews' rejection of Jesus (8:11–12; 21:43; 27:25). The principal conflict within that scheme, however, is between Jesus, on the one hand, and the rulers in Jerusalem who virtually include the Pharisees, on the other (e.g., Matt 21:45–46; 27:62; and 23:6–38, esp. the ending in 23:37–38). Just as the crowds are separate from the rulers or Pharisees, so also the synagogues, that is, the local assemblies, are not implicated.

In fact, Matthew's attitude toward the synagogues appears to be roughly the same as Mark's and Luke's, except for the special stab at the scribes and Pharisees in 23:34. Matthew 6:2, 5 and 23:6 are

---

56. Recently, e.g., Kee, "The Transformation of the Synagogue after 70 C.E.," 15–24; earlier, e.g., Douglas R. A. Hare, *The Theme of Jewish Persecution of Christians in the Gospel according to St. Matthew,* SNTSMS 6 (Cambridge: Cambridge University Press, 1967), 104–5; review of scholarship on Matthew in relation to Judaism in Graham N. Stanton, "The Origin and Purpose of Matthew's Gospel: Matthean Scholarship from 1945–1980," in *ANRW* 2.25.3, 1911–21.

simple references to local assemblies (without a pronominal gen-
itive "their" or "your"). Matthew's (like Mark's or Josephus's)[57]
use of "their" some or much of the time (but not consistently) may
simply be stylistic or may indicate historical distance from the period of Jesus' ministry in Palestine and/or a sense of distance or
difference from the ethos of Galilean assemblies. Matthew 4:23
and 9:35 are summary passages about Jesus' teaching "in their
assemblies," preaching the kingdom and healing, with no polemical overtone.[58] Matthew's change of "the" to "their" synagogue
in the story of Jesus' rejection at Nazareth in "his own country"
in Matthew 13:53–54 does not appear to sharpen the "distance"
in comparison with Mark's version. Nor does Matthew's similar
change at 12:9 appear to heighten the Markan polemic in the sequence of challenges by the Pharisees in Matthew 12:1–14.[59] Similar
to Mark 13:9 (and perhaps dependent on it), Matthew 10:17 clearly
refers to *synagōgai* as courts, as indicated by the juridical language,
and apparently to courts above the local village level, as suggested
by the parallel to *synhedria, hegemonas,* and *basileis.* The assemblies in Matthew 23:34 are part of a distinctive, contemporizing
Matthean formulation, that represents the "prophets, sages, and
scribes" of the Matthean group as subject to the discipline of the
assembly courts. In none of these passages can some sort of nascent
development of a religious institution or organization of the supposed "Jewish synagogue" be discerned. Nor is there anything in
the only two Matthean passages that mention the *ekklēsia* (i.e.,
its founding and its discipline, respectively, in Matt 16:17–18 and
18:15–18) to suggest that Matthew is setting the church over against
the synagogue(s).[60]

---

57. The same variation occurs in Josephus, who has "their synagogue" in one of
his three reports (*J.W.* 7.43–44).

58. Is Matthew's "their synagogues" in these passages dependent on Mark 1:39, or
is the canonical text of Mark 1:39 secondary and possibly influenced from Matthew?

59. Cf. Anthony J. Saldarini, *Matthew's Christian-Jewish Community* (Chicago:
University of Chicago Press, 1994), 66. Saldarini finds the assemblies in both Matthew 12:9 and 13:54 hostile to Jesus or Matthew's group, but without noting how
similar the tone in Matthew is to Mark in both cases. The hostility comes from other
features of the stories in both cases, including sharpening the polemic by the addition
of Matthew 12:5–7.

60. Both *synagōgē* and *ekklēsia,* as mentioned at the outset above, have their background in Israelite tradition, as illustrated in the use of both to translate *qahal* and
edah in the Septuagint. Saldarini, *Matthew's Christian-Jewish Community,* lays out
a multifaceted argument for Matthew as standing within Israel (including interaction
with the assemblies), but opposed to the Judean rulers and, apparently, contemporary
"Jewish leaders." L. Michael White, "Crisis Management and Boundary Maintenance: The Social Location of the Matthean Community," in *Social History of the*

Recognition both that the Pharisees are separate from the local *synagōgai* in the synoptic Gospels and that there is no conflict between Jesus or his movement and the local assemblies may even open up a new appreciation for the process of social formation and an otherwise obscured concern in the Gospel of Matthew. It is highly likely that the emergent communities of Jesus followers, including the Matthean *ekklēsiai* (assemblies) were informed by the customary patterns of the *synagōgai* (assemblies). Indications also show, on the other hand, that the Matthean community in particular was developing its own scribal leadership: "scribes trained for the kingdom," 13:52, and "sages and scribes (as well as prophets) sent," 23:34. Indeed, key features of the Gospel itself, particularly the formula quotations and schematic discussion of the Torah in the Sermon on the Mount, manifest just such scribal leadership, which has been compared with the scribal activities of the Pharisees or the (proto-) rabbis at "Yavneh." Thus one of the concerns expressed at points in Matthew (esp. the insertion of 23:8–12 after introduction to the woes against the scribes and Pharisees!) may be to maintain the more democratic and egalitarian relations within the community that the Jesus movement(s) inherited from the village and town assemblies over against the emerging specialized leadership of scribes desirous of special recognition and status in the new movement (cf. how Matt 20:20–28 closely follows Mark 10:35–45).

The Gospel of John, finally, like the Gospel of Matthew, has been read recently as involved in a post-70 conflict between "the (Johannine) church" and "the synagogue." Indeed, the dialogue in chapter 9, particularly the explanatory statement in 9:22 that "the *ioudaioi* had already agreed that anyone who confessed Jesus to be the Messiah would be put out of the synagogue" (cf. 12:42; 16:2), has been seen as the key to the situation of the Johannine community and the origins of the Gospel.[61] The argument that the drama of chapter 9 refers to "ordinary members of a local synagogue in John's city,"[62] however, cannot be based on the actual terms used in the Gospel. *Synagōgē* is simply not an important term in John. In the

---

Matthean Community: Cross-Disciplinary Approaches, ed. David L. Balch (Minneapolis: Fortress, 1991), 211–47, esp. 215–17, 238–40, lays out a reading of "their synagogues" and the relation between Matthew's community and contemporary Judaism somewhere between that of Kee and that of Saldarini.

61. In particular see the nuanced argument by J. Louis Martyn, *History and Theology in the Fourth Gospel,* 2d ed. (Nashville: Abingdon, 1979), 37–62. Still accepted and even developed by M. de Boer, *Johannine Perspective on the Death of Jesus* (Kampen: Kok Pharos, 1996).

62. Martyn, *History . . . in the Fourth Gospel,* 40.

only occurrences of *synagōgē* in John, Jesus reminds the high priest that he has always taught openly, that is, publicly "in assembly and (the public area of) the temple" (18:20), and in an awkward transition in the discourse about bread, we are informed that he said these things while "teaching in assembly (i.e., publicly) at Capernaum" (6:59). Moreover, once we are aware that *synagōgē* can be used for the assembly of the whole people, Israel, as well as for a local assembly, then the term unique to John, "to become/be made *aposynagōgos/oi*," must be read as exclusion from the (assembly of the) people, not from "the synagogue." That it is "the *ioudaioi*" or "the Pharisees," that is, Judean officials who held power in Jerusalem (and not as officers of local assemblies), who would effect this exclusion clinches this as the necessary primary-level reading (whatever the symbolic value). Neither Jesus in his teaching and action nor the Johannine community stands in conflict with the synagogue in John.

In summary, both the synoptic Gospels and tannaitic literature understand the "synagogues" or "houses of assembly" as local village and town assemblies. The *synagōgē* or *bet haknesset* was the principal form of local self-governance in which the communal life was expressed and local problems dealt with. People of each locality gathered for communal concerns and activities of all sorts, including religious expressions of community identity, solidarity, and loyalty. Socioeconomic life was guided and social conflicts handled according to the people's customs and cultural traditions. Guidance of community activities and implementation of decisions was done by recognized indigenous leaders. Like the later rabbis (according to their own self-representation), the scribes and Pharisees of synoptic Gospel traditions were apparently not members of these local communities, much less of their assemblies. The Pharisees, like the later rabbis, were apparently attempting to influence local community life from a position outside of the local communities. Finally, not only do the synoptic Gospels portray Jesus as preaching and healing typically in the village and town assemblies of Galilee, but pre-Markan and pre-Q "mission" traditions represent Jesus' envoys as sent to preach and heal while temporarily living in those local communities. Far from opposing the synagogues of the Galilean villages and towns, Jesus is portrayed by the synoptic Gospels as teaching and healing precisely in those synagogues, particularly on the sabbath, when they would have gathered for communal prayers and other village business. Once we recognize that the synagogues in Galilee were the local village assemblies, it should be possible to correct yet another misunderstanding rooted in Christian theological con-struction of Jesus' ministry and "early Christianity" as opposed to "Judaism." As portrayed by the Gospels, Jesus appears to have been engaged in a renewal of Israel based in village and town commu-nities that gathered in synagogues / assemblies on sabbath days. He challenges and is opposed to the Jerusalem rulers and their scribal and Pharisaic representatives, who visit but do not belong to, much less control, the local synagogues.

Part Two

THE DEVELOPMENT OF THE SYNAGOGUE IN THE DIASPORA

CHAPTER FOUR

The Synagogue of Dura-Europos
A Critical Analysis

Joseph Gutmann
Wayne State University, Detroit

Howard Carter's discovery of Tutankhamun's tomb on November 26, 1922, was a dazzling, spectacular find. The incredible riches in the tomb finally confirmed theories and speculations long held by Egyptian archaeologists. Clark Hopkins's discovery of the synagogue of Dura-Europos ten years later, on November 22, 1932, was equally sensational, although the works of art unearthed from what was a provincial Roman military outpost in Syria hardly compare with the costliness and splendor of Tutankhamun's tomb. Far from confirming hypotheses and theories formulated by late antique historians and archaeologists, Hopkins's unique and startling discovery has engendered controversy and has rudely shattered dearly held scholarly conceptions. Many vital areas of scholarship have been affected, and scholars have been busy revising and reconsidering solutions that had been accepted as proven and incontestable. The revolutionary nature of the Dura synagogue discovery has also been treated with benign neglect by scholars unwilling or unable to come to terms with its far-reaching implications. Among the many scholarly questions raised by this amazing find are the following:

1. When and how were the final Dura synagogue murals painted?

2. What are the stylistic and iconographic sources of the Dura synagogue paintings?

3. What were the hypothetical models of the paintings?

Essays mentioned in this article are in J. Gutmann, ed., *The Dura Europos Synagogue: A Re-evaluation (1932–1992)* (Atlanta: Scholars Press, 1992).

4. What were the architectural sources of the Dura synagogue building?

5. What do the individual painted panels in the Dura synagogue depict?

6. What is the meaning and purpose of the entire cycle of paintings?

7. What type of Judaism flourished in Dura-Europos?

8. Is the Dura synagogue with its complex cycle of paintings a local, isolated phenomenon, or does it represent a widespread practice?

9. Why was the so-called Second Commandment ignored at Dura?

10. Do the Dura synagogue murals serve as evidence for the Jewish origins of Christian art?

1. When and how were the final Dura synagogue murals painted? Most scholars have now accepted the date Carl Kraeling proposed for the rebuilt synagogue, 244/45 c.e., although several publications mistakenly give other dates.[1]

Whether a Sassanian attack on Dura occurred in 253/54 has been debated, but not convincingly resolved in several articles. Scholars base some of their conclusions on the dipinti and graffiti of Iranian writers in the Dura synagogue, as well as on coin hoards and a Sassanian mural.[2]

The Middle Persian dipinti and graffiti in the Dura synagogue recording visitations and viewings by Iranians, who may have been Jews, appear to have little relevance for substantiating a Sassanian occupation in 253/54.[3] The Dura coin hoards, according to David

1. The date 243/44 given in Clark Hopkins's posthumous writings on the excavations at Dura should be corrected. Cf. C. Hopkins, _The Discovery of Dura-Europos,_ ed. B. Goldman (New Haven and London, 1979), 140, 142. The date 245/46 given by J. Goldstein, "The Central Composition of the West Wall of the Synagogue of Dura-Europos," _Journal of the Ancient Near Eastern Society_ 16/17 (1984–85): 100, should also be rectified.

2. Cf. B. Goldman, A. M. G. Little, "The Beginning of Sassanian Painting and Dura-Europos," _Iranica Antiqua_ 15 (1981): 289–98. R. Altheim-Stiehl, "Die Zeitangaben der mittelpersischen Dipinti in der einstigen Synagoge zu Dura-Europos," _Boreas_ 5 (1982): 152–59.

3. D. McDonald, "Dating the Fall of Dura-Europos," _Historia_ 35 (1986): 63. On pp. 61–63 McDonald discusses whether these Persian visitors were Iranian ambassadors, inspectors, artists, scribes in the service of the Persian army, and/or Jews or Jewish sympathizers.

Macdonald, "offer no genuine corroboration of the supposed capture of [Dura in] 253," and the date of the Sassanian mural is far from certain.[4]

The date of the final demise of Dura and its synagogue has been placed in 256 C.E. Although this dating is widely accepted, recent scholarship contends that 257 may be the more likely date for the capture of Dura by the Sassanians.[5]

Many publications continue to label the Dura synagogue paintings "frescoes."[6] However, as the late Clark Hopkins has pointed out in the introductory essay to *The Dura Europos Synagogue,* "The Excavations of the Dura Synagogue Paintings," they are not frescoes painted on wet plaster: "rather, the paint is powdery tempera which was brushed onto dry plaster."[7]

2. What are the stylistic and iconographic sources of the Dura synagogue paintings? Richard Brilliant's "Painting at Dura Europos and Roman Art" is a short synopsis of a promised book on the stylistic and iconographic aspects of the Dura paintings. Unfortunately, the book has been abandoned. While a detailed stylistic and iconographic study of the Dura synagogue paintings is a scholarly desideratum, some progress has been made in the last fifteen years. Scholars still debate whether the unique stylistic features found in the Dura synagogue paintings should be attributed to Roman provincial art — a pejorative term usually denoting an inferior art that naively and crudely copied the art emanating from the Roman imperial capital — or whether it was a development of Parthian art. Although some scholars glibly speak of Parthian art, we actually know little about art in Iran during the Parthian period, somewhat more about that in outer Iran, and almost nothing about Parthian painting.

The attempt of several studies to link Dura synagogue art to Western Asian (so-called Near Eastern) sources is not convincing. Examples chosen for comparison, such as the relief of the seventh century B.C.E. Assyrian King Ashurbanipal reclining on a high couch as he drinks from a bowl, or the tenth-century B.C.E. (?) sarcophagus showing King Ahiram of Byblos (in Phoenicia) banqueting,

---

4. Ibid., 53, 55.

5. Ibid., 63–68.

6. Cf. K. Weitzmann and H. L. Kessler, *The Frescoes of the Dura Synagogue and Christian Art* (Washington, D.C., 1990).

7. J. Goldstein, "Central Composition," 101 and pp. 15, 17 of Hopkins's essay in *The Dura Europos Synagogue: A Re-evaluation (1932–1992),* ed. J. Gutmann (Atlanta: Scholars Press, 1992).

are not only removed in time from the Dura synagogue by over a thousand years, but reveal no stylistic and hardly any significant iconographic parallels. One need only compare the many figures reclining on couches and the triumph of Mordecai panel in the Dura synagogue with the contemporary Palmyrene depictions to realize that the artistic sources of the Dura synagogue are close at hand.[8]

Recent research has demonstrated that the hieratic, frontal, rigid, impersonal, two-dimensional figure with large staring eyes, so common in the Dura synagogue paintings, represents an artistic mode of presentation that began to develop in first-century C.E. Syria. It undoubtedly grew out of an artistic syncretism of such diverse elements as the Hellenistic-Roman, Parthian-Iranian, and native Arab-Syrian. This novel compositional technique demanded a spiritual confrontation and interaction of the figures on the synagogue wall with the Jewish worshiper viewing them. Spiritual-theological, sociocultural, aesthetic, and political aspirations in the Syrian region were probably responsible for these new artistic practices.[9] Whether the art of such Western Asian cities as Dura and Palmyra directly inspired similar artistic renditions in later Roman and Christian art of western Europe or whether both cultures adopted it in response to similar sociocultural, spiritual-theological, propagandistic-political, and aesthetic needs remain to be fully examined.[10]

Dura was primarily a military headquarters on the Parthian/Roman frontier, where soldiers, merchants, and others with diverse and colorful costumes from the East and the West were seen commingling in the streets. These costume differences are reflected in the Dura synagogue paintings. Bernard Goldman in his "The Dura Costumes and Persian Art" examined why and when the tailored costume of Western Asia and the robe of the Greco-Roman world were worn in the Dura synagogue paintings. His fine analysis of

---

8. M. A. R. Colledge, *The Art of Palmyra* (London, 1976), figs. 61, 62, 69, 100, 102, 107, 109, and H. J. W. Drijvers, *The Religion of Palmyra* (Leiden, 1976), plates LXIX, LI. Cf. Goldstein, "Central Composition," 131–41. R. D. Barnett, "Ashurbanipal's Feast," *Eretz Israel* 18 (1985), 1*-6*; Cf. also J. Gutmann, "Early Synagogue and Jewish Catacomb Art and Its Relation to Christian Art," in *Sacred Images: Studies in Jewish Art from Antiquity to the Middle Ages,* ed. J. Gutmann (Northampton, 1989), 7:1332.

9. B. Goldman, "A Dura-Europos Dipinto and Syrian Frontality," *Oriens Antiquus* 24 (1985): 279–300, and J. Gutmann, "The Dura Synagogue Paintings: The State of Research," in *The Synagogue in Late Antiquity,* ed. L. I. Levine (Philadelphia, 1987), 64. Cf. also H. J. W. Drijvers, "The Syrian Cult Relief," *Visible Religion* 7 (1990): 69–82.

10. W. Tronzo, *The Via Latina Catacomb: Imitation and Discontinuity in Fourth-Century Painting* (University Park and London, 1986), 42–45.

dress should be followed up by such iconographic studies as the military uniforms worn, the type of animals employed, and the furnishings depicted.[11]

3. What were the hypothetical models of the paintings? Mary Lee Thompson's suggestion in "Hypothetical Models of the Dura Paintings" that "pattern books, panel painting and cartoons must have been standard equipment of ancient artists" — to inspire such programs as that of the Dura synagogue — has won additional support in studies by such scholars as Malcolm Colledge, Katherine Dunbabin, Thomas Stevenson, Harald Mielsch, Friedrich Deichmann, Ernst Kitzinger, and William Tronzo, among others.[12] These scholars are convinced that pictorial guides — pattern, model, or motif books — served as transmitters of similar iconographic and formal elements found in various media and workshops in the diverse and widely scattered Roman imperial provincial cities.

4. What were the architectural sources of the Dura synagogue building? Andrew Seager discusses the architectural sources of the Dura synagogue building in "The Architecture of the Dura and Sardis synagogues." Evaluating the Dura synagogue building complex in light of new synagogal excavations and scholarly studies should now augment his study.[13]

5. What do the individual painted panels in the Dura synagogue depict? Following Carl Kraeling's numbering, I have summarized

11. B. Goldman, "Greco-Roman Dress in Syro-Mesopotamia," in *The World of Roman Costume*, ed. J. Sebesta and L. Bonfante (Madison, 1994), 67–74.

12. Tronzo, *Via Latina Catacomb*, 2, n. 6, 31. Gutmann, "Dura Synagogue Paintings," 68, and M. L. Heuser, review of B. Brenk, *Die frühchristlichen Mosaiken in S. Maria Maggiore zo Rom*, in *The Art Bulletin* 61 (1979): 476. J. Gutmann, "Revisiting the 'Binding of Isaac' Mosaic in the Beth-Alpha Synagogue, *Bulletin of the Asia Institute* 6 (1992): 85, n. 34.

13. Cf. now A. Seager, "The Recent Historiography of Ancient Synagogue Architecture," in R. Hachlili, ed., *Ancient Synagogues in Israel Third–Seventh Century C.E.*, BAR International Series 499 (Oxford, 1989), 85–91. The following corrections should be made in Seager's "Architecture of the Dura and Sardis Synagogues" article: The building at Stobi referred to on p. 94 is now understood to be a church (called the Central Basilica) rather than a synagogue. Evidence of two superimposed synagogues was found in strata below the church, but these are not known to have had frontal forecourts. Page 108, n. 35, line 19 should read: *Tarbiz*, 32. Cf. F. Hüttenmeister and G. Reeg, *Die antiken Synagogen in Israel*, 2 vols. (Wiesbaden, 1977); M. J. C. Chiat, *Handbook of Synagogue Architecture* (Chico, Calif., 1982); J. Gutmann, ed., *The Synagogue: Studies in Origins, Archaeology and Architecture* (New York, 1975); J. Gutmann, ed., *Ancient Synagogues: The State of Research* (Chico, Calif., 1981); L. I. Levine, ed., *The Synagogue in Late Antiquity* (Philadelphia, 1987); A. Kasher et al., *Synagogues in Antiquity* (Jerusalem, 1987) [Hebrew with English summaries]; R. Hachlili, *Ancient Jewish Art and Archaeology in the Land of Israel* (Leiden, 1988); A. Seager et al., *The Sardis Synagogue and Its Setting* (forthcoming).

what the individual scenes in the Dura synagogue portray. Several new interpretations and identifications should be added to this list.[14]

Lower Central Panel: David as Orpheus, the messianic king (Goldstein)

Upper Central Panel: King David, the Messiah, flanked by Moses and Elijah (Goldstein); David, King over all Israel, flanked by Samuel and Nathan (Weitzmann)

Wing Panel III: Moses (Goldstein), Gamaliel ha-Zaken (Dequeker), Jeremiah (Kessler)

Wing Panel IV: Moses (Goldstein), Judah ha-Nasi (Dequeker), Isaiah (Kessler)[15]

WC 3: Samuel anointing David before the six brothers (Gutmann)[16]

WC 4: Nude princess rescues Moses (Gutmann)[17]

WB 1: Miriam's Well (Gutmann)[18]

WA 3: Armed Israelites and Twelve Paths at the Crossing of the Red Sea (Gutmann)[19]

SC 1: Ahab and Elijah (Weitzmann)

---

14. Cf. J. Gutmann, "Early Synagogue and Jewish Catacomb Art," 7:1315–22, and C. Kraeling, *The Synagogue. Excavations at Dura Europos,* Final Report viii.1 (New York, 1979; augmented edition).

15. Cf. Goldstein, "Central Composition," 113–31; L. Dequeker, "Le Zodiaque de la Synagogue de Beth Alpha et le Midrash," *Bijdragen, tijdschrift voor filosofie en theologie* 47 (1986): 26, claims that Judah ha-Nasi is proclaiming the Oral Law and Gamaliel is announcing the liturgical calendar. H. L. Kessler, "Prophetic Portraits in the Dura Synagogue," *JAC* 30 (1987): 129–33.

16. The six brothers present at the anointing appear to be in consonance with a Midrash preserved by Christian tradition, J. Gutmann, "The Illustrated Midrash in the Dura Synagogue Paintings: A New Dimension for the Study of Judaism," in Gutmann, *Sacred Images,* 8:96–98.

17. J. Gutmann, "Josephus' *Jewish Antiquities* in Twelfth-Century Art: Renovatio or Creatio?" in Gutmann, *Sacred Images,* 9:434–38. Idem, "Illustrated Midrash," 7:93–94.

18. The Koran and Byzantine traditions best explain the details of this aggadic story. Gutmann, "Illustrated Midrash," viii, 98–100. Although Kraeling, *The Synagogue,* 120, noted that the Dura artist is following the biblical description (Numbers 2) of dividing the Israelite tribes into four groups of three, he failed to note that the twelve streams of water flowing from the rock also divide into four groups of three. Cf. H. P. Staehli, *Antike Synagogenkunst* (Stuttgart, 1988), 81.

19. These legendary traditions are found in Christian art and literature. Gutmann, "Illustrated Midrash," viii, 102–4.

SC 3: Hiel hides in the altar of the Baal prophets (Gutmann)[20]

SB 1: David's transport of the Ark to Jerusalem (Weitzmann)

NC 1: Mattathias killing the apostate Jew (Gutmann, Weitzmann)[21]

The Torah shrine and the panels above it have been the subject of several recent discussions. This Torah shrine with its depiction of Abraham's sacrifice of Isaac is interpreted by Archer St. Clair as an "evocation of the Feast of Tabernacles.... [T]he feast is presented not only as it will be celebrated in the future, but as it is celebrated in the past as well, when at the Sacrifice of Isaac, Abraham's obedience resulted in the future deliverance of Israel."[22] The conclusion presented is not convincing, because it is not viewed in the context of the entire Dura synagogue program and because the author uses citations from the Bible, the Book of Jubilees, and late rabbinic sources without determining whether these sources were relevant to and/or known to contemporary Dura Jews. The substitution of the hand of God for the biblical angel in Abraham's Sacrifice of Isaac depiction and the ram placidly standing next to a tree, instead of being entangled in the biblical thicket, have also been considered in several current studies.[23]

The methodological problem outlined in the St. Clair study is also found in an article by Herbert Kessler. He quotes biblical and apocryphal statements to support a theory that in Wing Panel III–IV it is Isaiah and Jeremiah who are depicted. This interpretation is problematic since the Durene Jews, as I have indicated, did not read the Bible literally, but saw it filtered through the exegetical

---

20. The Church Father Ephraem also records this legend. Gutmann, "Illustrated Midrash," viii, 95–96.

21. A third-century Antioch synagogue was built upon the supposed remains of the "Maccabean" martyrs, indicating reverence for these heroes by Syrian Jewry; cf. E. Bickerman, "Les Maccabees de Malalas," *Studies in Jewish and Christian History* 2 (Leiden, 1980), 200–209.

22. A. St. Clair, "The Torah Shrine at Dura-Europos: A Re-evaluation," *JAC* 29 (1988): 109–17.

23. J. Gutmann, "The Sacrifice of Isaac: Variations on a Theme in Early Jewish and Christian Art," in Gutmann, *Sacred Images,* 13:115–22. Idem, "The Sacrifice of Isaac in Medieval Jewish Art," *Artibus et Historiae* 16 (1987): 67, 69. See corrections to the above articles in Gutmann, "Revisiting the 'Binding of Isaac' Mosaic in the Beth-Alpha Synagogue," 83, n. 6. For a detailed analysis of the Torah niche and its relation to similar depictions in Greco-Roman, Jewish, and Christian art, cf. F. Rickert, *Studien zum Ashburnham Pentateuch* (Bonn, 1986), 32–93, esp. 51–52. Idem, "Review of E. Revel-Neher, *L'art juif et chretiénne du second au dixième siècles,*" in *JAC* 29 (1986): 218–22.

eyes of the Midrashim and the Targumim. Any identification of these prophetic figures must reflect how biblical personages were understood and how they functioned in contemporary third-century Jewish thought and literature.[24] Several scholars have commented that, in Jacob's blessing of Joseph's sons in the Lower Central Panel, Jacob cannot be deemed to cross his hands since the artists would have wished to avoid the obvious christological implication. Dieter Korol challenges this reconstruction and suggests that Jacob may indeed be crossing his hands when blessing Joseph's sons.[25]

David Goldstein in his detailed study of the entire central composition on the west wall makes many valid observations and shows that Henri Stern's thesis that Christians borrowed from Jews the figure of Orpheus as the royal King David, however attractive, is unproven.[26] Even so, the author's conclusions, that Christians may have "Christianized iconographic patterns that were originally Jewish," and that there are "too many parallels between the apses [of Byzantine churches] and the tradition exemplified in the synagogue [of Dura] for the resemblance to be coincidental" are neither proven nor convincing.[27] In the first place, there is a three-hundred-year difference between the Justinianic Byzantine monuments and the Dura synagogue. In the second place, the programs of the Byzantine mosaics emanate from the imperial Byzantine capital, while the Dura program comes from a Western Asian provincial desert caravan outpost. Third, the biblical figures in the Byzantine churches function within a Christian liturgical-theological context aimed to give meaning to the "liturgy of the Eucharist." Within this context the Christian altar is the focal point where the divine mystery of Christ is unveiled and revealed. In the Dura synagogue the biblical figures function within a Jewish liturgical-theological context. Here the focal point is the Torah ark housing the divine mystery of Torah, whose wisdom is also unveiled and revealed to the congregation. In both programs we simply have the visual accompaniment of the liturgical movements and audial prayers uttered and sung below.[28]

---

24. Kessler," Prophetic Portraits," 129–33. *Mekhilta de Rabbi Ishmael,* Tractate *Wa-Yassa'* 6, 51b, an early tannaitic source for instance, mentions that Jeremiah exhorted his contemporaries to busy themselves with the study of Torah.

25. D. Korol, *Die frühchristlichen Wandmalereien aus dem Grabbauten in Cimitile/Nola* (Münster, 1987), 100–129.

26. Goldstein, "Central Composition," 113–18.

27. Ibid., 130–31.

28. Goldstein, "Central Composition," 118–31. The author completely overlooks the basic work by F. W. Deichmann, *Ravenna. Hauptstadt des spätantiken Abendlandes* (Wiesbaden, 1969–76) 3 vols., on Justinian's artistic programs.

Although some of the prophetic and other figures used by both religions may have some similarities in iconography and compositional arrangement, their meaning and function are entirely different and do not necessarily point to borrowing by Christians from Jews. The central section of the Dura synagogue is in any case badly damaged, making any interpretation difficult. In addition, no one has provided a satisfactory explanation why the paintings in the central panels have been changed three times.

6. What is the meaning and purpose of the entire cycle of paintings? Until a similar synagogue is unearthed, we will not be able to decipher the entire program of the Dura synagogue, as only about sixty percent of the paintings have survived. Any interpretation of the meaning and purpose of the cycle of paintings, as indicated in my essay "Programmatic Painting in the Dura Synagogue," must begin with trying to recover the now lost active liturgical functions — the rites, ceremonial movements, and prayers — that the Dura synagogue building and its art were intended to shelter.[29] The apparently discontinuous series of pictures in the Dura synagogue appear organized around a set of ceremonies, liturgical prayers and midrashic ideas, dependent on or bound to specific sacred texts and a congregation, a community praying and performing religious rites within that sacred space. The paintings, moreover, are linked to the life and thought of the congregation, and any interpretation must reflect this reality. One cannot arbitrarily force or read some proposed theory into the paintings, as has been done by several of their interpreters.[30] These paintings must be understood as theological advertisements or religious propaganda perhaps intended to win converts. They also served as visual accompaniments to the ongoing audial prayers recited and sung, and to the ceremonies carried out by the congregation below. They had messianic implications in that they united the worshipers with the pious heroes of a glorious biblical past. The congregants would again encounter these heroic biblical figures in the promised messianic future. In fact, the biblical stories, torn from their biblical moorings, simply serve here as prooftexts of new theological ideas, spiritual lessons, moral teachings, and ethical conduct. These painted stories follow a mode of presentation found in written Palestinian midrashic works and the Talmud, where verses and stories drawn from different books of

---

29. Cf. also my essays, "Early Synagogue and Jewish Catacomb Art," 7:1324–28, and "Dura-Europos Synagogue Paintings," 62–63. Page 141, line 6, of my essay should read: *Sura* 7.160.

30. Cf. Gutmann, "Early Synagogue and Jewish Catacomb Art," 7:1322–24.

the Bible, often with aggadic elaborations, are now used to make the point of an identical lesson and to prove the essential unity and timelessness of the Torah, God's entire revelation to Israel.

In the second band of the Dura paintings, the largest of the three figurative bands, the substitution of the biblical ark-box for the prominent yellow Torah ark-chest is, I believe, done purposely. All the panels in the second band reveal the long history of the Ark — how it sustained Israel in the desert, performed miracles in the land of the Philistines and finally came to rest in the synagogal Torah shrine, where it continued to assure the faithful that they would be granted the salvation of the soul and the bodily resurrection they craved. This latter fact is made amply clear by a graffito in the Dura synagogue, "Praise to God, praise! For life, life eternal he gives (. . . ?)," and by the prayer on the Dura synagogue ceiling tile, "Their reward, all whatever . . . that the world which is to come . . . assured to them."[31]

Although following no narrative sequential order, the scenes in the second and largest band are bound together, not by the Bible, but by the words of a contemporary Palestinian hymn that may have been sung during an actual liturgical procession when the Torah ark-chest, kept outside the synagogue proper, was brought in for synagogal worship. Hence the congregation in a liturgical procession recounted and relived through a song what is depicted in the second band of the Dura synagogue wall. This second band no doubt affirmed the continued efficacy of Torah (symbolized by the Torah ark-chest) for all believers and hence guaranteed salvation and resurrection in the messianic future. The four figures flanking the central panels on the west wall are also likely to have had specific meanings. The two top figures, identified as Moses, may represent the revelation and giving of Torah — the Written and the Oral Law. The two bottom biblical figures are difficult to interpret; they may embody the two basic components of synagogal worship: recitations of prayer and reading of Scripture (Torah). They may be placed next to the two sanctuaries — the ancient Wilderness Tabernacle and the Jerusalem Temple — to underscore that prayers are a fitting substitute for sacrifices and that reading Torah in the synagogue is equal to performing cultic Temple rites.[32]

---

31. Kraeling, *Synagogue,* 315, 264, and L. H. Kant, "Jewish Inscriptions in Greek and Latin," in *ANRW,* ed. H. Temporini and W. Haase, 20.2 (Berlin, 1987), 916–19. The wealthy Jewish patrons probably viewed the synagogue not only as a source of divine salvation, but also as a means of worldly recognition by the community.

32. Gutmann, "Early Synagogue and Catacomb Art," 7:1326–28.

7. What type of Judaism flourished in Dura-Europos?

A. We have no evidence of Jewish literature from such Syrian cities as Dura, and few literary citations alluding to these communities from the Palestinian / Babylonian Talmuds or from patristic literature. We are almost totally dependent on archaeological and epigraphical evidence for a reconstruction of the Judaism that may have flourished at Dura and in neighboring communities. We find no mention of Philo, or any reference to Talmudic or Midrashic writers, or the existence of any yeshivot in these areas. We do not even know the extent to which the Palestinian patriarch or other leaders exercised authority, exacted taxes, or controlled the Diaspora Jewish communities.[33]

B. We can be fairly certain that the popular Philonic "mystic Hellenistic" Judaism that Erwin R. Goodenough imposed on or read into the Dura synagogue paintings would have been totally incomprehensible to the small congregation of probably unsophisticated and unintellectual Jewish merchants and other Jewish inhabitants residing at Dura. The late Michael Avi-Yonah in his study of "Goodenough's Evaluation of the Dura Paintings: a Critique" and Morton Smith in his excellent article have made this quite clear.[34]

C. The artificial distinction once made between Hellenistic and Rabbinic Judaism (especially Palestinian Judaism) by nineteenth- and twentieth-century scholarship offers no solution for interpreting the Judaism at Dura-Europos, as Jacob Neusner's essay, "Judaism at Dura-Europos" demonstrates.[35] This distinction is gradually being abandoned in light of the Dura and other archeological and epigraphical discoveries, as well as the analysis of literary and linguistic evidence through newer historical methodologies. Such terms as "normative" and "orthodox" to characterize Judaism are also gradually being eliminated. These terms are value judgments imposed by later Jewish generations to intimate (or to claim) that Judaism was always essentially a monolithic, non-changing entity. It is now realized that all the Jews of Greco-Roman antiquity, no matter whether they spoke Aramaic or Greek, were subject to the process of Hellenization, although each Jewish community may have responded differently to the Hellenistic environment, which was also not uni-

---

33. Cf. L. H. Feldman, "Proselytes and 'Sympathizers' in the Light of the New Inscriptions from Aphrodisias," *Revue des études juives* 148 (1989): 265–305.

34. M. Smith, "Goodenough's *Jewish Symbols* in Retrospect," in *The Synagogue,* ed. Gutmann, 194–209, and xxvi, n.19.

35. J. Neusner, "Judaism at Dura-Europos," in *History of Religion: An International Journal for Comparative Historical Studies* 4, no. 1 (1964): 81–102.

form throughout the region. It would be better to speak of major
and minor Jewish movements — multiform and diverse Judaisms —
that, though they may have shared certain fundamental concepts
of God and Torah, differed often radically not only in their interpretation of these concepts, but in liturgy, customs, practices and
theological emphases.[36]

D. At this juncture, we cannot determine the kind of Judaism
that may have existed in third-century Dura — we cannot even
delineate with any degree of assurance the Jewish religious movements that were at home in third-century Palestine. We can say that
the concern with salvation, resurrection, the Messiah and the em-
ployment of painted Midrashim bespeak a Judaism that appears to
bear some kinship to the Judaisms described in Palestinian rabbinic
literature.

The sacred texts that supply most of the visual materials at Dura
are not biblical narratives, but contemporary liturgy, Targumim and
midrashic works. The Judaism found on the walls of the Dura synagogue was one that dispensed with historical reality and temporal
accident. Time was God-directed: it was considered cyclical and
repetitive. Within this time schema, time-future was simply a return
to time-past (to the glorious restoration of the biblical Solomonic
Temple and the resurrection of the righteous Jews in the Land of
Israel): the new was the old revisited. Though rooted in history,
time-future-past-and-present, as envisioned by the rabbis, was non-
historical. Time-present was insignificant — a rupture with a divine
past, a period of limbo, of suffering, of punishment for past and current sins — yet with the hope that moral reconstitution and spiritual
regeneration and/or the divine forgiveness of sins with the miracu-
lous coming of the Messiah, would usher in time-future and bring
an end to the cycle. Within this timeless schema, biblical personages
like David, Moses, and Elijah, though historically centuries apart,
were united through the exegetical interpretations of the Midrash
and the liturgy (as we see in the Dura paintings) and could converse
with its worshipers (in time-present) and allow them to experience
and be united with their Jewish past, which they would relive in the
glorious messianic future.[37]

8. Is the Dura synagogue with its complex cycle of paintings a
local, isolated phenomenon, or does it represent a widespread prac-

---

36. Gutmann, "Dura-Europos Synagogue Paintings," 62.

37. Cf. L. A. Hoffman, *Beyond the Text: A Holistic Approach to Liturgy* (Bloom-
ington, 1987), 84–113 and J. Yahalom, *Poetic Language in the Early Piyyut of the
Land of Israel* (Jerusalem, 1985), 33–36 [in Hebrew].

tice? Many scholars working on the Dura paintings have, on the basis of the poor reproductions in books, given them crude and unsophisticated labels. Actual examination of the murals by researchers, however, has revealed a surprising professional quality in their execution. Notwithstanding the quality of its paintings, its iconographic program is far too complex to have been developed in that small Jewish community. The elaborate cycle of paintings may stem from a synagogue in a nearby but larger, more prosperous, and prominent Jewish center such as Palmyra, Nisibis, or Edessa. Dura must have been part of a widespread Jewish artistic tradition whose remains are largely unknown. Only a future archaeological discovery of another painted synagogue in a major Jewish center will resolve this perplexing issue.[38]

9. Why was the so-called Second Commandment ignored at Dura? Jewish and non-Jewish scholars largely ignored Jewish art up to very recent times on the grounds that Jews had no talent or capacity for the visual arts. Following either dogmatic and fundamental Jewish interpretations or essentially Hegelian metaphysical racial ideas, these scholars went so far as to conclude that Jews had an inherent congenital incapacity for the visual arts — their talents were thought to lie in the domain of the audial and not the visual. Even so distinguished a Jewish historian as Heinrich Graetz affirmed that "paganism see its god, Judaism hears him." It is still not unusual to read that the strict biblical prohibition was formulated because the God of the Hebrews was an implacable enemy of images. Yet we need only look at the Bible itself to realize that within the Book of Exodus, the clear mandate "You shall not make yourself a sculptured image or any likeness" (Exodus 20:4–5) is juxtaposed eleven chapters later with the story of Bezalel, who "was endowed with a divine spirit of skill, ability, and knowledge in every kind of craft" (Exodus 31:1–3) to fashion the very images condemned in the earlier section of Exodus. In spite of the above, writers still claim that, in most periods of history, the Second Commandment hampered Jewish artistic expression, while in other periods Jews simply ignored this prohibition. What was operative among Jews, according to some scholars, was either attraction or revulsion towards the visual arts.

---

38. Gutmann, "Dura-Europos Synagogue Paintings," 61–62, 64–65. B. Goldman, "The Iranian Elements in the Dura Synagogue," *Irano-Judaica Third International Conference,* Jerusalem, 1994 [in press]. A. J. Wharton, *Refiguring the Post-Classical City* (Cambridge, 1995), 42.

Current studies have demonstrated that one cannot speak of
one Second Commandment — an unchanging concept that never
transcended its original biblical context. Thus, in the course of
Jewish history, multiple versions of the Second Commandment appeared. The Jewish attitude to art reflects not so much inherent
forces of revulsion or attraction, of observance or disobedience to
a static, biblical divine command; instead it is largely conditioned
by a dynamic interaction with the dominant official attitude towards art expressed in the non-Jewish Greco-Roman and other
societies, and by the official treatment accorded Jews in these places
of residence. Thus we find that first-century Palestinian Jewry is
known to have objected violently to the placement of a statue of
the hated Roman emperor Caligula in the Jerusalem Temple (Josephus, *Antiquities* 18.8.2 [264]); the biblical Second Commandment
was cited to undergird the political affront and grievance. Third-
century Babylonian Jewry, on the contrary, offered no objection
to the placement of a royal statue in the important synagogue of
Nehardea (Babylonian Talmud, *Rosh ha-Shanah* 24b and *Avodah
Zarah* 43b). Again, we find no figural art in first-century Roman
Palestine, but in the third century — the very century of the Dura
paintings — the Palestinian Rabbi Jochanan records that "they began to paint pictures on walls [of synagogues (?)] and he did not
hinder them" (Palestinian Talmud, *Avodah Zarah* 3, 3, 42d). Thus,
each Jewish involvement with new societies or changing conditions
in old societies demanded a reevaluation and reinterpretation of
the original biblical prohibition.[39]

10. Do the Dura synagogue murals serve as evidence for the Jewish origins of Christian art? Scholars supporting a hypothesis that
the elaborate cycle of paintings at the Dura synagogue was one of
the sources for later biblical scenes in Christian and Jewish art base
their contention on a putative existence of earlier illustrated Jewish
manuscripts stemming from such large Hellenistic Jewish centers as
Alexandria, the iconographic parallels between the Dura synagogue
paintings and later Christian and Jewish art, and the appearance of
Jewish legends in later Christian, Islamic, and Jewish art.

---

39. Cf. J. Gutmann, "The 'Second Commandment' and the Image in Judaism,"
in *No Graven Images: Studies in Art and the Hebrew Bible,* ed. J. Gutmann (New
York, 1971), xiii–xxx and 1–14. Idem, "Deuteronomy: Religious Reformation or
Iconoclastic Revolution?" in *The Image and the Word: Confrontations in Judaism,
Christianity and Islam,* ed. J. Gutmann (Missoula, Mont., 1977), 5–25. J. M. Baum-
garten, "Art in the Synagogue: Some Talmudic Views," in *The Synagogue,* ed.
J. Gutmann, xii, 79–89.

A. The existence of illustrated Jewish Septuagint manuscripts in antiquity is an *argumentum ex silentio* that has little substantive evidence to support it. The earliest extant illustrated narrative biblical Christian manuscripts or illustrated narrative manuscript cycles based on Greco-Roman mythology date only from around the fifth century C.E.; illustrated Jewish manuscripts have survived only from the tenth century C.E. No illustrated literary manuscripts are mentioned in surviving ancient sources. The few Greco-Roman manuscript fragments that have come down to us reveal in the main sketches that they served a didactic function in ancient mathematical and natural science books. No continuous classical literary cycle of painted figural illustrations in manuscript scrolls is known from Greco-Roman antiquity. Certainly precious manuscripts would not customarily have been exposed to dirty workshops, and a provincial atelier at Dura would not very likely have had access to a library of biblical books ranging from Genesis to Maccabees.

The Dura synagogue paintings do not reflect the Alexandrian style that would have been in the assumed illustrated Jewish Septuagint scrolls. The Hellenistic-Roman attitude toward books differed radically from what typified the later Judeo-Christian world. No canonical book like the Bible secured recognition as an authoritative moral guide in the Hellenistic or Roman cultures. No one book in the Greco-Roman world was considered so holy or was so celebrated as the Gospels or the Bible. The Greco-Roman book was not holy in itself; it was simply a utilitarian object, a vehicle of information, and not a conveyor of God's sacred words. Depictions from Hellenistic-Roman societies never show the gods — Zeus-Jupiter, for instance — with a sacred book in their hands, though such a scene is common enough in depictions of Jesus, the evangelists and the prophetic figures in Christian art. Authors, philosophers, and pedagogues are usually depicted holding or reading scroll texts; they are never transcribing or writing holy words, as is the case in the Judeo-Christian world. The very transmission of the written sacred word is assigned to God at Mount Sinai in Judeo-Christian traditions, and the recording of God's holy words, considered an act of great religious merit, was assigned to people of high status such as priests, scholar-scribes, or monks. In the Hellenistic-Roman civilization, the inferior task of reading and writing was often assigned to slaves.

In the Roman world, fresco painting, not illustrated manuscripts, served as the preferred mode of artistic expression. Rhetoric was regarded as the highest form of communication in the Greco-

Roman world, while writing and reading were an inferior mode
of communication. As the manuscript had no sacred value, it seems
improbable that the Romans would have gone to the expense of
commissioning costly illuminated manuscripts. All of these factors argue against the existence of Jewish or non-Jewish illustrated
manuscripts in Greco-Roman antiquity.[40]

B. It is also highly doubtful that convincing iconographic parallels
can be drawn between the scenes found in the Dura synagogue and
those in later Christian and Jewish art. The iconographic comparisons made by scholars are of such a superficial and general character
that no direct and indisputable connections can be established. The
compositional layout, the stances, the costumes, and the expressions
of the figures used for examination are often quite different from
the Dura paintings, thus ruling out a concrete and definite association. Furthermore, the Dura synagogue paintings could hardly have
influenced later Christian and Jewish art, as they were buried after a
brief existence of maybe a dozen years, were located in a provincial
back country, and were probably themselves derivative.[41]

C. We now generally accept that aggadic elaborations, originally
drawn from such works as the Targums and Midrash, exist in illustrated Christian manuscripts. The appearance of these Jewish legends — extrabiblical stories — in later Christian, Jewish, and Muslim
art does not automatically underwrite the existence of illustrated, but
lost, Jewish manuscripts. Jewish legends adapted by Christians and
Muslims are found extensively in their writings, so the appearance of
a Jewish legend in Christian and Muslim art does not warrant posit-
ing a direct Jewish inspiration that would at the same time support
the existence of lost ancient illustrated Jewish manuscripts.[42]

On the whole, then, the incredible discovery of the synagogue
of Dura-Europos has widened our scholarly horizons: it has posed
many questions, some of which have been answered, while others
await solution.[43]

40. Gutmann, "Dura-Europos Synagogue Paintings," 66–69.

41. Weitzmann and Kessler, *The Frescoes of Dura Synagogue and Christian Art*
should be read in light of the evidence presented in J. Gutmann, "The Dura Synagogue Paintings and their Influence on Later Christian and Jewish Art," *Artibus et
Historiae* 17 (1988): 25–29, my review of the Weitzmann-Kessler book in *Speculum*
67 (1992): 502–4, and B. Goldman, *Bulletin of the Asia Institute* 6 (1992): 187–92.

42. Cf. J. Gutmann, "Illustrated Midrash," viii, 92–104. Idem, "The Testing of
Moses: A Comparative Study in Christian, Muslim and Jewish Art," in Gutmann,
Sacred Images, 14:107–17. J. Gutmann, "On Biblical Legends in Medieval Art,"
Artibus et Historiae 38 (1998): 137–42.

43. I am greatly indebted to Profs. Stanley F. Chyet and Bernard M. Goldman for
reading this essay and offering suggestions for its improvement.

CHAPTER FIVE

Were Pharisees and Rabbis the Leaders of Communal Prayer and Torah Study in Antiquity?

The Evidence of the New Testament, Josephus, and the Early Church Fathers

Shaye J. D. Cohen

Brown University, Providence, Rhode Island

Were the Pharisees before 70 C.E. and the rabbis after 70 C.E. the leaders of Jewish communal prayer and Torah study? Since "the synagogue" was home to Jewish communal prayer and Torah study, the question can also be formulated as follows: Were the Pharisees before 70 C.E. and the rabbis after 70 C.E. the leaders of the synagogue? Aside from a few skeptics, until recently most scholars had no doubt, and many scholars still have no doubt, that the Pharisees and their rabbinic continuators were in charge of synagogues,[1] but

This is a revised version of an essay that originally appeared in *The Echoes of Many Texts: Essays in Honor of Lou Silberman*, ed. William G. Dever and J. Edward Wright, Brown Judaic Studies 313 (Scholars Press, 1997), 99–114. The original version benefited from the comments and suggestions of Steve Mason (York University), Catherine Hezser (King's College, Cambridge; now Institut für Judaistik, Free University of Berlin), and Saul Olyan (Brown University). I also benefited from the discussions that ensued after I presented the original version of this paper at the World Congress for Jewish Studies in Jerusalem (June 1993) and, through the courtesy of Bernadette Brooten, at a seminar at Brandeis University (May 1994).

1. George F. Moore, *Judaism in the First Centuries of the Christian Era* 1.287, writes; "[I]t is certain that they [the Pharisees] took possession of it [the synagogue] and made most effective use of it. Through it, more perhaps than by any other means, they gained the hold upon the mass of the people which enabled them ... to establish such power as Josephus ascribes to them.... The synagogue in the hands of the Phar-

as far as I know, no one has yet collected and evaluated the evidence
that supports this view. In my conclusion, I briefly touch upon negative evidence, that is, evidence that the Pharisees and rabbis were
not the leaders of Jewish communal prayer and Torah study, but
in the body of my presentation I cite and discuss only positive evidence, or that which is regarded by some as positive evidence. I
focus on evidence from the first two centuries C.E.

This essay stands at the intersection of three difficult and complicated questions — the origins and history of the synagogue, the
origins and history of the Pharisees, the origins and history of the
rabbis — and space does not permit the treatment of these topics
in this essay.[2] In order to keep the essay to reasonable length, I am
excluding rabbinic and archaeological evidence, since each requires
sustained treatment in its own right.[3] Even if I cannot discuss the

---

isees was doubtless the chief instrument in the Judaizing of Galilee." Martin Hengel
writes, "[D]as Synagogeninstitut...sich im Mutterland vor allem aufgrund phari-
saischer Initiative verbreitete"; see his "Der vorchristliche Paulus," *Paulus und das
antike Judentum,* ed. Martin Hengel and Ulrich Heckel (Tübingen: Mohr-Siebeck,
1991), 177–291, at 260 (I owe this reference to Gunther Stemberger). He writes
further, "It is therefore no wonder that the Pharisees were especially interested in
introducing the institution of the synagogue as a place for worship and teaching";
see Martin Hengel and Roland Deines, "E. P. Sanders' 'Common Judaism,' Jesus,
and the Pharisees," *JTS* 46 (1995): 1–70, at 32. "They [the Pharisees] thus fostered
the synagogue as a place of worship, study, and prayer, and raised it to a central
and important place in the life of the people," writes M. Mansoor, *Encyclopaedia
Judaica* 13:363–66, s.v. Pharisees, at 366. Even Howard Kee, for all of his skepticism, assumes that the development of the synagogue should somehow mirror the
development of Pharisaism (as outlined by Jacob Neusner). See Kee, "The Transformation of the Synagogue after 70 C.E.: Its Import for early Christianity," *NTS*
36 (1990): 1–24. Scholars skeptical of Pharisaic dominance include E. P. Sanders,
Jewish Law from Jesus to the Mishnah (Philadelphia: Trinity Press International,
1990), 79–81; *Judaism: Practice and Belief 63 BCE–66 CE* (Philadelphia: Trinity
Press International, 1992), 398; and Lester Grabbe, "Synagogues in pre-70 Palestine: A Re-assessment," *JTS* 39 (1988): 401–10 On p. 408, Grabbe writes: "There
is nothing particularly Pharisaic about the institution of the synagogue.... The early
sources on the Pharisees mention nothing in particular about them in relationship to
synagogues." Grabbe's article is reprinted in *Ancient Synagogues: Historical Analysis and Archaeological Discovery,* ed. Dan Urman and Paul V. M. Flesher, 2 vols.,
Studia Post-Biblica 47 (Leiden; Brill, 1995), 1:17–26 (where the quotation appears
on p. 23).

2. I do not discuss here questions such as the following: When did communal prayer and Torah study become localized in synagogues? Where did communal
prayer and Torah study take place before being localized in synagogues? What other
activities took place in the synagogues of antiquity? What is the relationship between
communal leadership and synagogal leadership?

3. See my "Pagan and Christian Evidence on the Ancient Synagogue," in *The
Synagogue in Late Antiquity,* ed. Lee Levine (Philadelphia: American Schools of
Oriental Research, 1987), 159–81.

history of the synagogue, I must comment briefly on the range of meanings of the word "synagogue."

The basic meaning of the Greek *sunagōgē* is "a gathering, a collection," and can be used either of people or of things, such as water or utensils. In Jewish contexts the word may designate either the Jewish community of a certain place, or a gathering of Jews, or the place where Jews are gathered or habitually gather. The English "synagogue" is narrower than Greek *sunagōgē* in three respects: the English word does not mean "community," while the Greek often does; the English word implies the existence of a building, while the Greek does not;[4] the English word designates a gathering of Jews or a place where Jews gather for the sake of communal prayer and/or Torah study, while the Greek can refer to a gathering of various sorts. This last point is important: as discussed below, the Greek word *sunagōgē* sometimes is used to designate a gathering of Jews for judicial or communal or political purposes, but if in these passages the word is translated "synagogue," the point is lost. Not every (Greek) *sunagōgē* is necessarily a (English) synagogue, because not every gathering or assembly is necessarily for the sake of prayer and Torah study.[5] Jews gathering for judicial, communal, or political purposes likely gathered in the same places in which they would have gathered for the sake of communal prayer or Torah study,[6] but we must recognize the range of social activities that took place in a *sunagōgē*. Perhaps to resolve at least some of this ambiguity, Diaspora Jews in antiquity coined the word *proseuchē* to designate a place (usually a building) of prayer, and used *sunagōgē* to refer to the community (or the meeting of the community).[7] In recognition of this ambiguity, in my discussions of the evidence I leave

---

4. In the synoptic Gospels it is not always clear whether *sunagōgē* necessarily means a building; only Luke 7:5 clearly refers to a building. Kee, "Transformation," makes much of this ambiguity and of Luke's exceptional usage, but many of his arguments are effectively dismissed by Richard Oster, "Supposed Anachronism in Luke-Acts' Use of *sunagōgē*," *NTS* 39 (1993): 178–208, esp. 182–91.

5. Similarly, the rabbis can speak of a *kenesiyah* (equivalent to *sunagōgē*) "not for the sake of heaven," M. Avot 4:11.

6. Thus Josephus *Vita* 277, 280, 290–303, describes a meeting in the "prayer house" in Tiberias to discuss the war; in general see Sidney B. Hoenig, "The Ancient City-Square: The Forerunner of the Synagogue," *ANRW* 2.19.1 (1979), 448–76.

7. The best discussion of these terms remains the classic article of Martin Hengel, "Proseuche und Synägoge: Jüdische Gemeinde, Gotteshaus, und Gottesdienst in der Diaspora und in Palästina," *Tradition und Glaube: Das frühe Christentum in seiner Umwelt*, Festschrift für K. G. Kühn, ed. G. Jeremias, H. Kühn, and H. Stegemann (Göttingen: Vandenhoeck & Ruprecht, 1971), 157–83, reprinted in J. Gutmann, *The Synagogue: Studies in Origins, Archaeology and Architecture* (New York: KTAV, 1975), 27–54. See too Schrage, *"sunagōgē,"* *TDNT* 7:798–841, and Emil Schürer,

sunagōgē untranslated and discuss whether the intent of the word is "assembly" in general or specifically an assembly for the sake of communal prayer and Torah study, that is, a "synagogue." I am attempting to locate evidence that specifically and unambiguously states that Pharisees/Rabbis lead communal prayer and/or Torah study, activities that in both common and scholarly parlance are associated with (English) synagogues.[8]

I have found seven passages that indicate (or might be thought to indicate) Pharisaic or rabbinic leadership of Jewish communal prayer and/or Torah study. They are: (1) Matthew 12:9–14 (and parallels); (2) Matthew 23:2; (3) Matthew 23:6–7 (and parallels); (4) Matthew 23:34; (5) Josephus, *Ant.* 18.15; (6) John 12:42; and (7) Justin Martyr, *Dialogue with Trypho* 137.2. I treat each of these in turn.

1. Matthew 12:9–14: "And he [Jesus] went from there and entered their *sunagōgē*." The meaning of *sunagōgē* in this case is fairly clear: the assembly is meeting on the Sabbath (12:10–11), presumably for communal Torah study; the Lukan parallel reads that "he went to the *sunagōgē* and taught" (Luke 6:6) — this assembly is clearly a "synagogue." The problem is the referent of "their" (*autōn*). The nearest previous masculine plural noun, the Pharisees of 12:2, is seven verses away; thus it is possible, even if syntactically unlikely, that the Pharisees of 12:2 are the "they" of 12:9–14. It is more likely, however, that "they" are the Jews en bloc. The phrase *sunagōgē/ai autōn* recurs four other times in Matthew (4:23, 9:35, 10:17, 13:54) and in all four the referent of "their" is not the Pharisees but — even if the syntax is not always clear — the Jews as a whole.[9] (Similarly 11:1 refers to "their cities.") In three of these passages (4:23, 9:35, 13:54) *sunagōgē* clearly means, as it

---

The History of the Jewish People in the Age of Jesus Christ, rev. by G. Vermes et al. (1979), 2:429–31 and 439–41.

8. Scholars have long recognized the diversity of functions that were filled by "the synagogue," but it is the merit of Kee, "Transformation," to insist that not every New Testament *sunagōgē is* equivalent to a "synagogue" in its fullest sense. For a recent discussion of the relationship between communal prayer and communal Torah study, and the relationship between *bate keneset* and *bate midrashot,* see D. Urman, "The House of Assembly and the House of Study," *JJS* 44 (1993): 236–57 (=in *Ancient Synagogues: Historical Analysis and Archaeological Discovery* 1:232–55).

9. Douglas R. A. Hare, *The Theme of Jewish Persecution of Christians in the Gospel according to St. Matthew,* SNTSMS 6 (Cambridge University Press, 1967), 104–5; W. D. Davies and Dale Allison, *A Critical and Exegetical Commentary on the Gospel according to St. Matthew,* 3 vols., ICC (Edinburgh: T. & T. Clark, 1988–97), 1:413 on 4:23, "The fixed nature of the expression is shown by 4.23; 12.9; and 13.54, where 'their' has no proper grammatical antecedent."

does here, a synagogue. The fourth passage (10:17), and a passage with a related expression (23:34), is discussed below. If *autōn* refers to the Jews taken as a whole, the passage is no evidence for Pharisaic leadership of communal Torah study. If *autōn* refers to the Pharisees specifically, only Matthew implies that the synagogue was theirs, the Pharisees'; the parallels in Mark and Luke omit *autōn* (Mark 3:1; Luke 6:6).[10]

2. Matthew 23:2: "The Pharisees and the scribes sit [or sat] on the seat of Moses." This verse, unique to Matthew, opens a long polemic against the Pharisees. The theme of the polemic is that the Pharisees are powerful and influential, but hypocritical and wrong.[11] This verse can be used as direct evidence for our subject by means of the following chain of argumentation: (a) "the seat of Moses" is not a metaphor but a real chair or seat; (b) the existence of this seat is confirmed by a reference to it in Pesiqta de Rav Kahana; (c) this seat was located in the synagogue in a place of honor in front of the congregation; (d) such seats have actually been found in the archaeological excavations of various synagogues; (e) therefore Matthew 23:2 is evidence for Pharisaic (and rabbinic) leadership of synagogues: the Pharisees sit on seats of honor in the synagogue and there exercise their authority. Each link in this chain is weak.

(a) Does the phrase "the seat of Moses" identify an actual item, or is the phrase metaphoric? In all likelihood the latter.[12] Most commentators on the passage, ancient (including Origen, Cyril of Jerusalem, and Jerome), medieval, and modern, understand "seat of Moses" as metaphor or symbol: the Pharisees have inherited, or claim to have inherited, the authority of Moses to teach law to the people. "To sit on the seat of Moses" means to teach like Moses,

---

10. *Sunagōgē/ai autōn* is typically Matthean; the phrase occurs only twice in Mark (1:23 [note the variants] and 1:39//Matthew 4:23) and only once in Luke (4:15 [note the variants]).

11. For the social setting of this polemic see David Garland, *The Intention of Matthew 23*, NovTSup 52 (Leiden: Brill, 1979); Anthony Saldarini, "Delegitimation of Leaders in Matthew 23," *CBQ* 54 (1992): 659–80; see now Kenneth G. C. Newport, *The Sources and* Sitz im Leben *of Matthew 23*, JSNTSup 117 (Sheffield, 1995). Sanders, *Jewish Law* 80, thinks that Matthew 23:2 gives the impression that "synagogues were generally dominated by Pharisees," even if Sanders doubts that this impression is correct. I am arguing that Matthew 23:2 does not have to give this impression at all.

12. The singular *kathedra* might suggest that the metaphorical interpretation is preferable, for how can the Pharisees and the scribes (!) sit on a single seat? Contrast the plural *protokathedriai* in verse 6. This argument is at best suggestive, since verse 6 also has the singular *protoklisia* (but see the variants!). Davies and Allison 3:268 n. 17 offer LXX Psalms 106:36 as a parallel, *en kathedra presbuterōn*.

since teachers sit when they teach.[13] The phrase says nothing about the actual seats of the Pharisees.

(b) In 1897 Wilhelm Bacher observed that the term "seat of Moses" occurs in Pesiqta de Rav Kahana.[14] In a discussion of the throne of the kings of Israel the midrash quotes 1 Kings 10:19, "and the throne had a back with a rounded top." R. Aha comments, "like the seat of Moses" (*kahada qatedra demoshe*). The manuscripts provide several variants, and the parallel passage in Esther Rabbah 1:12 provides yet additional variants. It is not impossible that the text is corrupt, but on the assumption that *qatedra demoshe is* the correct reading, what does it mean? Numerous rabbinic texts have rabbis sitting on *qatedratot*,[15] and the rabbis may well have imagined Moses "our rabbi" doing likewise when he taught.[16] In Exodus Rabbah R. Drosai says, "He [God] made for him [Moses] a *qatedra* like the *qatedra* of *scholastikoi.*"[17] Thus the Pesiqta passage confirms the *qatedra* as a piece of contemporary rabbinic furniture but

---

13. Origen, *Matthauserklärung: Series Commentariorum,* ed. E. Benz and E. Klostermann, GCS 38 (Leipzig: Hirzel, 1933), 16–17; Cyril of Jerusalem, *Catechesis* 12:23 (a reference I owe to Oded Ir-Say); Jerome, commentary on Matthew 23:1–3 (Corpus Christianorum series Latina 77, p. 210), *per cathedram doctrinam legis ostendit.* Reflecting the consensus of patristic and medieval interpretation, Cornelius à Lapide writes, "Per *cathedram* metonymice intelligit honorem, gradum, dignitatem, auctoritatem docendi et iubendi, quam apud Iudaeos habuit Moyses quam scribae post Moysen acceperant"; see *Commentarius in quattuor Evangelia* (1639) 422, commentary on Matthew 23:2. For a list of modern commentators who interpret the phrase metaphorically see I. Renov, "The Seat of Moses," *IEJ* 5 (1955): 262–67 (reprinted in *The Synagogue,* ed. Joseph Gutmann [New York: KTAV, 1975], 233–38), at 264 n. 13. See too Frank W. Beare, *The Gospel according to Matthew* (Oxford: Blackwell, 1981), 448: "Moses' seat — the post of teaching authority. This is hardly to be taken as a reference to a special chair in the synagogue for the chief elder. It is simply a metaphor." A similar view is articulated in *Anchor Bible Dictionary* 4:919. Davies and Allison 3:268 cannot decide.

14. Wilhelm Bacher, "Le siège de Moise," *Revue des études juives* 34 (1897): 299–301. The reference is PdRK 1:7 7b Buber = 12 Mandelbaum.

15. Renov 266, drawing on M. Ginsburger, "La 'chaire de Moise'," *Revue des études juives* 90 (1931): 161–65. Hans-Jürgen Becker, *Auf der Kathedra des Mose. Rabbinisch-theologisches Denken und antirabbinische Polemik in Matthäus 23:1– 12* (Berlin: Institut Kirche und Judentum, 1990; Arbeiten zur neutestamentlichen Theologie und Zeitgeschichte, Band 4) 31–49; and Meir Bar-Ilan, "The Rock, the Seat, and the *qatedra* on Which Moses Sat," *Sidra* 2 (1986): 15–23 (Hebrew). I am grateful to Samuel Byrskog of Lund University for bringing Becker's book to my attention.

16. According to Sifrei Numbers 140 (p. 186 ed. Horovitz), Moses sat on a bench (*safsal*) when he taught. Cf. Assumption of Moses 12:2. Some scholars connect these passages with rabbinic ordination; see E. Lohse, *Die Ordination im Spätjudentum und im Neuen Testament* (Göttingen: Vandenhoeck & Ruprecht, 1951), 25 and 30. I owe these references to Dr. Catherine Hezser.

17. Exodus Rabbah 43:4. Avigdor Shinan, who is preparing a critical edition of Exodus Rabbah, informs me that there are serious variants here, too. For an alter-

says nothing about the *qatedra demoshe* as a piece of contemporary rabbinic furniture.

(c) No matter how "the seat of Moses" is construed in Matthew and the Pesiqta, neither text locates the seat in the synagogue. Indeed, to the best of my knowledge no ancient text places a *qatedra* in a synagogue.[18]

(d) In the synagogues of Chorazin, En Gedi, Hammath Tiberias, Delos, and Dura-Europos archaeologists discovered ornate stone objects resembling chairs. These chairs were identified as "seats of Moses" and juxtaposed to Matthew 23:2 by Eleazar Sukenik in an influential article published in 1930.[19] Sukenik's conjecture is attractive, but not without problems. The function of these objects is not clear; some archaeologists have suggested that they were not chairs but stands (or tables or platforms).[20] Furthermore, the synagogues of Chorazin, En Gedi, Hammath Tiberias, and Dura-Europos postdate Jesus and the Gospel of Matthew by at least 150 or 200 years, and these later buildings cannot readily be cited as evidence to elucidate circumstances of a much earlier time. The synagogues of Delos (perhaps first century B.C.E.) and Dura-Europos are diaspora synagogues, and they cannot readily be cited as evidence to elucidate circumstances of a much different place. It is also worth noting that only five "seats of Moses" have been discovered — a tiny percentage of the dozens and dozens of synagogues excavated. If archaeological remains really were to confirm the Matthean statement, "seats of Moses" should have been discovered in large numbers.

(e) I conclude that Matthew 23:2 clearly regards the Pharisees as a powerful and influential group, but whether or not this power and influence extended to the "synagogue" the text says not a word. Perhaps we should conclude that a group that sits "on the seat of Moses," in other words, that claims Mosaic authority, will,

native to the transcription *scholastikoi* see D. Sperber, *A Dictionary of Greek and Latin Legal Terms in Rabbinic Literature* (Bar-Iran, 1984), 22.

18. The text that comes closest is T. Sukkah 4:6 p. 273 Lieberman (and parallels), a description of the *diplostoon* of Alexandria. For an *exedra* at the *proseuchē* of Athribis, see *CIJ* 1444 = William Horbury and David Noy, *Jewish Inscriptions of Graeco-Roman Egypt* (Cambridge University Press, 1992), no. 28 (with full discussion of the meaning of *exedra*).

19. E. L. Sukenik, "The Seat of Moses in Ancient Synagogues," *Tarbiz* 1 (1930): 145–51. For recent discussion and bibliography see Hachlili *Ancient Jewish Art and Archaeology* 193–94; L. Y. Rahmani, "Stone Synagogue Chairs: Their Identification, Use, and Significance," *IEJ* 40 (1990): 192–214; Lee Levine, "From Community Center to 'Lesser Sanctuary': The Furnishings and Interior of the Ancient Synagogue," *Cathedra* 60 (1991): 36–84, at 60–63 (Hebrew).

20. See Renov and Rahmani.

like Moses, teach the community and lead communal Torah study. However, this conclusion is not necessary, for Mosaic authority might express itself more in judicial verdicts than in synagogal study. In any case the archaeologically attested "seats of Moses" are irrelevant to the question.

3. In its indictment of the Pharisees and scribes, Matthew 23 continues (23:6–7): "They love (a) the first couch at feasts (b) and the first seats in the *sunagōgai,* (c) and salutations in the market places, (d) and being called rabbi by men." The parallels in Mark (12:38–39) and Luke (11:43; 20:46) offer minor variants but only one item of significance for our purposes: In Mark and in the second Lukan parallel the polemic is directed against scribes, while in the first Lukan parallel it is directed against the Pharisees; only Matthew combines the Pharisees and scribes.[21] *Sunagogai* in this case parallels feasts and market — places — and therefore seems to mean "assemblies" (just as it does in Matthew 6:2, where it parallels "streets"). The verse is concerned not with leadership of communal prayer and Torah study but with social prominence.[22] This interpretation receives some support from Josephus in *Jewish Antiquities* 15.21 (a parallel duly noted by several commentators). Herod greeted Hyrcanus "with every honor, assigned him the first place in assemblies (*sullogoi*), gave him the first couch at banquets, and called him father." The only thing Herod could have done to make the parallel with Matthew complete would have been to salute Hyrcanus in the market place. Josephus's *sullogoi* corresponds to Matthew's *sunagōgai,* and clearly means "assemblies."

Even if this explanation is incorrect, and *sunagōgai* here means

---

21. See Renov and Rahmani. Parallels: Mark 12:38–39, different order (c, b, a; om. d); Luke 20:46 (c, b, a; om. d); Luke 11:43 (b, c; om. a and d). I cannot discuss here the much debated question of the relationship of the scribes to the Pharisees.

22. For what it may be worth I note that the rabbinic expression *leshev barosh,* as far as I have been able to determine, is not used in synagogal contexts. Prominent seating in the synagogue is described in other terms; see T. Megillah 3:21 p. 360 Lieberman. B. Brooten appositely cites *CIJ* 738 = B. Lifshitz, *Donateurs et fondateurs* 13, an inscription from Phocaea (third century C.E.?) which honors a woman named Tation. She donated "to the Jews" a building and an enclosure around a courtyard, and in return was honored by the *sunagōgē* with a golden crown and the right to sit in front (*proedria*). See Brooten, *Women Leaders in the Ancient Synagogue,* BJS 36 (Scholars Press, 1982), 143–44. Brooten assumes that the *proedria* is to be exercised in the synagogue (that is, assemblies for the sake of prayer and Torah study), but the point is not clear; the word *sunagōgē* in the inscription means "community," not "synagogue" (it is correctly translated by Lifshitz, but incorrectly translated by Brooten 157) and the *proedria* might have been exercised at nonreligious meetings. Brooten assumes that both Matthew and the inscription are referring to synagogues; I am suggesting that both are referring to assemblies.

synagogues, that is, assemblies for the sake of communal prayer and/or Torah study, Matthew 23:6–7 and its parallels would merely demonstrate that when Pharisees attend synagogues they are given (they take?) prominent seats befitting their social prominence. The verse does not claim that Pharisees lead the prayer or the study.[23] Similarly, Matthew 6:2 and 5 decry the prominence that "the hypocrites" arrogate to themselves when giving alms and praying in the *sunagōgai* and the streets / street corners; even if here too *sunagōgai* means "synagogues," these verses attribute prominence, not leadership, to "the hypocrites," a Matthean synonym for Pharisees. Indeed Matthew 6:5 strongly implies that "the hypocrites" are not communal prayer leaders; the accusation that they do what they do "in order that they may be seen by men," makes far more sense if "the hypocrites" are private individuals eager to flaunt their piety rather than communal leaders performing a legitimate communal function.

4. In its indictment of the Pharisees and scribes, Matthew 23 continues (Matt 23:34), "Therefore I send you prophets and wise men and scribes, some of whom you will kill and crucify, and some you will flog in your *sunagōgai* and persecute from town to town." The motif of persecution in the *sunagōgai* recurs several times in the synoptic Gospels, although Matthew 23:34 is the only passage to link this motif with the Pharisees.[24] Cf. Matthew 10:17, "Beware of men; for they will deliver you up to councils (*sunedria*), and flog (*mastigosousin*) *you* in their *sunagōgai*," paralleled by Mark 13:9, "But take heed to yourselves: for they will deliver you up to councils (*sunedria*); and you will be beaten (*darēsesthe*) in *sunagōgai*," and Luke 21:12, "... they will lay their hands on you and persecute you, delivering you up to the *sunagōgai* and prisons." Cf. Luke 12:11, "And when they bring you before the *sunagōgai*. ... " All of these parallel passages continue with reference to how the disciples should behave when brought before kings and governors. In these passages *sunagōgai*, parallel to *sunedria* and prisons (and kings and governors), seems to refer to assemblies with a judicial function, rather than assemblies for prayer and study.[25]

---

23. I owe this observation to Dr. Catherine Hezser. Similarly, even in Brooten's reading, the Tation inscription does not state that she is a leader of the synagogue (see previous note). Hengel and Deines, "E. P. Sanders," 33 n. 85, think that Matthew 23:6 proves that "the Pharisees... played an important role" in synagogues.

24. Persecution in the *sunagōgai* is missing from the parallel in Luke 11:49, and may have been an addition to Q by Matthew; see Hare, *Jewish Persecution* 92.

25. Wellhausen correctly translates *sunedria* "judicial assemblies," "courts." See

5. In his description of the Pharisees Josephus writes the following (*Ant.* 18.15): "On account of these (views) they happen
to be most persuasive to the people; of prayers and sacred rites,
whatever is considered divine happens to be conducted according
to their interpretation."[26] The Greek is very difficult, but the basic
meaning seems clear.[27] The only real ambiguity is the word *euchai,*
which can mean either "prayers" (as translated here) or, as Feldman correctly notes in his translation in the Loeb edition, "vows."
Given the Pharisees' reputed expertise in matters connected with
vows (Matt 23:16–22),[28] the latter translation cannot be ruled out.
Certain kinds of vows, especially Nazirite vows, involved a sacrifice in the temple (cf. Acts 21:23–26; Josephus, *Jewish War* 2.313),
and these sacrifices, if not the vows themselves, certainly could be
considered "sacred rites" and "divine." The pairing of *euchai* with
hierdōn poiesis ("sacred rites") gives a slight edge to the translation
"prayers," because this pair of nouns seems to be the equivalent of
euchai kai thusiai (or *hierourgiai),* a common Josephan pair that
means "prayers and sacrifices."[29] Regardless of the way *euchai* is
understood, this passage is unique in the Josephan corpus. In many
places Josephus emphasizes that the Pharisees are powerful and influential, whereas the Sadducees are powerless and ineffective (*Ant.*
18.17),[30] but this is the only passage to highlight the Pharisees'

W. Schrage, *TDNT* 7:834, n. 230. *Sunagogai* probably has the same meaning in
Acts 22:19. Similarly, *keneset* in M. Makkot 3:12 (flogging is administered by *haz-
zan hakeneset)* means either "community" (so Rashi) or "court" (so R. Ovadya
Bartenora).

26. Steve Mason, *Flavius Josephus on the Pharisees* (Leiden: Brill, 1991), 305.

27. The crucial clause is *kai hoposa theia eukhōn te ekhetai kai hierōn poiēseōs
exēgēsei tēi ekeinōn tugkhanousin prassomena.* Feldman's translation in the Loeb is
a bit freer: "Because of these views they are, as a matter of fact, extremely influential among the townsfolk; and all prayers and sacred rites of divine worship are
performed according to their exposition." Schürer-Vermes 2:402 takes the Greek
as referring to three categories: "They held the greatest authority over the congregations, so that everything to do with worship, prayer, and sacrifice took place
according to their instructions." This translation misses the mark.

28. See too M. Nazir 3:6.

29. *euchai kai thusiai: Jewish War* 7.155; *Ant.* 6.19, 6.24 (note *euchai, thusiai,
horkoi),* 6.102, 14.260, 20.112; *euchai kai hierourgiai: Ant.* 1.231. In *Ant.* 11.9
euchai kai thusiai appears to mean "vows and sacrifices," but there each noun is the
object of a separate verb (*tas euchas apedidosan tōi theōi* means, as translated in
the Loeb edition, "they made the offerings vowed to God"; cf. 11.77). It is not clear
whether *euchon* in 18.15 is dependent on *poiesis* (parallel to *hieron*) or not; in either
case, the meaning is ambiguous, because Josephus uses the phrase *eukhen/euchas
poiein/poieisthai* to mean either "to pray" (*Jewish War* 7.128; *Ant.* 3.191, 6.128,
11.134–35, 12.55) or "to vow" (*Ant.* 1.284, 11.77).

30. For references and discussion, see note 44 below.

power in religious matters, specifically prayers / vows and sacred rites. The passage refers to Pharisaic power not just in the temple (no matter what *euchai* means, surely all temple rituals would be considered "sacred rites" and "divine") but also among "the people" (*demoi*) and "the cities" (*poleis*). If, then, *euchai* means "prayers," this passage is important evidence for our subject: the passage claims that public prayers are conducted according to the instruction of the Pharisees. If, however, *euchai* means "vows," this passage remains important evidence, but not for our subject.

6. John 12:42, "Nevertheless many even of the authorities believed in him, but because of the Pharisees they did not confess it, lest they should be put out of the *sunagōgē*" (literally, lest they should become out-of-the-*sunagōgē*). As many commentators have noted, the term *aposunagogoi* is unique to John in the New Testament. It recurs in 9:22, in the story of the healing of the blind man, in a very similar passage: "His parents [i.e., the parents of the blind man healed by Jesus] ... feared the Jews, for the Jews had already agreed that if any one should confess him to be Christ, he was to be put out of the *sunagōgē*" (literally, he was to become out-of-the-*sunagōgē*). In 16:2 Jesus tells his disciples, ... they shall make you out-of-the-*sunagōgē*." Who is the "they" who have the power to put people out of the *sunagōgē*? In 12:42 it is the Pharisees. In 9:22 it is "the Jews," who are probably to be identified with the Pharisees of 9:13–17. For John, as for Matthew 23, the distinction between "the Jews" and "the Pharisees" has all but disappeared.[31] John 12:42 distinguishes between the rulers (*archontes*) and the Pharisees: were it not for fear of the Pharisees many of the *archons* would have confessed Christ.[32] This statement closely resembles the view of Josephus that the Sadducees are unable to accomplish anything because they must perforce obey the dictates of the Pharisees.

What is the meaning of "out-of-the-*sunagōgē*?" Many recent scholars have taken it to refer to exclusion from the synagogue (assemblies for the sake of prayer) and have connected the exclusion with the rabbinic institution of the "benediction against heretics" (*birkat ha-minim*).[33] However, as I discuss below in connection with Justin Martyr, in all likelihood these Johannine passages have noth-

---

31. "Pharisees" and "the Jews" are parallel also in John 1:19//1:24 and 7:32//7:35 (perhaps).

32. Archons and Pharisees form a contrasting pair also at 7:48 (although Nicodemus is both a Pharisee and an archon, 3:1).

33. Even Grabbe, for all of his skepticism about Pharisaic dominance of the syn-

ing to do with the *birkat ha-minim*. If this is correct, *sunagōgē* should in this case simply be understood as "community." Those who confess Christ will be excluded from the Jewish community. Presumably exclusion from the community would manifest itself most immediately in exclusion from assemblies for the sake of prayer and Torah study, but the synagogue *per se* is not the focus of the statements. According to John the Pharisees have great power over the community.

7. In his dialogue with Trypho, Justin Martyr (c. 140–50 C.E.) writes as follows (137.2), "Agree with us, therefore, and do not revile the Son of God, nor, obeying Pharisaic-teachers (*Pharisaioi didaskaloi*), ever mock the King of Israel, as the rulers of your synagogues (*archisunagōgoi*) teach you after the prayer (*meta tēn proseuchēn*)." Two groups demand of Trypho and the Jews that they revile and mock Christ: Pharisaic teachers, and rulers of synagogues. In response Justin asks of Trypho and the Jews to ignore their leaders and never to mock Christ.

What is the relationship between the Pharisees, teachers, and the rulers of synagogues? Justin mentions the Pharisees seven times in his *Dialogue;* five of these seven refer unambiguously to the Pharisees (and scribes) of Jesus' time.[34] The sixth reference occurs in a list of seven Jewish sects (*haireseis*), among them the Pharisees (80.4); this list has caused great difficulties for interpreters and requires separate discussion.[35] The seventh reference is our passage. In the light of the five unambiguous references, surely it is best to understand our passage as a reference to a group of the Second Temple Period. The same conclusion emerges from a study of Justin's references to teachers (*didaskaloi*). The rulers of the synagogues (*archisunagōgoi*) are mentioned only here in the Dialogue, but teachers (*didaskaloi*) are mentioned frequently. They were and are the leaders of the Jews; they teach and interpret Scripture, cite tradition, and establish law. The Jews in turn seek to understand and perform the dictates of these teachers.[36] Insofar as the teachers were the leaders of the Jews in the time of Jesus, Justin can identify or associate them with Phar-

---

agogue (see note 1 above), writes, "Only one New Testament passage suggests any particular connection [between the Pharisees and the synagogue]: John 12:42."

34. 51.2, 76.7, 102.5, 103.1, 105.6.

35. Shaye J. D. Cohen, "The Significance of Yavneh," *Hebrew Union College Annual* 55 (1984): 27–53, at 34–35 and 52 n. 70.

36. Adolf Harnack, *Judentum und Judenchristentum in Justins Dialog mit Trypho,* Texte und Untersuchungen 39 (Leipzig: Hinrichs, 1913) 56–57. *Didaskaloi* are mentioned, aside from 137, in Dialogue 9, 38, 43, 48, 62, 68, 71, 83, 94, 102, 103, 110, 112, 114, 117, 120, 134, 140, and 142.

isees, scribes, and priests.[37] Insofar as the teachers are the leaders of contemporary Jewry, Justin can ascribe to them some of the same negative qualities that the Gospels ascribe to the Pharisees.[38] The faults of the Pharisees of Jesus' time remain the faults of the teachers of Justin's, but Justin nowhere labels contemporary teachers as Pharisees. Thus our passage probably should be interpreted as follows, "Do not mock Jesus as the Pharisaic teachers once taught you and as the rulers of the synagogues teach you now." If this is correct, our passage says nothing about the influence of Pharisees on the synagogue of Justin's time. In any case, it is worth noting that Justin clearly distinguishes between Pharisees, teachers, and heads of synagogues.

This passage might be thought to provide evidence of another sort for Pharisaic-rabbinic control of synagogues. In a series of passages Justin accuses the Jews of cursing or anathematizing either Christians (93.4, 123.6) or Christ and Christians together (95.4, 108.3, and 133.6). He specifies in three additional passages that the cursing (of Christians) takes place in the synagogues (16.4, 47.4, 96.2).[39] In our passage he states that the rulers of the synagogues teach the Jews to scoff Christ after the prayer.[40] Many scholars have connected these reports, various other patristic passages, and the passages from the Gospel of John cited above) with the *birkat ha-minim,* a prayer reportedly instituted or formulated by Rabban Gamaliel and the sages of Yavneh and directed against "heretics."[41] If this identification were correct, it would provide good evidence for the adoption of a rabbinic liturgical innovation by the Jews in their synagogues, thus for rabbinic influence on the synagogues of late antiquity.[42]

---

37. Pharisees and scribes: 102.5 and 103.1–2 (perhaps inspired by Matthew 15:1–7//Mark 7:1–6 and Luke 5:17; see next note). Priests: 117.

38. For example: in 38.2, 48.2, and 140.2 Justin implicitly connects Isaiah 29:13 with the teachers; this polemic comes from Matthew//Mark (see previous note). Teachers want to be called "rabbi, rabbi" (112.5); cf. Matthew 23:7.

39. In these passages "synagogues" almost certainly means "places of communal prayer and study"; see 72.3.

40. Does "after the prayer" modify the verb "teach" (after the prayer the rulers of the synagogues teach the Jews to mock Christ) or the verb "mock" (the rulers of the synagogues teach the Jews: mock Christ after the prayer)? The syntax is ambiguous.

41. Schrage, *TDNT* 7:848–52, s.v. *aposunagogos;* W. Horbury, "The Benediction of the Minim and Early Jewish-Christian Controversy," *JTS* 33 (1982): 19–61; Oskar Skarsaune, *The Proof from Prophecy,* NovTSup 56 (Leiden: Brill, 1987), 290–91; and many others.

42. Thus it would be much better evidence than that provided by the Greek Jewish prayers contained in book 8 of the Apostolic Constitutions, because those prayers

In all likelihood, however, *birkat ha-minim* has no connection either with John or Justin Martyr. The *birkat ha-minim* was a curse against heretics in general. It was not, and was not intended to be, a curse specifically against Christians, and it certainly was not a curse against Christ. John claims that Jews who believe in Christ will be ejected from the Jewish community; John had any number of reasons for making this claim, whether the claim be true or false. He says nothing about a prayer or a curse. Justin speaks of scoffing after the prayer, which is not the same thing as cursing during the prayer. At some point in its history the *birkat ha-minim* became a curse directed against "Jewish Christians" (Nazoreans), perhaps, as Jerome thought, a curse against all Christians, but originally it was not so. These passages have nothing to do with the *birkat ha-minim* and offer no evidence concerning rabbinic influence over synagogues.[43]

In conclusion: I have surveyed seven passages from the New Testament, Josephus, and the church fathers of the first two centuries of the common era. These passages constitute the major nonrabbinic literary evidence for the view that communal Jewish prayer and Torah study were led by Pharisees before 70 C.E. and rabbis after 70 C.E. The most striking fact to emerge from this survey is the paucity of relevant evidence. None of the seven passages gives explicit and unambiguous testimony. Perhaps there is other relevant evidence that I have missed, especially in the church fathers, but even with some additional evidence I do not think that the overall picture will change.

According to Matthew and Josephus, the Pharisees are the most powerful and influential Jewish "school:" they control prayers (vows?), sacred rites, sit on the seat of Moses (a metaphor), and sit on seats of honor (not a metaphor) in public assemblies. According

---

may well attest not rabbinic liturgical innovations but the standard Sabbath prayer of pre-rabbinic times.

43. For studies that deny, or at least question, the relevance of the *birkat ha-minim* to John and Justin see: Peter Schafer, "Die sogenannte Synode von Jabne. Zur Trennung von Juden und Christen im 1./2. Jh. n. Chr.," *Studien zur Geschichte und Theologie des rabbinischen Judentums* (Leiden: Brill, 1978), 45–64; A. Finkel, "Yavneh's Liturgy and Early Christianity," *Journal of Ecumenical Studies* 18 (1981): 231–50; Reuven Kimelman, "*Birkat ha-minim* and the Lack of Evidence for an anti-Christian Prayer in Late Antiquity," *Jewish and Christian Self-Definition II*, ed. E. P. Sanders et al. (Philadelphia: Fortress, 1981), 226–44; Cohen, "Yavneh"; Johann Maier, *Jüdische Auseinandersetzung mit dem Christentum in der Antike* (Darmstadt: Wissenschaftliche Buchgesellschaft, 1982), 136–41; T. G. G. Thornton, "Christian Understandings of the *Birkath Ha-Minim* in the Eastern Roman Empire," *JTS* 38 (1987): 419–31; and others.

to John, Pharisees have the power to exclude from the community whomever they wish. The reliability and purpose of Matthew's and Josephus's assertions of Pharisaic dominance have been much debated,[44] but even if they are largely accurate we should not simplify a complicated situation. Texts of, or about the Second Temple Period, including Matthew and Josephus, do not locate Pharisees in or near synagogues (that is, assemblies for the sake of communal prayer and Torah study).[45] Matthew places the Pharisees on the seat of Moses, but does not place the seat of Moses in the synagogue. Matthew (and parallels in Mark and Luke) and John use the word *sunagōgē* in connection with Pharisaic power, but the word is ambiguous and seems to refer to public "assemblies," whether judicial or communal, rather than "synagogues." Some synagogues, like the Theodotus synagogue of Jerusalem, were controlled not by Pharisees but by priests.[46] The office of *archisunagōgeus is* known from the New Testament, inscriptions, and rabbinic literature (where the office is called *rosh hakeneset),* but not a single Pharisee or rabbi can be shown to have been an *archisynagogue.* Justin, as we have seen, distinguishes Pharisees from *archisynagogues.*[47]

Since the synagogue has its ultimate origins not in sectarian piety but in the social ethos and political forms of the Hellenistic Period, it was predominantly a democratic lay organization, not beholden to a single group or party. In antiquity no central synagogue organization — no "United Synagogue," no chief rabbinate, and no pope — ever existed. No office was empowered to enforce standards (for example, *birkat ha-minim)* in all synagogues, and no political mechanism existed to enforce standards.[48] The liturgy was not stan-

---

44. David Goodblatt, "The Place of the Pharisees in First Century Judaism," *Journal for the Study of Judaism* 20 (1989): 12–30; Mason 372–73 and "Pharisaic Dominance before 70 C.E. and the Gospels' Hypocrisy Charge (Matt *23:2–3),"* HTR 83 (1990): 363–81, esp. 371–79. See Hengel's long critique of Sanders (above n. 1).

45. In Josephus *Vita* 276–303, four delegates from Jerusalem, three of whom are Pharisees, take a prominent role in a series of meetings that take place over a Shabbat-Sunday-Monday in the large synagogue (*proseuchē*) of Tiberias. However, these were exceptional times and events, and hardly indicate anything about Pharisaic power generally in synagogues.

46. On priests in the synagogue, see Sanders, *Judaism: Practice and Belief* 201.

47. Nicodemusts the Pharisee (John 3:1) is an archon, not an *archisynagogue.* For a discussion of the title and the office see Brooten, *Leaders* 15–33. For a full survey of synagogue officers in antiquity, see James Burtchaell, *From Synagogue to Church* (Cambridge University Press, 1992), 228–71. On *archisynagōgos,* see now Tessa Rajak and Dov Noy, "*Archisynagōgos:* Office, Title, and Social Status in the Greco-Jewish Synagogue," *JRS* 83 (1993): 75–93.

48. Contrast William Horbury, "Extirpation and Excommunication," *Vetus Tes-*

dardized. These facts are no less true for the period after 70 C.E. than for the Second Temple Period. Aside from the synagogue of Rehov, with a piece of the Yerushalmi spelled out in mosaic tile on its floor,[49] not a single synagogue excavated in the land of Israel is demonstrably rabbinic. Synagogue inscriptions do not place rabbis in positions of leadership; neither does the Theodosian code, which refers to the patriarch, patriarchs, archisynagogues, and various other officials.[50] How to reconcile synagogal art and architecture with rabbinic law and piety is a well known and enduring problem.

The widely held notion that Pharisees and rabbis led communal prayer and study seems to derive ultimately from rabbinic literature, on the Jewish side, and from the writings of Jerome, on the Christian side. Rabbinic literature conceives of the rabbis and their predecessors as *the* leaders of Judaism, indeed as synonymous with Judaism itself. If rabbinic Judaism is Judaism, and if the synagogue is the central institution of Judaism, then surely the rabbis, and their predecessors the Pharisees, will have been the leaders of all that took place in the synagogue! However, both this conception and the conclusion that derives from it are flawed, because neither the Judaism nor the synagogue of antiquity should be conceived in monistic terms. Pharisaic Judaism and rabbinic Judaism are not synonymous with Judaism.

This rabbino-centric (or Pharisaeo-centric) perspective receives its first nonrabbinic attestation in the writings of the church father Jerome (c. 380 C.E.), who knows the rabbinic *birkat ha-minim*,[51] clearly identifies the Pharisees of old with the rabbis (or sages, *sophoi*) of his own time, and sees them both as the leaders of the Jews.[52] Some of these sages (*sapientissimi*), as the heads of synagogues (*praepositi synagogis*), render decisions on questions of

tamentum 35 (1985): 13–38, who ascribes to Jewish communities a much higher degree of organization and centralization than is warranted by the evidence.

49. J. Naveh, *On Stone and Mosaic: The Aramaic and Hebrew Inscriptions from Ancient Synagogues* (Jerusalem: Israel Exploration Society, 1978), 79–85.

50. On the inscriptions see Shaye J. D. Cohen, "Epigraphical Rabbis," *JQR* 72 (1981): 117; on the Theodosian code see Cohen, "Pagan and Christian Evidence."

51. See Thornton, "Christian Understandings." Epiphanius, sometime before Jerome, may also have known the *birkat ha-minim*.

52. Cohen, "Yavneh," 52–53. A full study of Jerome's knowledge of contemporary Judaism is a desideratum; the fullest study remains that of Samuel Krauss, "The Jews in the Works of the Church Fathers: Jerome," *JQR* 6 (1894): 225–61; Adam Kamesar, *Jerome, Greek Scholarship and the Hebrew Bible* (Oxford: Clarendon Press, 1993), 176–91 ("Jerome and his Jewish Sources") deals with Jerome's knowledge of Jewish Bible exegesis.

Jewish law.[53] The evidence of Jerome is important and awaits full scholarly assessment. It may tell us more about Jerome's conception of Judaism than about Jewish society and institutions of Jerome's time and place. At most it tells us something about the synagogues with which Jerome was familiar, and not about all synagogues everywhere in antiquity.

The seven passages that I have treated do not provide sufficient evidence for the view, still held in many circles, that the synagogue was the main institutional base of Pharisaic and rabbinic piety and power. No doubt some, perhaps many, synagogues in antiquity will have been under the religious influence of the Pharisees / rabbis, but many will not have been. As their name indicates, synagogues belonged to the community.[54]

---

53. Epistle 121.10.19 (*CSEL* 56:48): *quantae traditiones pharisaeorum sint, quas hodie deuteroseis vocant, et quam aniles fabulae, revolvere nequeo ... dicam tamen unum in ignominiam gentis inimicae: praepositos habent synagogis sapientissimos quosque foedo operi delegatos, ut sanguinem virginis sive menstruatae mundum vel inmundum, si oculis discernere non potuerint, gustatu probent.* ("How many are the traditions of the Pharisees, which today they call [in Greek] *deuteroseis,* and how foolish are their stories, I am unable to recount. ... Nevertheless, I shall say one of them, in order to shame that hateful people: they have as the heads of their synagogues certain very learned men who are assigned the disgusting task of determining by taste, if they are unable to discern by the eyes (alone), whether the blood of a virgin or a menstruant is pure or impure.") Cf. M. Niddah 2:6–7. I see no reason to think that *synagoga* in Jerome means anything other than "synagogue," but I have been unable to locate any study of the subject; on *sunagōgē* in the church fathers, see Schrage, *TDNT* 7:838–41.

54. B. Shabbat 32a, *"bet am."*

CHAPTER SIX

The Jewish Community
of Ancient Sardis
Deconstruction and Reconstruction

Marianne Bonz

Harvard Divinity School, Cambridge, Massachusetts

The archaeological discoveries at Sardis and their subsequent interpretation by George Hanfmann, Thomas Kraabel, and others from
the initial Sardis synagogue excavation team have made a significant contribution to our understanding of the social, economic,
and political position of diaspora Judaism in general, and especially with respect to the Jews of Asia Minor.[1] Generally lauded
was their emphatic rejection of some previous characterizations of
diaspora Jews as socially and culturally isolated in the Roman world
and frequently relegated to the lowest socioeconomic strata.[2] How-

1. David G. Mitten, *The Ancient Synagogue of Sardis,* Archaeological Explorations of Sardis (New York: Archaeological Exploration of Sardis, 1965); G. M. A.
Hanfmann, "The Ancient Synagogue of Sardis," *4th World Congress of Jewish Studies* (1967), 1:32–42; A. Thomas Kraabel, "Judaism in Western Asia Minor under
Roman Rule, with a Preliminary Study of the Jewish Community of Sardis, Lydia,"
(Th.D. diss., Harvard University, 1968); idem, "Melito the Bishop and the Synagogue at Sardis: Text and Context," in *Studies Presented to G. M. A. Hanfmann,*
ed. David G. Mitten et al., Fogg Art Museum Monographs in Art and Archaeology
2 (Cambridge, Mass.: Harvard University Press, 1971), 77–85; idem, "The Diaspora
Synagogue: Archaeological and Epigraphic Evidence since Sukenik," *ANRW* 2.19.1
(1979), 475–510; and Andrew R. Seager and A. Thomas Kraabel, "The Synagogue
and the Jewish Community," in G. M. A. Hanfmann et al., *Sardis: From Prehistoric
to Roman Times* (Cambridge, Mass.: Harvard University Press, 1983). It should be
emphasized, however, that the analysis of the evidence by excavation architect Seager was, from the beginning, at some variance with the historical interpretation put
forth by Hanfmann and particularly by Kraabel. See esp. Andrew R. Seager, "The
Building History of the Sardis Synagogue," *AJA* 76 (1983): 425–35.

2. Since Jean Juster's magisterial study (*Les Juifs dans l'empire romain* [Paris:
Geuther, 1914]) emphatically contradicts such simplistically negative characteriza-

ever, the wealth of evidence provided by the immense synagogue, which enabled Hanfmann and Kraabel to dispel all excessively pessimistic misconceptions, also gave rise to their own overly optimistic and essentially uncritical assessment. Unfortunately, this equally misleading interpretation continues to enjoy wide acceptance among historians of antiquity, particularly among religious historians. One notable example of its continued acceptance is Paul Trebilco's study of the Jewish communities in Asia Minor.[3] Trebilco rejects the earlier dating of the Sardis synagogue assumed by Kraabel in favor of excavation architect Andrew Seager's late third-century date,[4] but he does not seem to take into account the possible significance of this later dating in his subsequent analysis of the synagogue's members and their status within the broader context of Sardian civic life. A more recent study to systematically discuss the Sardis synagogue evidence is that of L. Michael White.[5] White's study represents another judicious attempt to reconcile the Hanfmann-Kraabel historical interpretation with Seager's seemingly incompatible architectural analysis and John Kroll's more recently completed epigraphic work. White's analysis also seeks to reconcile the original historical interpretation with more recent historical analyses that were to a great extent inspired by Seager's work and particularly by Kroll's research.[6]

The Linear Interpretation of Historical Development

The original historical interpretation set forth by Hanfmann and some (but not all) of the initial Sardis excavation team appears to

tions, however, one wonders how widespread these misconceptions really were, at least in the scholarly world.

3. Paul Trebilco, *Jewish Communities in Asia Minor,* Society for New Testament Studies 69 (Cambridge: Cambridge University Press, 1991).

4. Ibid., 40.

5. L. Michael White, *The Social Origins of Christian Architecture,* vol. 2: *Texts and Monuments for the Christian Domus Ecclesiae in Its Environment,* Harvard Theological Studies (Valley Forge, Pa.: Trinity Press International, 1997), 310–24.

6. John H. Kroll, "The Greek Inscriptions," (1974; rev. 1989; 2d rev. 1994). Unfortunately, this major study remains unpublished, although it is still listed as forthcoming in *The Synagogue at Sardis,* ed. Andrew R. Seager et al., Archaeological Explorations of Sardis R5 (Cambridge, Mass.: Harvard University Press). For the revisionist interpretations, see Helga Botermann, "Die Synagoge von Sardes: Eine Synagoge aus dem 4. Jahrhundert?" *ZNW* 81 (1990): 103–21; Marianne P. Bonz: "The Jewish Community of Ancient Sardis: A Reassessment of Its Rise to Prominence," *HSCP* 93 (1990): 343–59; and eadem, "Differing Approaches to Religious Benefaction: The Late Third-Century Acquisition of the Sardis Synagogue," *HTR* 86, no. 2 (1993): 139–54.

rest upon an erroneous application of the essentially valid concept of the historical continuity of society and culture in Greco-Roman antiquity. According to this view the historical development from Hellenistic and early Roman times, through the Roman imperial period, and into the early Christian era of late antiquity is characterized by prevailing elements of continuity. The rise and fall of rulers, the periodic outbreak of natural and human disasters, and the creation and decline of ideologies merely serve to form the rich pattern of an essentially unified tapestry. Although the fundamental wisdom of this understanding of the history of antiquity is unassailable, it does not justify, much less necessitate, a linear conception of socioeconomic development, such as the Hanfmann team originally constructed for the Sardis Jewish community and then extrapolated as a plausible model for other Jewish communities in Asia Minor.

This particular developmental model began with the end point of the late antique synagogue, with its impressive size and equally impressive decoration. It took as its starting point the land allotments and tax concessions granted by the Hellenistic ruler Antiochus III, who settled Jews in this area as part of a larger effort to secure his borders and stabilize his kingdom. Josephus's extensive reporting of decrees from the later Hellenistic period affirming Roman support for a variety of Jewish rights indicates that these Jewish communities took root and flourished. From their modestly favored beginnings as Seleucid *katoikoi* to their ultimate display of communal wealth and social integration in late antiquity, the original interpretive model simply assumed a linear progression of continually rising social, political, and economic status.

The evidence for such a pattern of development is, however, very weak indeed. First, although the Sardis decrees quoted in Josephus indicate that the Jewish community enjoyed considerable autonomy, the references (Josephus *Ant.* 14.235, 259) to their status as Greek citizens (*politai*) are regarded by many scholars as either misrepresentations or interpolations,[7] since the contexts of both references describe the conditions of a people organized as a *politeuma* (an autonomous social and civic entity), not as full Greek citizens. Indeed, a generation earlier Victor Tcherikover cast suspicion on Josephus's claims regarding Jewish citizenship in cities founded by the Seleucid kings (Josephus, *Ant.* 12.119–20, 125–26;

---

7. See, for example, the discussion in Trebilco, *Jewish Communities*, 169–71.

16.160).[8] The issue, according to Tcherikover, may be summarized as follows:

> There is no doubt that the Jews had rights.... The question is whether, besides these, the Jews had all those municipal rights which every Greek member of the city had; in other words, whether the Jewish community took part in the town's public life, for example, in the conduct of municipal affairs, the election of magistrates, and the like.[9]

Tcherikover notes that Josephus is the only ancient source that claims full Greek civic rights for the Jews and that even his assertions of Greek citizenship are not supported by his more detailed descriptions. In case after case what Josephus actually describes is a historical situation in which the Roman rulers of late Hellenistic and early Roman times affirm and uphold the autonomous privileges allowing the Jews to function as self-contained communities and permitting them to live according to their ancestral customs, unhindered by the civic laws of the Greek majority.[10] Scholars beginning with Harold Bell have noted that Josephus's purported quotation of an imperial edict affirming Jewish citizenship and rights in Alexandria (*Ant.* 19.280–85) stands in marked contrast to an authentic imperial letter addressing similar concerns.[11] In this letter, the emperor Claudius refers to the Alexandrians as Ἀλεξανδρεῖς μὲν ... (in the case of the *Alexandrians*)[12] and the Jews as Ἰουδέοις [*sic*] δὲ ... (whereas the *Jews*),[13] with the contrast clearly marked by the μὲν and the δὲ. Another crucial phrase appears in line 95 of the same letter, in which Claudius refers to the Jews as living "in a city not their own" (ἐν ἀλλοτρίᾳ πόλει).

Even though Greek citizenship was not generally considered a prerequisite for Roman citizenship,[14] there is likewise little evidence

---

8. Victor Tcherikover, *Hellenistic Civilization and the Jews* (Philadelphia: Jewish Publication Society of America, 1959), 328–29.

9. Ibid., 310.

10. Ibid., 296–332, esp. 330.

11. Victor A. Tcherikover and Alexander Fuks, *Corpus Papyrorum Judaicarum,* 3 vols. (Cambridge, Mass.: Harvard University Press; Jerusalem: Magnes, 1957–64) 2, no. 153, dated 41 c.e.; see Harold I. Bell, "Anti-Semitism in Alexandria," *JRS* 31 (1941): 1–18.

12. Tcherikover and Fuks, *Corpus Papyrorum Judaicarum,* 2. no. 153, ln. 82.

13. Ibid., ln. 88.

14. In a letter from Pliny to the emperor Trajan (*Ep.* 10.6), it is clear that only in the case of Egyptians was it necessary that provincials be Greek citizens before being granted Roman citizenship. Other categories of noncitizens could be granted Roman citizenship, provided only that they were not slaves.

to suggest that Jews were Roman citizens before the third century C.E. Indeed, in his study of the question of Roman citizenship, Trebilco cites only five possible examples of Jews from Asia Minor who were Roman citizens before 212 C.E., and in two of his five examples the evidence is either suspect or undated.[15] Although, therefore, the Jews of Sardis and elsewhere throughout the Greek diaspora may have enjoyed a degree of economic prosperity and considerable civic and religious autonomy in the Hellenistic and early Roman eras, they probably did not possess full citizenship. The lengthier of the two so-called God-fearers inscriptions from Aphrodisias, the one dated most securely by Joyce Reynolds and Robert Tannenbaum to the early third century, indicates that while a number of Gentile God-fearers of relatively humble social status and occupation had been incorporated into the city's governing council (*boulé*) as *bouletai* (council members), none of the Jews of comparable status and occupation had received this mark of civic acceptance.[16] Indeed, the repeated attestation of citizenship status in the mid-to-late fourth-century Sardis synagogue donor inscriptions indicates that Sardian Jews still regarded their Greek citizenship as a distinction and status worth mentioning.[17]

In short, all of the evidence suggests that, with few exceptions, the Jews of Asia Minor did not receive full citizenship (Roman or Greek) before the enactment of the *Constitutio Antoniniana* in the early third century. Thus, with rare exceptions, second- and early third-century members of the various Jewish communities would not have been city councilors, nor would they have had access to important imperial posts, nor would they have participated in provincial assemblies. Before 212, therefore, regardless of their economic status, Sardian Jews remained at best marginally influential in the social and civic affairs of their city.

This conclusion further calls into question the relevance and significance of the pervasive anti-Jewish polemic of the *Peri Pascha* homily, traditionally attributed to the late second-century Christian bishop Melito of Sardis. Although questions concerning the authorship and purpose of this rhetorical piece are treated more fully

---

15. Trebilco, *Jewish Communities*, 173.

16. Joyce Reynolds and Robert Tannenbaum, *Jews and Godfearers at Aphrodisias*, Supp. 12 (Cambridge: Cambridge Philological Society, 1987), esp. 93–123. On the probable fifth-century dating of the shorter inscription, see Marianne P. Bonz, "The Jewish Donor Inscriptions from Aphrodisias: Are They Both Third-Century, and Who Are the *Theosebeis?*" *HSCP* 96 (1994): 281–99.

17. Kroll, "Greek Inscriptions" (1989), 6.

elsewhere in this volume, several points deserve special emphasis within the context of the present discussion. Those who have argued that the motivation for the author's harsh anti-Jewish attack lies in Christian envy of the power and influence of the Sardis Jewish community have not only ignored the relevant historical realities noted above,[18] but also underestimated the hyperbolic elements that diatribe preaching typically employed.[19] That this sort of excessive and offensive invective was characteristic of the genre and a rhetorical feature that was quickly incorporated into early Christian preaching has long been noted.[20] Moreover, the virulence of the anti-Jewish attack in the second-century *Peri Pascha* is no greater than that of the late fourth-century *Adversus Iudaeos* homilies of John Chrysostom, clearly written at a time when the Church had little to fear socially or politically from diasporan Jewish communities.[21] Indeed, all of these excesses of anti-Jewish rhetoric can be understood much more

---

18. Fundamental to the preceding discussion as well as the more lengthy analysis that follows is acceptance of the findings of Seager and Kroll, namely, that the large, elegantly-appointed Sardis synagogue was originally a Greek civic basilica, which was converted to use as a synagogue only toward the end of the third century, with work continuing well into the fourth century. With one possible exception (a floor inscription dated sometime after 270 c.e.), all of the synagogue's donor inscriptions are dated to the fourth century or later (Kroll, "Greek Inscriptions" [1994], 11–12). With respect to the interpretation of the material and epigraphic evidence from this synagogue, therefore, one must focus on the social and economic context of the fourth and fifth centuries.

This is not to say, however, that there is no evidence for the existence of synagogues at Sardis prior to this time. On the contrary, an early third-century inscription lists a synagogue as one of the buildings located near a city fountain (William H. Buckler and David M. Robinson, *Greek and Latin Inscriptions*, American Society for the Exploration of Sardis 7 [Leiden: Brill, 1932], ins. no. 17). Unfortunately, excavators have never located this earlier synagogue.

Finally, it is well to remember, as Tessa Rajak recently noted, that any large Greek city would have had several synagogues and thus several (possibly diverse) Jewish communities (Tessa Rajak, "The Jewish Community and Its Boundaries," in *The Jews among Pagans and Christians*, ed. Judith Lieu et al. [London and New York: Routledge, 1992], 10–11). All efforts to reconstruct "the Sardis Jewish community," therefore, are limited by the term's inherent complexity.

19. See, for example, Kraabel, "Melito the Bishop and the Synagogue at Sardis," 77–85.

20. See Rudolf Bultmann, *Der Stil der paulinischen Predigt und die kynisch-stoische Diatribe*, FRLANT 13 (Göttingen: Vandenhoeck & Ruprecht, 1984 [1910]), 32–66, 103–5. More recently, Hans Dieter Betz has noted this stylistic feature in his interpretation of Gal 5:12, speaking of such invective as characteristic of the genre (*Galatians*, Hermeneia [Philadelphia: Fortress, 1979], 270).

21. For an informed and balanced discussion of the gradual ascendancy of the Christian majority and its correlative restrictions against the pagan and Jewish minorities, see Fergus Millar, "The Jews of the Greco-Roman Diaspora between Paganism and Christianity, AD 312–438," in *Jews among Pagans and Christians*, 97–123.

readily as motivated by clerical concern over the powerful attraction that the Jewish synagogue and Jewish festivals continued to exert on impressionable Christian converts than by fear of excessive Jewish political power or civic influence.[22]

The Sardis Synagogue Evidence and Its Late Antique Context

If, as I have argued, the evidence supporting the original interpretation of the historical development of the Sardis Jewish community is at least open to question, then perhaps it is time to consider an alternative hypothesis based upon a revised interpretation of the synagogue evidence itself. Every student of the archaeological record agrees that the physical evidence clearly attests to a Jewish community of the fourth and fifth centuries that is large and affluent, as well as socially and politically secure within the late antique city. A more refined and nuanced analysis of both the strengths and limitations of the community's success is possible, desirable, and indeed necessary, however, if a consensus is to be reached as to its true historical significance. To my knowledge this task remains largely unfulfilled because Clive Foss's work on late antique Sardis eschews incorporation of the synagogue evidence, and Kraabel's interpretation of the Sardis Jewish community, which assumes an early dating of the synagogue, is predicated to a large extent on the historical context of the late second and early third centuries.

Placing the Sardis synagogue evidence within its proper historical context is essential, however, for a realistic appraisal of its meaning. For example, much has been made of the fact that nine separate inscriptions attest to members of the synagogue as having been *bouletai*. Clearly this rank indicates a relatively high level

---

22. Although the emperor Julian (361–63 C.E.) had made plans to reconstruct the Jerusalem Temple and in other ways had endeavored to strengthen Jewish power and prestige throughout the empire, his intention was to use the Jews as a means of checking the growing dominance of the Christian church throughout society. By these means Julian hoped to enable a resurgence of paganism, which had been increasingly on the defensive. Far from affirming the menacing power of the Jews, therefore, Julian's efforts on their behalf should be interpreted as further evidence of the increasing social and political power of the Christians relative to both pagans and Jews. This interpretation is largely borne out by Millar, "Jews of the Graeco-Roman Diaspora," 105–8. However, Helmut Castritius ("Zur Konkurrenzsituation zwischen Judentum und Christentum in der spätrömisch-frühbyzantinischen Welt," *Aschkenas: Zeitschrift für Geschichte und Kultur der Juden* 8 [1998]: 29–44) rightly observes that in the early Christian empire of late antiquity, religious policies cannot be wholly separated from political and economic consequences.

of economic prosperity for the individuals who held it, since sub-stantive property requirements remained the defining qualification for this post, even in the fourth and fifth centuries. It also at-tests to a high degree of social and political integration for Sardian Jews, because the council remained the chief governing body of the city. Nevertheless, in order to arrive at a more realistic assessment of the significance of this designation in the late antique period, many caveats need to be supplied, especially since it is generally acknowledged that the *boulé* had suffered a measure of decline.

First, in discussing the decline of the *boulé* in late antiquity, a distinction must be drawn between the difficulties of the third cen-tury and those of the fourth and fifth centuries. As early as the end of the second century, and increasingly so in the third, the *boulai* of the Greek cities in Asia Minor experienced difficulty in filling their vacancies. In these earlier centuries, however, the problem was al-most entirely economic. Indeed, already by the beginning of the third century the combination of intermittent war and economic decline had taken its toll on many provincial landowners. Thus an imperial decree by the early third-century jurist Callistratus ruled that shopkeepers and traders of sufficient wealth should be allowed to fill the increasing number of vacancies in the council chambers.[23] Moreover, as the third century progressed, the economic troubles, particularly in the Greek East, deepened and became a widespread crisis. Although earlier historical interpretations of ancient Sardis, such as those of Hanfmann and Foss, had been predicated upon the assumption that the economic crisis of the later third century had not seriously affected the Lydian city, significant numismatic evi-dence brought to light subsequent to their analyses does not support their optimistic assumptions.[24]

Nevertheless, despite the broadly based economic crisis that by the later third century had engulfed most of the Greek East, in-cluding Sardis, the local *boulai* retained their prestige because, as

---

23. *Dig. Just.* 50.2.12. "It is not proper to ignore as base persons who deal in and sell objects of daily use, even though they are people who may be flogged by the aediles. Indeed, men of this kind are not debarred from seeking the decurion-ate." (*Eos qui utensilia negotiantur et vendunt, licet ab aedilibus caeduntur, non oportet quasi viles personas neglegi. denique non sunt prohibiti huiusmodi homines decurionatum.*)

24. According to the highly respected numismatic study of C. J. Howgego, the only area of Asia Minor that managed to survive the severe monetary crisis of the 260s was the south central portion, specifically, the regions of Pisidia and Pamphylia (*Greek Imperial Countermarks: Studies in the Provincial Coinage of the Roman Empire* [London: Royal Numismatic Society, 1985], esp. 65–70.

Kenneth Harl's study of Greek imperial coinage has shown, civic pride and traditional civic values continued throughout the third century. Harl maintains, however, that it is precisely these traditional civic values of piety and pride in the social and political integrity of the *polis* that disappeared after 300 C.E. and that for this reason no subsequent attempt was ever made, not even by the emperor Julian, to revive the local coinage, the quintessential symbol of those no longer extant civic values.[25]

By contrast, in the fourth and fifth centuries the vacancies in the city councils were no longer created primarily by the less affluent decurions; increasingly they were created by the voluntary exodus from the council of its wealthier and more influential members. That is to say, those decurions with sufficient wealth and social or political connections used these assets to purchase careers and offices in the imperial service in order to gain equestrian and ultimately senatorial rank. This, in turn, would guarantee their immunity from local council service.[26] Many also went into the Christian clergy in order to escape service on the local councils and the economic burdens such service imposed. Although this religious loophole was periodically plugged by imperial decree, it must have been routinely ignored. Otherwise there would have been no need for the repeated rulings on this matter found in the Theodosian Codes.[27]

Thus by the mid-fourth century, membership in the city council no longer necessarily implied high social status. Nor were all council members extremely wealthy. On the contrary, although some councilors were still recruited from the ranks of the very wealthy landowners, many were only moderately affluent. Indeed, in extreme cases, city councils might include humble and even illiterate traders and artisans.[28] According to Libanius, our most informed contemporary source, when the very wealthy few did choose to remain in the *boulē* instead of acquiring honorific posts in the imperial bureaucracy, they tended to aggregate the institution's dwindling power into their own hands, forcing the less prominent members to bear the more burdensome liturgies.[29]

With respect to the erosion of civic institutions in late antique

25. Kenneth Harl, *Civic Coins and Politics in the Roman East, A.D. 180–275* (Berkeley: University of California Press, 1987), 95.

26. *Cod. Theod.* 12.1.11.

27. *Cod. Theod.* 12.1.49, 99, 104, 115, 121, 123; 16.2.1, 2, 3, 6, 17, and 19.

28. *Cod. Just.* 10.32.6 293, cited in A. H. M. Jones, *The Later Roman Empire 284–602* (Baltimore: Johns Hopkins University Press, 1986 [1964]), 69, n. 60.

29. Libanius *Or.* 48.40; 49.8–12.

Sardis, one funerary inscription attributed to the fourth century is of particular significance. It refers to the sepulchre and coffins contained therein as belonging to Aurelia Hesychion and her husband Aurelios Zoticos, a municipal baker who was also a member of the formerly prestigious city *gerousia* (council of elders).[30] Although Foss has argued with some justification that access to the *gerousia* affirms that municipal bakers must have become socially and economically important, this argument is certainly open to qualification in the light of Libanius's references to the flogging of bakers in Antioch,[31] a punishment that was both illegal and politically impossible with respect to people of consequence in late antique society. Indeed, it is equally valid to emphasize that this inscription illustrates the erosion of the prestige of the *gerousia*, a civic institution like the *boulē*, whose status and importance relative to the imperial bureaucracy had declined, beginning in the third century and markedly so in the fourth and fifth centuries.[32]

Although the *boulē* remained necessary and important in the day to-day running of the city, it made no major policy decisions, these having been usurped by the provincial governor and his appointees. The power and prestige of city government was further compromised because the cities no longer possessed significant sources of discretionary income. Having already lost their endowments to the inflation of the late third century, their situation steadily deteriorated under the Christian emperors of the fourth century. With the exception of the pagan emperor Julian, the imperial governments of the fourth century confiscated city tax and land revenues, returning only a fraction of this money to enable the cities to maintain public buildings and defray public expenses.[33] Again these trends that A. H. M. Jones documented back in the 1960s are corroborated independently by the inscriptional evidence from Sardis. At Sardis during this period it is no longer the council and people who erect

---

30. Buckler and Robinson, *Greek and Latin Inscriptions,* ins. no. 166. Cf. Clive Foss, *Byzantine and Turkish Sardis* (Cambridge, Mass.: Harvard University Press, 1976), 110.

31. Libanius *Or.* 1.206–8, 228.

32. Indeed, three graffiti, crudely inscribed on the floor of the Marble Court of the fifth or sixth centuries, designate this place, now enclosed by crude rubble walls, as the meeting place of Sardis' *boulé* and *gerousia* (Archaeological Exploration of Sardis, inv. ins. 71.6a, b, and c). See *BASOR* 206 (1972): 25, fig. 27; Foss, *Byzantine and Turkish Sardis*, 41, fig. 2.

33. Regarding fourth-century confiscation of lands and revenues: Libanius *Or.* 30.6.37. See also *Cod. Theod.* 4.13.7; 5.13.3; 5.14.35; and 15.1.18. For their temporary restoration under Julian: Libanius *Or.* 13.45; *Cod. Theod.* 10.3.1; *Cod. Just.* 11.70.1. See Jones, *Later Roman Empire,* 732–33, nn. 44–45.

and restore buildings. Rather, it is the vicar, the governor, or the
pater poleos acting as the governor's agent.[34] Charlotte Roueché
affirms the same situation for late antique Aphrodisias, as does
Foss for Ephesus.[35] Additional evidence that the rank of *bouletēs*
no longer retained its former degree of power or distinction comes
from a late fourth-century provision in the Theodosian Codes in
which urban workers and decurions are lumped together as seeking
the protection of powerful patrons in an effort to avoid oppressive
and unjust civic liturgies.[36]

On the other hand, the synagogue inscriptional evidence also
suggests that some members of the Jewish community may have
achieved genuine prominence and acceptance into the higher ranks
of the imperial hierarchy. Two donor inscriptions, one identifying
a former procurator and the other a *comes*,[37] are possible evidence
of the social and political prominence of a few Sardian Jews of the
fourth century.[38] This possibility is given further credence by evidence from nearby Aphrodisias. Roueché cites an inscription, which
she dates to the second quarter of the fourth century, designating its
Jewish donor as the holder of high imperial office.[39] Equally possible in the case of the two Sardis inscriptions, however, is that they
refer to powerful Gentile patrons of the Sardis Jewish community.
Either possibility is commensurate with the evidence of an affluent
and centrally located late antique synagogue.

Moreover, if the prestige and importance of civic offices such as
that of *bouletēs* was in fact declining, the importance and economic
fortunes of artisans and successful traders were, relatively speaking, rising, particularly in the larger *metropoleis* such as Sardis.
Indeed, the emperor Constantine granted personal exemptions (pre-

---

34. Buckler and Robinson, *Greek and Latin Inscriptions*, 83; Fikert Yegül, *The Bath-Gymnasium Complex at Sardis*, Archaeological Exploration of Sardis R3 (Cambridge, Mass.: Harvard University Press, 1986), 171–72.

35. Charlotte Roueché and Joyce M. Reynolds, *Aphrodisias in Late Antiquity: The Late Roman and Byzantine Inscriptions* (Oxford: Society for the Promotion of Roman Studies, 1989), xxiv; Clive Foss, *Ephesus After Antiquity: A Late Antique, Byzantine, and Turkish City* (Cambridge and New York: Cambridge University Press, 1979), 25.

36. *Cod. Theod.* 12.1.146.

37. By the fourth century this term had come to refer to either a senior officeholder in the imperial service or a military commander of a small regional army. If the *comes* of the synagogue inscription refers to a regional military commander, then he may have represented a powerful Gentile "friend" or protector of the synagogue and its members.

38. Kroll, "Greek Inscriptions" (1989), 6, ins. nos. 5, 70.

39. Roueché and Reynolds, *Aphrodisias*, 23, ins. no. 10.

viously reserved for elite occupations, such as rhetors, or necessary ones, such as doctors) to all sorts of skilled labor needed for the rebuilding of the cities of his empire. The types of laborers specified in Constantine's decree included painters, sculptors, stone carvers, mosaicists, plasterers, gilders, metal workers, potters and glass workers, fullers, and purple dyers.[40] Personal exemption from compulsory public services must have enabled some of these workers to make the transition to prosperous entrepreneurs. Indeed, some traders became wealthy merchants, and some silversmiths became rudimentary bankers. They, along with jewelers and goldsmiths, although seldom counted among the local aristocracy, could acquire considerable wealth and could aspire to city council positions or minor court sinecures.

Although the Sardis synagogue inscriptions reveal their donors' occupations in only a few instances, these instances identify them as skilled craftsmen and tradesmen — several goldsmiths, a marble sculptor, and possibly some mosaic workers.[41] In addition, material evidence and inscriptions found in the fifth-century shops that adjoin the south wall of the synagogue identify Jewish owners of several small paint and dye shops and of a glass shop.[42] Indeed, a wealth of non-Jewish evidence for this period suggests that late antique Sardis was an important center for manufacture and commerce, as well as a center for highly skilled artisans. In addition to the shops that have been identified as Jewish, excavators have found evidence for the existence of several restaurants, a wine shop, several hardware stores, a grinding and weighing room, and a small business office.[43] These modest establishments serving only a small sector of the city doubtless represent a widespread pattern of city retail business and trade.

More important is the evidence that late antique Sardis benefited significantly from being the seat of the provincial governor and an important supply center for the imperial army. Sardis's wealth had always owed much to its strategic location along major trade routes. Although Sardian trade must certainly have suffered in the late third century because of the disrepair of the roads,[44] the city resumed

---

40. *Cod. Theod.* 13.4.2.

41. Kroll, "Greek Inscriptions" (1989), 5–15.

42. Hanfmann et al., *Sardis*, 164–66.

43. Ibid.

44. Numerous inscriptions marking the completion of road repairs to all of the major trade routes passing through Sardis attest that restoration of these vital trade routes was an important priority in Diocletian's reign. See, for example, *CIL* 3.

its former prosperity in late antiquity because the imperial government's continued reliance upon the army necessitated the repair and
maintenance of these very roads. Furthermore, Sardis's manufacturing and metal crafts benefited because the army needed weapons and
clothing. An important inscription from the time of Diocletian designates a major imperial weapons and shield manufacturing plant in
Sardis. Such a plant would have employed numerous skilled metal
workers and would also have enabled the flourishing of domestic
metal products.[45] Although we have no direct evidence of the establishment of an imperial weaving mill for wool and linen clothing,
we do have evidence that these trades also flourished at Sardis. Two
presumably fourth-century tomb inscriptions from the area attest to
the presence of clothes sellers and tailors.[46] Moreover, excavation of
the late antique House of Bronzes in the northwestern sector of the
city revealed equipment most likely used for the bleaching of wool.
According to Foss, the work area was sufficient in size to qualify as
a commercial establishment.[47]

Not limited solely to the practical arts, material evidence from the
synagogue and elsewhere in the city indicates that the workshops
for the decorative arts had achieved (or perhaps merely retained) a
high level of sophistication and refinement in late antique Sardis.
One need only compare the mid-fourth-century peacock mosaic
from the earliest known church in Philippi with the early fourth-
century peacock in the apse of the Sardis synagogue to appreciate
the vastly superior quality of the latter and the skill and sophistication of the workshop that produced it.[48] Here again, Sardis
workshops for the decorative arts would have benefited from the
demand created by the city's status as a provincial capital and by
the infusion of imperial money that such cities naturally attracted.

Thus with the decline in status and wealth of the less affluent
members of the decurion class and the comparable rise of the more
skilled and successful artisans and traders, a certain democrati-

---

7196–99; *CIG* 3449; and Buckler and Robinson, *Greek and Latin Inscriptions*, ins.
no. 84.

45. Foss, *Byzantine and Turkish Sardis*, 15.

46. Ibid., 110, ins. nos. 12 and 13.

47. Ibid., 15.

48. For a description and account of the synagogue mosaic, see *BASOR* 174
(1964): 30–33, fig. 17; Hanfmann et al., *Sardis*, 170, figs. 260–61. For a description
of the early Christian mosaic, see Charalambas Bakirtzis, "Philippi," in *Archaeological Resources for the New Testament,* ed. Helmut Koester and Ann Brock
(Valley Forge, Pa.: Trinity Press International, 1994), Philippi A 49; Stylianos M.
Pelekanides, "Excavations in Philippi," *Balkan Studies* 8 (1967): 123–26.

zation and social mobility emerges as characteristic of the fourth century. This change did not affect the extremely wealthy and socially privileged, whose position became, if anything, even stronger and more dominant as late antique society progressed. Nevertheless, a new and much larger segment of the urban population clearly gained broader access to society's economic and civic benefits and an accompanying rise in social, economic, and political opportunity. Many members of the Sardis Jewish community were probably part of this dramatically increasing class of prosperous and moderately well-to-do artisans and tradespeople.

The community's wealth and assets need not have been limited, however, to business and commerce. As has often been noted, in addition to the less reliable literary evidence from Josephus, epigraphic evidence shows that some Jewish families had been offered land grants and temporary tax exemptions to settle in the areas around Sardis during Hellenistic times.[49] These modest allotments would have provided sufficient acreage to establish small, independent farms.[50] Although conditions would probably not have permitted much opportunity for significant upward mobility during the first two centuries of the common era, considerable evidence (much of it legislative) supports the contention that land began to change hands as early as the end of the second century and that this trend gained momentum throughout the third and fourth centuries. Although scholars generally believe that the extremely wealthy estate owners most benefited from this transfer of agricultural assets, it is not at all impossible that others, particularly those willing and able to pool their resources into a common effort, might also have taken advantage of this new opportunity brought on by economic instability.

The agricultural troubles had already begun in Marcus Aurelius's late-second-century reign, when Roman armies brought back the plague from their involvement in the war with Parthia. Plague and zealous army recruitment drew workers away from the land, which then could not be harvested. During the subsequent reign of Commodus many estates, particularly the less fertile ones, fell into disuse

49. Josephus *Ant.* 12.147–51; Louis Robert, "Appendix on Inscriptions of 213 B.C.," in Hanfmann et al., *Sardis*, 111–12. The critical relevance of these inscriptions for the founding of the Jewish community is further dramatically attested by virtue of the fact that these Hellenistic spoils were built into the foundation piers when the south hall was converted into the synagogue in the late third century. See *BASOR* 174 (1964): 30.

50. Here one must rely mainly on Egyptian parallels. For example, Tcherikover and Fuks, *Corpus Papyrorum Judaicarum*, 1, nos. 28, 31.

and were abandoned by their owners. Accordingly, in his brief reign in the spring of 193, Pertinax issued a decree inviting anyone who wished to do so to cultivate deserted land (both private and imperial) in exchange for tax immunity and full ownership.[51] Again in the late third century, when high inflation and barbarian invasions had added to the farmers' troubles, the emperor Aurelian (270–75 C.E.) had offered favorable terms for those willing to buy or lease lands in exchange for temporary tax immunity and firm title.[52]

Although the administrative measures of Diocletian (284–305 C.E.) and the renewed unity of the empire under the later Christian emperors brought a measure of economic stability and eventual prosperity, agriculture still suffered. This difficulty was partly the result of the continued threat of wars and barbarian invasions; but also, as Libanius's petition to Theodosius clearly illustrates, powerful army officers quartered in the countryside enabled or encouraged tenant farmers to desert their landlords, these officers then offering protection from the landlords and the courts in exchange for payments in kind from the farmers' harvests.[53] Presumably as a result of all of these factors, a fourth-century census from Asia Minor shows that agriculture suffered from an acute shortage of labor.[54] Indeed, a series of legislative measures recorded in the Theodosian Codes and extending throughout the fourth century indicates that agricultural lands continued to change hands and that the imperial government's concern in addressing this problem was limited to the prevention of a loss of its own tax revenues.[55] As much as twenty percent of the land devoted to agriculture changed hands during the third and fourth centuries.[56]

Toward an Alternative Historical Reconstruction

Although the evidence remains insufficient to trace with certainty the fortunes and development of the Jewish communities of Asia Minor in general or even those of the Jewish community of Sardis in particular, the evidence assembled in the preceding pages at

---

51. Herodian, 2.4.6.

52. *Cod. Just.* 11.59.1, cited in Jones, *Later Roman Empire*, 812.

53. Libanius *Or.* 47.13–19.

54. A. H. M. Jones, "Census Records of the Late Roman Empire," *JRS* 43 (1953): 53–62.

55. *Cod. Theod.* 11.1.4 (337 C.E.); 7.20.11 (368 C.E.); 5.14.30 (386 C.E.); 5.14.33 (393 C.E.); and 5.14.34 (394 C.E.).

56. Jones, *Later Roman Empire*, 822.

least permits the construction of a reasonable alternative to the still commonly accepted hypothesis of a steady rise in the Jewish community's prosperity and influence, beginning in early Hellenistic times and culminating in the impressive affluence and social acceptance revealed by the material evidence of the late antique synagogue. Such an alternative historical reconstruction may be summarized as follows: The Jewish community of Hellenistic Sardis, which probably originated with the Seleucid settlements of the late third century B.C.E.,[57] consisted primarily of yeoman farmers, petty traders, and skilled artisans. With rare exceptions, these Jews did not possess Greek or Roman citizenship, nor would many of their number have likely risen socially or economically through military service, especially after the mid-first century B.C.E.[58] Therefore, generally speaking, their social status would have remained modest and their political influence marginal throughout the late republican and high imperial eras.

At least some members of the Jewish community, however, may have achieved a relatively high economic status by the second century C.E. and events of the third century may have accelerated this trend relative to their Greek neighbors. Although the vast majority of the Jewish community would have achieved Roman citizenship in 212, along with all other free subjects, Sardian Jews may nevertheless not have been nominated to serve in the council or in the city's magistracies until somewhat later in the third century.[59] Given the heavy financial burden of serving in these offices during a period of increasing inflation and other economic woes, their possible exclusion from these posts at the beginning of this period may actually have helped them to prosper after the crisis years had ended.

When stability returned sometime during the reign of Diocletian, many members of the Jewish community may have been in a po-

---

57. The evidence that Kraabel cites for earlier settlement is very problematic and its credibility is further undermined by the demonstrable importance with which those who converted the south hall into a synagogue accorded the Hellenistic inscriptions attesting to a *synoikismos*. For Kraabel's arguments, see Hanfmann et al., *Sardis*, 178–79.

58. Nonetheless, some may have prospered, since Jews were never actually prohibited from serving in the army until early in the fifth century C.E. (*Cod. Theod.* 16.8.24).

59. The absence of the title of *bouletēs* from the names of any of the Jews and the abundant presence of this title among the list of Gentile Godfearers makes the early third-century Aphrodisian inscription mentioned previously (see n. 16) a very important piece of evidence in evaluating the civic status of the Jews of Asia Minor during this period.

sition to educate their sons in the professions,[60] take advantage of
the economic opportunities of agricultural land on very favorable
terms, or capitalize on restored trade routes and renewed demands
for skilled labor and artisans.[61] Similarly, the altered political power
structure of the fourth century would have afforded Sardian Jews
a new opportunity for civic participation. While in this later period service on the city council may have held little appeal for the
well-to-do Greek citizens, particularly those who had converted to
Christianity and were being lured into more rewarding opportunities in the church and imperial bureaucracies, the Jewish community
may have recognized that having representatives on the city council would help to ensure its security and continued prosperity in the
face of the increasingly hostile Christian imperial rulings of the later
fourth and fifth centuries. Although the Sardis evidence is not alto-
gether unique in this regard, it is nonetheless noteworthy that the
city's Jewish community remained prosperous and secure throughout this period, retaining and continuing to repair and renovate its
monumental synagogue in the fifth and even into the sixth century,
apparently in open defiance of the hostile Christian imperial rulings
of this later period.

---

60. An early fifth-century decree indicates that many Jews were in the legal
profession (*Cod. Theod.* 16.8.24).

61. Although the government repeatedly attempted to make artisans and shopkeepers into a hereditary cast in the western part of the empire, in the East such
drastic measures were tried only briefly. While it is true that Diocletian's census and
taxing measures had the intended effect of binding the rural population to the land,
in the East this system was extended to the urban population only during the reign of
Galerius. After his death, the urban workers of the Eastern provinces were exempted
once again from this control, as indeed they had been under Diocletian (*Cod. Theod.*
13.10.2 [311 c.e.]).

CHAPTER SEVEN

Melito's *Peri Pascha*

Its Relationship to Judaism and Sardis in Recent Scholarly Discussion

Lynn H. Cohick

Nairobi Evangelical Graduate School of Theology

Much has been written on the Sardis synagogue and how it helps enlarge the picture of the socioeconomic development of that Jewish community. I would like to explore how various reconstructions of the synagogue material are used in creating contexts for and interpretations of the *Peri Pascha* (*PP*) attributed to Melito, bishop of Sardis. For example, the author's anti-Judaism,[1] which receives extensive attention in the literature, is often explained by reference to the Sardis synagogue archaeological data. Yet it has been suggested recently that the excavated synagogue, part of a gymnasium complex, is too late (i.e., fourth century C.E.) to have any direct bearing on decoding the second- or third-century C.E. homily's message about Jews and Judaism. A careful look at Sardis and diaspora Judaisms in the Roman world should caution the reader against the assumption that the homily's antagonism towards Judaism reflects a religious conflict. One should consider seriously broader social concerns and developing Christian thought, which may affect greatly the interpretation of the homily.

The Greek text of the *PP* was unknown until about sixty years

---

1. As defined by John Gager, anti-Judaism addresses the religious or theological distinctives of Judaism as a religion. In contrast anti-Semitism refers to racial attacks on Jews by Gentiles. John Gager, *The Origins of Anti-Semitism* (Oxford: Oxford University Press, 1983). A brief summary of the modern use of both terms is found in Judith Lieu, "History and Theology in Christian Views of Judaism," in *The Jews among Pagans and Christians,* ed. Judith Lieu, John North, and Tess Rajak (New York: Routledge, 1992), 79–96.

ago when, in 1936, it was identified by Campbell Bonner in the Chester Beatty / University of Michigan Greek papyrus codex, dated to the fourth century C.E.[2] The Greek is also preserved in the Bodmer Papyrus codex XIII, dated third to early fourth century C.E., edited by Michel Testuz.[3] More recently, James E. Goehring has edited the Coptic (Sahidic) Crosby-Schoyen codex MS 193 from the University of Mississippi, dated third century C.E.[4] All contain the name Melito, and the Bodmer Codex XIII includes the title "On Pascha" at the beginning of the homily, while the Coptic reverses the order of title and author ("Peri Pascha Melito") at the conclusion of the text. The textual evidence suggests the homily was written no later than the third century C.E.

While the text preserved is not anonymous, it does not provide any clear identification of this Melito. It is usually assumed by scholars, however, that the Melito who composed this homily is the same eunuch whom Polycrates (in Eusebius) says is waiting to rise from the dead in Sardis,[5] and who thus may be dated to the second century C.E. Eusebius's evidence,[6] however, is problematic. For example, his description of the author as a Quartodeciman is not obviously reflected in our homily, and his quotation allegedly from the *Peri Pascha* is not found in our homily.[7] Moreover, nothing in the homily itself hints of its provenance. With that in mind, and to prevent confusion, I will not refer to the homily's author as Melito. Thus while the primary focus of this paper will be on the use of the Sardis synagogue evidence in interpreting a Christian homily, there is some question as to whether this homily was written from Sardis.

---

2. Campbell Bonner, *The Homily on the Passion by Melito, Bishop of Sardis, and Some Fragments of the Apocryphal Ezekiel,* Studies and Documents 12 (Philadelphia: University of Pennsylvania Press, 1940).

3. Michel Testuz, *Papyrus Bodmer XIII Meliton de Sardes Homilie sur la Paque* (Geneva: Bibliotheca Bodmeriana, 1960).

4. The Crosby-Schoyen codex is also a Bodmer Papyrus. The Bodmer collection was probably from a Pachmonian monastery that was monophysite until Justinian changed it by force into a Chalcedonian monastery. The text begins at *PP* 46. *The Crosby-Schoyen codex MS 193,* ed. James E. Goehring, *Corpus Scriptorum Christianorum Orientalium,* vol. 521 (Lovanii: E. Peeters, 1990).

5. Eusebius, *E.H.* 5.24.2–6. Yet see Nautin, who suggests the homily is an anonymous text. Nautin, " 'L'Homelie de Melito' sur la Passion," *RHE* 44 (1949): 429–38.

6. Eusebius, *E.H.* 4.26.3–11, 13–14; 5.24.2–6.

7. Eusebius, *E.H.* (Frag. #4) reads, "In his book *On the Pascha* he indicates at the beginning the time when he composed it in these words, 'Under Servillius Paulus, proconsul of Asia, at the time when Sagaris bore witness, there was a great dispute at Laodicea about the Pascha, which had coincided according to season in those days;' and these things were written."

Andrew R. Seager and A. Thomas Kraabel reported on the synagogue in George M. A. Hanfmann's *Sardis, from Prehistoric to Roman Times*.[8] The synagogue was originally part of the city's gymnasium complex, located on its southeast side. Shops lined its long outer wall along the Main Avenue. When first built, the space now occupied by the synagogue consisted of three rooms; the same configuration has remained on the northern side of the complex. Stage One was never completed, and instead, Stage Two divided the space into an apse at the eastern end and a long basilican hall at the western end. Seager labels this second stage as a Roman civil basilica. Stage Three is problematic, for there were only minor changes done to the building, offering little clue as to its function. Nothing suggests that it was used as a synagogue at this point, though one cannot rule out that possibility. The synagogue in its final form is represented in Stage Four. In this stage, new floors and walls were added, a forecourt created, and wall niches or shrines installed at the east end of the hall.[9]

The dating of these stages is debated, but Seager suggests that Stage One, the initial building of the complex, continued "well into the second century."[10] Stage Two might be dated to the early third century, while Stage Three can be dated to about fifty years later, about 270 C.E. Stage Four should be located in the early part of the fourth century, about 320–40 C.E. Kraabel advocates an earlier dating of the synagogue, one which puts it closer to the late second century C.E. He writes, "this building, originally a public structure, came under their [the Jews] control and was turned into a synagogue in the third century, if not before."[11]

---

8. George M. A. Hanfmann, *Sardis from Prehistoric to Roman Times* (Cambridge, Mass.: Harvard University Press, 1983).

9. For a description of the inscriptions at Sardis, see Louis Robert, *Nouvelles Inscriptions de Sardes* (Paris, 1964). For a description of the synagogue excavations and of the determination of the various stages' date, see Andrew Seager, "The Synagogue and the Jewish Community," in *Sardis from Prehistoric to Roman Times*, ed. George M. A. Hanfmann, 168–78; and A. T. Kraabel, "Impact of the Discovery of the Sardis Synagogue," in *Sardis from Prehistoric to Roman Times*, ed. George M. A. Hanfmann, 178–90.

10. Andrew Seager, "The Synagogue and the Jewish Community," in *Sardis from Prehistoric to Roman Times*, ed. George M. A. Hanfmann, 172. It has been suggested by D. G. Mitten and others that the Jewish community built the synagogue beginning in the late second century, and continued to enlarge the structure in the following centuries. D. G. Mitten, "A New Look at Ancient Sardis," *Biblical Archaeologist* 29, no. 2 (1966): 38–68.

11. A. T. Kraabel, "Impact of the Discovery of the Sardis Synagogue," in *Sardis from Prehistoric to Roman Times*, ed. George M. A. Hanfmann, 179.

Of the more than eighty inscriptions found, only two are in Hebrew,[12] the rest in Greek.[13] Some interesting characteristics of these inscriptions include the use of "technical, philosophical vocabulary"[14] such as the term πρovoια, "Providence," shared by gentiles in the city. Some inscriptions highlight the donors' place in the larger Sardian community, not simply their status in the local Jewish community. For example, nine inscriptions identify donors as βουλευτης, members of the city council (one is from the city council of neighboring Hypaipa).[15] Both the placement of the synagogue as part of the larger gymnasium complex, and the numerous interior artifacts,[16] speak of a Jewish community at home with their non-Jewish Sardian neighbors.

Given the enormous weight assigned to the synagogue evidence when reconstructing a *milieu* for the homily's attitude toward Jews and Judaism, it is imperative to reassess the archaeological data when attempting to draw a picture of these Jews against whom our author raged. Useful as well is the archaeological material from other Jewish synagogues dated to the second century, as well as literary evidence about Jews in Sardis.

Using caution, one can draw upon the archaeological evidence from other Diaspora communities in re-creating a possible picture of the Sardian Jewish community in the second and third centuries C.E., realizing of course that each Jewish community had its own uniqueness, and that variety could exist within a given geographic context.[17] If the later dating of the synagogue gains favor, a revised picture of Judaism in second century Sardis could emerge, one

---

12. One reads "Shalom," the other "Verus," according to I. Rabinowitz, referring perhaps to co-Emperor Lucius Verus, 161–69 C.E. Seager notes that if this reading is accurate, then the inscription must have been removed from its original position and reinstalled, because it was found in a wall built about 150 years after Verus. Seager, "The Synagogue and the Jewish Community," 171.

13. For a list of the inscriptions found at Sardis, see Louis Robert, *Nouvelles Inscriptions de Sardes* (Paris, 1964). For a summary of the inscriptional evidence, see Paul Trebilco, *Jewish Communities in Asia Minor,* 43–52.

14. Kraabel, "Impact of the Discovery of the Sardis Synagogue," 185.

15. See Louis Robert, 55f.

16. Among the distinctive features in the synagogue is a large marble table, the "Eagle Table," so named because of the eagles carved on its end supports. On either side of this table stood a lion statue, and one (or a pair) of lions were placed outside the forecourt. The lion was not only an important biblical symbol, but also a significant one for the city of Sardis, accounting for about one-third of all sculpture produced in the Lydian and Persian periods of the city. See Kraabel, "Impact of the Discovery of the Sardis Synagogue," 184.

17. Sardis may have been the locale for more than one Jewish congregation, though no specific archaeological or literary evidence suggests this possibility.

which may not reflect the wealthy and politically influential Sardian Jews that the synagogue and its inscriptions seem to indicate existed in the fourth century C.E. It may be that the Jewish community's τοπος in the second century was in a private home converted for communal needs, or in a building not yet excavated or no longer recoverable. That there was a meeting place of the Jews in Sardis seems fairly certain, based on an early third century C.E. fountain inscription identifying it as the fountain of the synagogue.[18]

It may be that the second century Sardian Jewish community resembled two contemporary assemblies: the neighboring one in Priene (second century C.E.) or the much more distant one in Dura-Europos (ca. 150–200 C.E.). In both these cities, the excavated meeting places were in a house with a redesigned interior space. This may indicate a tendency toward using private homes for communal gatherings that was empire wide, rather than simply a regional practice. The excavated diaspora synagogues of Stobi, Delos, and Ostia were also probably built originally as family dwellings. In fact, Michael White has noted that of the synagogues excavated in the diaspora, all but the Sardis synagogue were converted domestic spaces.[19] It may be that during the second century in Sardis an adapted private home suited the needs of the community.

The literary evidence from Josephus[20] has been used to reinforce the image of a successful, integrated Jewish community in second century Sardis. Josephus presents in *Jewish Antiquities* three decrees concerning Sardis that he claims date to the first century B.C.E., about two or three centuries before the general period of our homily. Josephus cites a decree by Lucius Antonius (49–50 B.C.E.) which reads in part, "from the earliest times they have had an association (συνοδον) of their own in accordance with their native laws and a

---

18. W. H. Buckler and D. M. Robinson, *Sardis. Publications of the American Society for the Excavation of Sardis*, vol. 7, *Greek and Latin Inscriptions*. Part 1 (Leiden: Brill, 1932): 37–40, no. 17, line 7. This inscription does not clearly refer to the large fountain found at the excavated synagogue, but some scholars have used it to defend the early dating of the excavated synagogue. The inscription has been dated to ca. 200 C.E. by Buckler and Robinson (p. 40), "the presence of the name 'Aurelia' (l. 20), and the fact that the other individuals mentioned do not have 'Aur.' as a first name, indicate that the date of the document is about 200 A.D."

19. L. Michael White, *Building God's House in the Roman World* (Baltimore: Johns Hopkins University Press, 1990), 62.

20. See also Josephus, *Jewish Antiquities* 12.119–20, which includes a source claiming to be from the reign of Seleucus 1, and which speaks of Jews in Asia Minor becoming citizens as well as using suitable oil instead of gentile oil; and *Jewish Antiquities* 19.285–91, quoting a source allegedly from 40–41 C.E., referring to a general empire-wide announcement from Claudius of tolerance toward Jews.

place (τοπον) of their own, in which they decide their affairs and controversies with one another" (*Ant.* 14.235). From this quotation at least three points can be made. First, the Jews claim a long history of tradition in Sardis. Second, throughout this history, they have been able to meet together. Third, they have had a particular place (building perhaps?) in which to meet.

Josephus preserves comments allegedly from the people of Sardis that may be a response to the letter from Lucius Antonius (*Ant.* 14.259). Along with reiterating that the Jews should have a place of their own to settle disputes among themselves, to pray, and to offer sacrifices to God, they propose that the city provide suitable food for the Jews. Finally, Josephus includes a decree he claims was written in the early part of Augustus's rule from Gaius Norbanus Flaccus, proconsul. The latter informs the Sardis leaders, "Caesar has written to me, and commanded me not to forbid the Jews, however many they may be, from assembling together according to the custom of their forefathers, nor from sending their money to Jerusalem" (*Ant.* 16.171). This reference to Temple taxes is yet another possible piece of data useful in sketching a portrait of the Sardian Jewish community. Obviously, evidence from Josephus will not provide direct access into the second-century Jewish community of Sardis.[21] The value of his information is calculated in part by how unchanging one imagines the Sardis community to be. If one is able to show that the community's growth and prosperity continued on a rather straight line from the first century B.C.E. until the time of the excavated synagogue, then Josephus's information can be used to support the portrait of a rather prestigious, somewhat powerful, and certainly thriving Jewish community.

This is precisely what Paul Trebilco seeks to do, with some measure of success. He theorizes a "significant degree of continuity"[22] in the influential Sardian Jewish community from the first century B.C.E. until the seventh century C.E., and therefore projects information from the first century B.C.E. into the second century C.E. Yet a few important elements in his reconstruction

---

21. Another piece of literary evidence about Sardis is found in Rev 3:1–6. The Sardis church is described quite negatively; the author charges that most in the community were dead in their failure to live as Christians. Much has been written on the Johannine tradition's impact on Asia Minor, and even on its possible impact on the homily. See, for example, S. G. Hall, "Melito's Paschal Homily and the Acts of John," *JTS*, n.s. 17 (1966): 95–98.

22. Paul R. Trebilco, *Jewish Communities in Asia Minor* (Cambridge: Cambridge University Press, 1991), 52.

seem unsound. For example, though he makes some attempts at challenging Kraabel's early dating, he nevertheless proceeds with his analysis based on this possible early date of the synagogue. In addition, he presupposes that the building, when used by Jews as their synagogue, could not have had a door communicating to the gymnasium directly through the shared interior wall.[23] This claim appears to be based primarily on the implicit assumption that Jews would have had little or nothing to do with gymnasium activities. Nevertheless, this conjecture is not self-evident, as the very placement of the synagogue within the gymnasium complex and at the heart of the city, could reflect a Judaism which, at the very least, did not seek to isolate itself from its non-Jewish neighbors.

Having summarized the literary and archaeological evidence, it becomes unfortunately clear that most of the Sardis material does not come from the second century c.e. This should be underlined, for in assessing the homily as a second- or third century writing, one has little direct evidence from the Sardis provenance on which to make judgments.

We now will trace chronologically the development of scholarly interpretations and assumptions concerning the *Peri Pascha*'s anti-Judaism from the homily's identification by Bonner in the late 1930s to the present. Bonner's treatment of our author's perspective on Judaism in his edition is best characterized as minimal — he has only roughly a page on the idea. While classifying the homily as *adversus Judaeos* literature, he seems to contend that the text is not arguing against contemporary Jews directly, but against the Jews of the gospel stories.[24] Bonner is certainly not alone in his rather brief description of the homily's attitude toward Judaism.[25] Most scholars prior to the discovery of the synagogue were interested in the homily's Christology[26] or placement within the developing "orthodoxy."

With the discovery of the synagogue, a fresh look was taken at the homily's anti-Judaism. Kraabel in particular stressed the synagogue's importance in interpreting the *Peri Pascha* in its social

---

23. Trebilco, 40.

24. Bonner, 19–20.

25. For example, M. Testuz in his edition mentions nothing about anti-Judaism.

26. For example, see R. Cantalamessa, "Meliton de Sardes: Une christologie anti-gnostique du II siècle," *RevSR* 37 (1963): 1–26. See also T. Halton, "The Death of Death in Melito, *Peri Pascha*," *Irish Theological Quarterly* 36 (1969): 163–73.

context.[27] He suggests a very large, prosperous, influential second-century Jewish population that was angered by Melito's *Apology* to Marcus Aurelius,[28] wherein the bishop is said to have proposed that Christians should receive special treatment because as Christianity grew, the Roman Empire prospered. The Sardian Christians were in a sense jealous of the very size, wealth, and social prestige of the Jewish community as evidenced by its enormous synagogue. Our author's anathema against the Jewish community was fueled by a desire for more social or political influence.

Subsequent scholars have used this picture in a variety of ways. I. Angerstorfer builds on the early dating of the synagogue in her 1985 dissertation from Regensburg, "Melito und das Judentum."[29] She proposes that the synagogue changed from Roman hands to Jewish ones in 166–67 C.E., when Lucius Verus, on his way home from the Parthian wars, gave the building to the Jews.[30] In her reconstruction of Sardian Jewish life, she makes the interesting comment that the gift of the building allowed the Jews to practice their religion publicly, but does not explain further.[31] Adding to the early dating of the synagogue Josephus's claims about the Jews having Roman citizenship,[32] she suggests that Jews, as members of the local leadership, were part of the persecution against Christians mentioned in Melito's *Apology*. She cites Kraabel directly in postulating a Christian community made up of, at least in part, "converted" Jews, and suggests that this created even more tension between the communities.[33] Thus for Angerstorfer,

27. Kraabel, "Melito the Bishop and the Synagogue at Sardis: Text and Context," 83–85.

28. See Eusebius, *E.H.* 4.26.

29. Ingeborg Angerstorfer, "Melito und das Judentum," Ph.D. Dissertation, Universität Regensburg, 1985. She also speaks of Melito's typological method resulting in an anti-Jewish position. Andrew Manis likewise stresses both the politically motivated anti-Judaism as well as the anti-Jewish hermeneutic, "Melito of Sardis: Hermeneutic and Context," *Greek Orthodox Theological Review* 32 (1987): 387–401.

30. Angerstorfer, 213.

31. Angerstorfer, 215. She also mentions that Christians did not have a special building in Sardis during our author's time, and thus had no public visibility as a religious community. While it is to be expected that Christians in the second century had no public buildings because Christianity was not a recognized cult, her assumption that the community was therefore not visible fails to consider current archaeological evidence for the use of domestic buildings and their very "public" alterations into meeting places.

32. Josephus, *Jewish Antiquities* 14.10.17.

33. Angerstorfer, 219. Kraabel rightly points out the possibility that some Jews in the early centuries of the Common Era might have joined a Christian group.

Melito's polemic is driven by sociopolitical motives as much as by religious ones.[34]

In his essay, Lee Martin McDonald distorts the archaeological evidence, saying that the Jews "had built not only the largest synagogue known in ancient times, but also owned and operated one of the largest and most impressive gymnasiums."[35] It is this impressive Jewish presence in Sardis, as well as their strong, influential missionary activity that motivates our homilist's bitterness against them. He suggests that the Jews played an active role in fostering the Christian polemic.

Neither Angerstorfer nor McDonald has dealt with the evidence adequately. For example, Angerstorfer's suggestion that Lucius Verus "gave" the building to the Jews rests on a very shaky foundation. One has to assume that the Hebrew inscription is reconstructed accurately as "Verus." Next one must assume that the inscription was based on a donation made, and finally that the donation was the building itself! Again, there is no direct evidence that Lucius Verus visited Sardis; only his visit to Ephesus can be verified.[36] In a similar vein, the claim that Jews had political power over the Christians is at best an overstatement. Marianne Bonz has shown how limited Jewish political power was in Sardis in the late second century,[37] and even the spontaneous outbursts recorded in Christian literature (as in the martyrdom of Polycarp) were apparently localized, sporadic crises.

While Kraabel's dating continues to be very influential, some scholars have taken a second look at the synagogue dating, and suggested that the evidence provides a picture of only an early fourth-century Jewish community, about 150 years after the presumed date

He is careful to note, however, that no direct evidence in our homily confirms that possibility.

34. Angerstorfer, 187–89. She identifies our author's approach as a Jewish typological interpretational model.

35. Lee Martin McDonald, "Anti-Judaism in the Early Church Fathers," in *Anti-Semitism and Early Christianity,* ed. Craig A. Evans and Donald A. Hagner (Minneapolis: Augsburg Fortress, 1993), 241. McDonald does not support his claim with any specific evidence.

36. David G. Mitten, "A New Look at Ancient Sardis," *Biblical Archaeologist* 29, no. 2 (1966): 62. He notes that in the Sardis gymnasium is a statue base dedicated to Lucius Verus by Claudius Antonius Lepidus, who claims to be a priest of Asia and to have taken care of the gymnasium. Mitten suggests that Verus might have stopped in Sardis on his way home from the wars in Parthia.

37. See Marianne Palmer Bonz's contribution in this volume, "The Sardis Evidence and the Jewish Communities of Asia Minor: A Reappraisal." See also her article, "The Jewish Community of Ancient Sardis: A Reassessment of Its Rise to Prominence," *HSCP* 93 (1990): 343–59.

of the *Peri Pascha*.[38] Even though this new interpretation of the data limits the synagogue's relevance in discussing the homily, those who support the later dating often agree with Kraabel's suggestion that the homily seems to indicate that our author felt threatened by the Jewish community. It is still possible to build a strong case for our homilist's anti-Judaism being motivated by social or political concerns without relying upon an early dating of the synagogue.

Given the language used by Josephus (σuvoδov) and our knowledge about guilds and θιασoι in the Roman world during the early centuries C.E.,[39] it is entirely possible that Jewish communities understood themselves and were understood by others as collegial assemblies. Wealthy Jewish and non-Jewish benefactors could sponsor such an assembly. Often cited as evidence of non-Jewish interest or patronage is the Julia Severa inscription from Acmonia (*CIJ* 766).[40] While Severa is credited only with building the structure, and while there is no direct mention of her turning it over to the Jewish community, most scholars assume she gave the building to the Jewish community. Tessa Rajak's conclusion, "it was Julia Severa who built the synagogue in Acmonia,"[41] might go beyond the evidence; at the very least one can say that a non-Jew[42] is recognized in a synagogue inscription. The evidence from the Sardis synagogue inscriptions suggests a significant level of non-Jewish interest in the synagogue. Michael White writes that "competition for honors by both Jewish and non-Jewish donors resulted in the placement of the mosaic pavements in the [synagogue] hall and the forecourt."[43] Wealthy, generous pagans certainly could have supported their Jewish clients and suppliers with gifts to the latter's τοπος. Our homilist may have resented such endorsement.

---

38. George M. A. Hanfmann, 194. He notes that the first Christian church building also dates from the mid-fourth century, although it was built in a new section of the city developed during Constantine's rule.

39. For a brief summary of associations in the Greco-Roman world, see Helmut Koester, *Introduction to the New Testament* (Philadelphia: Fortress Press, 1982), 1:65–67.

40. Often the Julia Severa inscription (C. & B. 559; C.I.I. 766; M.A.M.A. 6, #264) is touted as an example of pagan benefaction toward Jews, but the inscription only seems to indicate that she built the building, not that she gave it to the Jewish community in Acmonia. The critical lines read, τὸν κατσκευασθυ[ν]τα ο[ἶ]κον ὑπὸ Ἰουλίς Σεουήρας Π. Τυρρώνιος Κλάδος ὁ διὰ βίου ἀρχισυνάγωγος.

41. Tessa Rajak, "The Jewish Community and its Boundaries," in *The Jews among Pagans and Christians in the Roman Empire,* ed. Judith Lieu, John North, and Tessa Rajak (New York: Routledge, 1992), 24.

42. Her status as either "pagan" or "Jewish" has been debated, though most scholars today would identify her as non-Jewish.

43. White, 84.

Another possible social impetus behind our author's remarks is postulated by F. W. Norris, who suggests our author's educational background as a window into the homily's anti-Judaism.[44] While he accepts more of Eusebius's information than I am prepared to do, an analysis of the homily's rhetoric certainly indicates an educated person. Norris asks whether our author came from a well-to-do family that sought to educate their son for a political future in the πολις. Thus our author's anger at the apparently favored status of the Jews could have more to do with personal expectations based on wealth and little to do with being a Christian. Norris also notes that the homilist might be a slave or freedperson who was educated, which would likely modify personal expectations. This type of theorizing is helpful because it recognizes that people in the ancient world were not simply identified by their religious affiliation.

Not all scholars, however, believe the homily's inflammatory remarks against Israel were sparked by social concerns. Writing after Kraabel's work on the Sardis synagogue, both D. F. Winslow and Stephen G. Wilson interpret the homily's anti-Jewish stance as springing primarily from the author's religious convictions. Winslow examines the phrase, "God has been murdered" (*PP 96*), a statement that has earned our homilist the dubious honor of "first poet of Deicide" by Eric Werner.[45] Winslow claims that this disturbing phrase epitomizes the anti-Jewish Christology of the text. Acknowledging that at one level the author's words are certainly an oxymoron, Winslow claims that at another level they sum up the homily's argument about Jesus being and doing all that is associated with God. This argument is directed against Jews primarily, though Winslow adds an interesting observation. He suggests that "Melito was not a happy man,"[46] that his tirade against Jews was only slightly more vindictive than his censure of humanity in general, as seen in the passages discussing sin (for example *PP 47–56*). Thus, for Winslow, our homilist's rhetoric expresses his profound

---

44. F. W. Norris, "Melito's Motivation," *Anglican Theological Review* 68 (1986): 16–24.

45. Eric Werner, "Melito of Sardis, the First Poet of Deicide," *Hebrew Union College Annual* 37 (1966): 191–210.

46. D. F. Winslow, "The Polemical Christology of Melito of Sardis," *Studia Patristica* 17 (1982): 774. The value of this observation lies in its reading the homily as an entire unit. Often scholars focus on only the first and last sections of the homily — where the author is most virulent against the Jews — and fail to incorporate the middle of the homily.

remorse at the human condition, as well as his religious argument against Israel.[47]

Although Winslow locates the homily's anti-Jewishness in the overall grim view of humanity, Wilson's primary thrust in exploring the development of Easter traditions is to show how our author's anti-Judaism is closely linked to his supersessionary theology and "modalistic" Christology. He also reflects on our homilist's use of rhetoric in exaggerating the distinctions between both the Christian and Jewish Passovers, as well as between Christians and Jews.[48] He notes that our homilist may have feared that some in the congregation were attracted to Judaism. Although he acknowledges that no firm proof supports this thesis, he cites as possible evidence Chrysostom's sermons against Judaizing[49] and the following excerpts:

> Ignatius, *Philadelphians* 6.1: But if any one propound Judaism unto you, hear him not: for it is better to hear Christianity from a man who is circumcised than Judaism from one uncircumcised. But if either the one or the other speak not concerning Jesus Christ, I look on them as tombstones and graves of the dead, whereon are inscribed only the names of men.

> *Epistle of Barnabas* 4.6: ... not to liken yourselves to certain persons who pile up sin upon sin, saying that our covenant remains to them also. Ours it is; but they lost it in this way for ever.

Thus, for Wilson, the impetus behind the homily's harsh words is not the larger social world of Sardis, but the religious problem of proselytizing and Judaizing.

Wilson's concern about Christianity's relationship to Judaism is shared by Andrew Manis, who postulates that our homilist's hermeneutic was created to handle the envisioned Jewish "menace." He advances the thesis that our author chose the typological approach both to maintain the validity of the "Christian" interpretation of the Jewish Bible, and to write "Israel out of salvation history."[50] He

---

47. For the homilist's use of the term "Israel," see *PP* 72–77, 81–82, 87.

48. Stephen G. Wilson, "Passover, Easter, and Anti-Judaism," in *To See Ourselves as Others See Us*, ed. J. Neusner and E. Frerichs (Atlanta: Scholars Press, 1985), 337–55. See also Wilson, *Related Strangers, Jews and Christians 70–170 C.E.* (Minneapolis: Fortress Press, 1995), 241–57.

49. Chrysostom, *Jud.* 3. See Wilson's summary of Chrysostom's arguments in "Passover, Easter, and Anti-Judaism," 342. See also R. Wilken, *John Chrysostom and the Jews* (Berkeley and Los Angeles: 1983).

50. Manis, 400.

postulates three influences on our author based on a presumed Sardian milieu: first, persecution (which the homilist felt was coming from Jews), second, "competition with the synagogue and a Judaizing tendency in the area,"[51] and third, our author's Quartodeciman stance.[52]

Suggesting that our author's polemic reflects primarily a religious tension between the two groups is problematic. For example, it is often assumed that behind the homily's invective lies Jewish missionary activity, but the alleged proselytizing is not secured by solid evidence.[53] Given the paucity of historical data, one should proceed cautiously when explaining apparent sympathetic attitudes towards Jews. What appears to be alleged by some early Christian authors (for example Chrysostom or Ignatius) is that, in their Antiochian communities, some Christians showed an interest in Jewish synagogue worship. Jews were not necessarily actively pursuing Christians with the intent to convert them. Any possible pagan interest in Jewish festivals or practices need not be interpreted as a result of a concerted Jewish effort to missionize.

A few scholars have suggested that our author's wrath may have been targeted not against Jews, but against other Christians, such as Marcionites or Gnostics. In defaming "Judaism," our author might have been hoping to exonerate the beliefs expressed in the homily from charges of Judaizing directed against them by Marcionites, for example. Winslow cites our homilist's stress both on the suffering of Jesus and on the historical Israel as possible anti-Gnostic polemics. Yet he concludes that the evidence only offers hints — no real clear picture of a Gnostic or Marcionite enemy emerges.[54]

---

51. Manis, 401.

52. Our author's Quartodeciman position is supported by Eusebius's evidence from Polycrates. If the author of our homily and the Melito mentioned by Polycrates are the same person, then the homily can be labeled Quartodeciman. However, I find little unambiguous material in the homily itself that suggests a Quartodeciman stance. Hall postulates the homily's structure is built upon the Passover Haggadah. S. G. Hall, "Melito in Light of the Passover Haggadah," *JTS* n.s. 22 (1971): 29–46. See also Judith Lieu, *Image and Reality, the Jews in the World of the Christians in the Second Century* (Edinburgh: T. & T. Clark, 1996), 232.

53. See Martin Goodman, "Jewish Proselytizing in the First Century," in *The Jews among Pagans and Christians in the Roman Empire*, 53–78; Scot McKnight, *A Light among the Gentiles* (Minneapolis: Fortress Press, 1991); Shaye J. D. Cohen, "Crossing the Boundary and Becoming a Jew," *HTR* 82, no. 1 (1989): 13–33; Kraabel, "Synagoga Caeca": Systematic Distortion in Gentile Interpretations of Evidence for Judaism in the Early Christian Period," in *To See Ourselves as Others See Us*, 219–46, see especially 226–27, "The Roman Diaspora: Six Questionable Assumptions," *JJS* 33 (1982): 445–64.

54. Winslow, 771.

D. Efroymson defends the need to examine anti-Jewish statements wherever they might be found in second-century (and later) Christian literature as potential arguments with Marcion. He notes that by the second century the Law is no longer an issue simply between Jews and Christians, but is now hotly debated among Christians themselves. "Marcion's challenge or threat placed all the anti-Judaic themes in a new apologetic context, appending them to ideas of God and Christ."[55] Efroymson concludes that often the themes of God, Christ, scripture and the Christian way of life are both directly attacked by Marcion's proposals and defended with an anti-Jewish rebuttal by the emerging "orthodox."

I am not proposing an either/or situation, where one must choose between anti-Jewish polemics or intra-Christian battles. Our author might have had several adversaries, and even more, those "adversaries" might have been "imagined." That is, our homilist's rhetoric could reflect an interest primarily in self-definition. Robert Maclennan claims that our homilist and the Sardian community "felt insecure in the face of such a well-developed and venerable sister tradition: Judaism."[56] This insecurity explains our author's choice of rhetorical polemics — like a man back against the ropes, he came out swinging.[57] Maclennan reminds readers that our author's Christianity may not have been the only form in and around Sardis. He concludes that "the *Homily* was not directed against the Jews of Sardis, or any other Jewish group in particular, but was written to Christians who defined themselves against the Israel of the Bible."[58]

Miriam Taylor in *Anti-Judaism and Early Christian Identity*[59] asserts forcefully that our homilist was concerned to prove the superiority of Christianity over the Judaism of the Bible and the New Testament traditions about Jesus and the Jews. She argues convincingly that the homily's descriptions and details about Jews / Judaism are biblical images, with little or no reference to second-century

---

55. David Efroymson, "The Patristic Connection," in *Anti-Semitism and the Foundations of Christianity*, ed. Alan T. Davies (New York: Paulist Press, 1979), 105.

56. Robert Maclennan, *Early Christian Texts on Jews and Judaism* (Atlanta: Scholars Press, 1990), 107.

57. Maclennan's assumptions that Jews were drawing Christians into their community and that Jews used the excavated synagogue in Sardis in Melito's time have been challenged above.

58. Maclennan, 112.

59. Miriam Taylor, *Anti-Judaism and Early Christian Identity* (Leiden: Brill, 1995).

Sardis. In examining the characteristics of "Israel" in the homily's anti-Jewish section, one is struck with the overwhelming number of biblical comparisons and the absence of examples of second- or third-century C.E. Jewish practices. "Israel's" crime seems to be that it did not recognize the miracles of Jesus or the person of Jesus as the Messiah (*PP* 84–90). Whereas Chrysostom's sermons against the Judaizers include ample examples of specific interactions between Christians and Jewish in fourth-century Antioch,[60] our homily offers only characteristics or incidents from biblical accounts.

In summarizing the various possibilities in interpreting our homilist's anti-Jewish rhetoric, the majority of scholars accent the social situation of Sardian Jews as a backdrop to explaining the homily's vitriol. Kraabel is credited as first focusing on the historical setting of the Sardian Jews to interpret the homily, and then concluding that the Jews' established position in the city led to our author's expressions of anger and resentment. Some scholars have interpreted the Sardis archaeological and literary evidence as indicating that Jews and Christians fought for converts, or that Christians felt persecuted by Jews, or that Christians desired the political clout attained by the Jewish community. They suggest that at least in some cases — as in the case of portraying Judaism as missionary — the existing evidence is likely stretched beyond its limits.

Other scholars have suggested that our homily does not reflect any second- or third-century rivalry between Jews and Christians in Sardis, but instead highlights the developing theological arguments about identity among Christians, who tended to define themselves over against a caricature of Jews / Judaism. This approach in no way discredits the evidence that Judaism in the early centuries was active, vibrant, and even prominent in some cities. It simply suggests that our homily's anti-Jewish rhetoric is not the place to find evidence for Jews or Judaism at this time.

One might argue that the homily was directed against several adversaries. The carefully elaborated typology from the Jewish scriptures may indicate some significant concern for the Israel of the Bible and Jews in Jesus' generation, and the rhetoric or tone of the homily might suggest that the issue is urgent, thus implying a current standoff with contemporary Jews. Stephen Wilson offers

---

60. For example, see *Hom. in Rom.* 12.20.3 on Sabbath practices, *Jud.* 1.2, 5 on festival practices, and *Jud.* 1.3 on oath taking.

such a model for interpreting the homily. He notes the importance of our author's attempt to articulate Christian belief, but also reminds readers that "the Jews in Sardis were, in short, a force to be reckoned with, and scarcely to be ignored by a Christian community attempting to establish a distinct identity and political standing.[61]

Taylor challenges this synthesis of the contemporary and historic Jews "in their determination to avoid the pitfalls of the theologically over-determined approach, and to uncover the social and political context of early Christian existence, scholars come to their interpretation of the Christian texts on Judaism with a preconceived notion of the level of reality revealed in the writings."[62] She maintains that for some texts, one is dealing only with a particular aspect of Christian identity, that is, with a view that does not allow one to extrapolate conclusions about the author's Jewish contemporaries.

Her admonition is an important one when dealing with our text, whose provenance is at best problematic. The significant level of diversity among Jewish communities in the ancient world cautions against any general assumptions about a particular Jewish community's makeup. If a text's provenance can be determined, however, one ought not to rule out the possibility that knowledge about Jews in that city could nuance or exacerbate a particular Christian's view about "biblical" Jews. For example, Chrysostom's fire against the Judaizers, Christians following certain "Jewish" practices, might have been stoked by his inability to remove from Antioch the positive presence of Jews. Yet such an assumption of a vibrant Jewish community and a Christian's direct attack against it might not always prove true. One need look no further than Theophilus in Antioch one century earlier for a Christian who seemed unaffected by the contemporary Jews. Within the same city — though with a century between them — two Christians express different attitudes about Jews and/or Judaism. Thus, archaeological, epigraphic, and even certain literary evidence (as from Josephus) about Jews might not help explain a particular Christian's attitude toward Judaism. In our homily the possibility that the author was speaking about

---

61. Stephen G. Wilson, "Passover, Easter, and Anti-Judaism," 350. See also Judith Lieu's statement concerning the second half of the homily, "the direct second-person address, you or O Israel, creates an implied hearer, or better an 'implied defendant', to be distinguished from the implied (Christian) audience of the *Peri Pascha* who are included in the contrastive we. Repeated hints bring this implied 'defendant' out from the past to be identified with an Israel today." *Image and Reality,* 217. Countering Lieu's position, see Cohick, "Melito of Sardis's PERI PASCHA and Its Israel," *HTR* 91, no. 4 (1998): 366–70.

62. Miriam Taylor, 140.

only Jews from the Bible should caution against drawing general assumptions about the possible impact the second- or third-century Jewish community might have had on our author.

In summary, at least four basic approaches to interpreting our homilist's attitude toward Judaism can be identified. The first approach proposes a conflict (real or imagined by our author) with contemporary Jews as the author's main reason for invective against Jews in the homily. The second approach attends to the social sphere in which our homilist and fellow Jews and Christians lived as a window into understanding the homily's tirade. This approach emphasizes the possible effect of wider Roman social structures on our homily.[63] The third approach postulates that our homilist might be motivated to write anti-Jewish rhetoric to counter other Christians' charges that our author is too "Jewish." A final option emphasizes that the homily's rhetoric was designed to strengthen our author's identity and that of the community. No direct interaction with or reference to contemporary Jews is behind our homilist's argument.

In evaluating the theories, one could argue that each of the four positions contributes to the writing of the homily, but not equally. Biblical images play an important role in defining Jesus in the homily — witness the critical role of the Exodus 12 passage in shaping the explanation of the Passion. Nevertheless, the religious context does not stand isolated from the larger social context. The forces of the larger social milieu need to be brought into focus in order to understand adequately the homily's "theology" — quite apart from attempts to evaluate its "orthodoxy" or even its coherence.

A careful interpretation of the homily's anti-Jewish statements must include in the equation the political and social ramifications of identifying oneself as Christian or Jewish in the late second century. Because most second- or third-century Christian groups held little power socially, any political influence of the Jewish community is likely to have been greater than our homilist's congregation. Social or political concerns, such as the pursuit of patrons, may have driven the homilist's fury against Jews. Yet there is no particular reason to assume that the homily's invective against Jews reflects the ranting of a sore loser in the game of finding proselytes.

---

63. For purposes of discussion, I have created distinct categories of "sacred" or religious and "secular." Yet there was no tidy division between these realms in the second-century Roman world, and any analysis of the homily should take this realization into account.

When accounting for possible social agenda, the redating of the synagogue must be considered. No longer can scholars assume that Jews in our author's day occupied center stage in Sardis, holding prime real estate and significant political power. Even more, because the evidence linking our author to Sardis has been called into question, our homily might be better interpreted without assuming its provenance. Careful focus on the homily's images of "Israel" drawn from biblical traditions and its supersessionary evaluation of Judaism, coupled with little or no contemporary descriptions of Jews, suggests caution in re-creating possible interaction between our author and second- or third-century Jews.

CHAPTER EIGHT

Jews, Slaves, and the Synagogue on the Black Sea

The Bosporan Manumission Inscriptions and Their Significance for Diaspora Judaism

J. Andrew Overman

Macalester College, St. Paul, Minnesota

At the start of this century Eastern Europe was emerging as a promising region for the study of the early Roman Empire and its various provincial manifestations. This region of the ancient world was also providing suggestive and important material evidence about ancient diaspora Jewish communities. Numerous Jewish communities had been established along the north and east coast of the Black Sea in the larger Greek-style cities from the first century B.C.E.[1] Scholars east and west had begun to piece together the compelling and enigmatic stories of these Pontic Jews.[2] M. I. Rostovtzeff and E. H. Minns are examples of scholars from the first two decades of this century who saw the importance of the material being unearthed along the north coast of the Black Sea for understanding the broader empire and various regional expressions within the same. E. Schürer, and to a lesser extent A. Deissmann, familiarized themselves with this material in a more cursory fashion in order to

---

1. Rostovtzeff, *Iranians and Greeks in South Russia* (Oxford: Clarendon Press, 1922), 150. Rostovtzeff suggests that these Jews were colonies settled by Mithridates the Great after Chersonesus ambivalently received him. See G. Glen, "Mithridates Eupator and Rome: A Study of the Background of the First Mithridatic War," *Athenaeum* 65 (1977): 380–404. Chersonesus and the other settlements of this region were particularly concerned with the threat of Scythian dominance.

2. I. Surgaja, "Der griechisch-ägyptische Kult im nördlichen Schwarzmeergebiet," *Klio* 61 (1979): 453–58. Also, Y. Vinogradov and M. Zolotarev, "La Chersonèse de la fin de l'archaïsme," in *Le Pont Euxine vu par les Grecs* (Paris, 1990), 85–119.

examine diaspora Judaism and emerging Christianity respectively.[3] These and a few other scholars from the west were trying to incorporate and interpret advances in Black Sea research by some outstanding Russian epigraphers and archaeologists. However, the analysis of this material in the west virtually stopped after 1920. Clearly one victim of the tragedies of the World Wars, the Stalin years, and more recently the Cold War has been the rupture between scholars east and west.[4] The post-Soviet period has provided us with an opportunity to renew these conversations. So-called *openness* has presented us with a chance to renew the investigation of this material and incorporate it into our transforming portrayal of emerging Judaism and Christianity within the Roman world. Furthermore, in this reunion between scholars after so many years, we have some new insights about diaspora Jews and Judaism to bring to our analysis and conversation. Our more recent appreciation of the diversity and attraction of diaspora Jewish communities in the early Roman period provokes us to interpret afresh this material from the Black Sea. These insights and data were not available to a significant degree when the Black Sea evidence was last scrutinized.[5] We can

3. E. Schürer, "Die Juden im bosporanischen Reich und die Genossenschaften der *Sebómenoi Theòn Hyphiston* ebendaselbst," *Sitzungsberichte der königlich preussischen Akademie der Wissenschaft zu Berlin* 12/13 (1897): 200–225. A. Deissmann, *Light from the Ancient East.* Translated by L. R. M. Strachan (London: Hodder and Stoughton, 1910).

4. E. R. Goodenough, F. Cumont and Rostovtzeff, understandably, were the leading examples of those few scholars who continued to promote the importance of this region during a period when it was receiving very little attention. Rostovtzeff had the advantage of having spent considerable time there as a young scholar. He traveled to the north coast of the Black Sea on several occasions to conduct research at Chersonesus and other Black Sea sites. He did this as a personal friend of the family of Count Veronsov whose estate was near Yalta. Goodenough's interest is reflected in the oft cited but now obviously dated article, "The Bosporan Inscriptions to the Most High God," *JQR* 47 (1956): 221–44.

Those interested in the history of scholars and scholarship from earlier in the century can find a number of prefaces of books that shed light on the difficulty and tragedies associated with the efforts to sustain scholarly discussions. The prefaces to Deissmann's *Light From the Ancient East,* both Deissmann's and the translator's, provide a sense of this struggle. The *Black Sea Project,* initiated in 1993, directed by the author, Douglas Edwards, Gary Lindstrom, Robert Maclennan, Jack Olive and Miron Zolotarev of Chersonesus has conducted in-depth archival research under the guidance of Dr. Maclennan with chief translator Prof. James von Geldern of Macalester College. This work has also detailed the life and work of several archaeologists and other scholars relating to Jews and Judaism in the Black Sea region over the last century which is outlined in a forthcoming article by Maclennan and von Geldern.

5. Scholars in the east had their own impediments to critical analysis of this material. Perhaps most prominent in this regard has been the anti-Semitism that was part of life under the Soviet regime in many cities and regions. The inscriptions from the north coast of the Black Sea deal explicitly with the ancient Jewish communities

now return to this material to investigate it anew and ask how it contributes to our understanding of the nature of diaspora Jewish communities more broadly.

The Inscriptions

Perhaps the most striking piece of material evidence for a significant Jewish presence in the Black Sea region dating from the Roman period is the Jewish manumission inscriptions from ancient Panticapaeum (modern Kerche) on the eastern edge of the Crimean peninsula, and from Gorgippia and Phanagoria, both located on the Taman peninsula across the straits of Kerche. These inscriptions will serve as the primary focus of this chapter.

The manumission inscriptions from the Bosporan kingdom have been largely neglected in western scholarship. Moses Finley did attempt to analyze these inscriptions with a view toward what they could tell us about the institution of slavery and the legal processes of manumission in the Greco-Roman world.[6] And few scholars since Schürer have attempted to study these manumission inscriptions in light of what we now know about ancient diaspora communities from the Roman period. The work of Irena Levinskaia stands as an exception to this second point.[7] For some of the reasons alluded to above, these inscriptions were not heavily studied in the for-

---

of that region. Secondarily, the inscriptions also deal with slavery, which was a topic of considerable interest during the Stalin years. In fact, on February 19, 1933, Stalin himself gave a paper on slave revolts in antiquity where he laid out the orthodox or "correct" historical understanding of slavery and slave revolts with special reference to the Roman period. This orthodox historical analysis by Stalin limited inquiry into this subject. See the article by Z. W. Rubinson, "Saumakos: Ancient History, Modern Politics," *Historia* 29 (1980): 49–70. Stalin's orthodoxy with respect to ancient history and even the ancient slave system and the obstacle that presented was expressed by G. G. Diligenskii, editor of *Vestnik Drevnei Istorii*, in a post-Stalin period when he wrote, "the cult of personality had exercised a determining negative influence on research work in the field of history and, in particular, ancient history. Such problems as the diverse forms of slave relations were sometimes resolved with the aid of schematic formulas applied without the requisite concrete analysis..." Quoted from M. Finley, *Ancient Slavery and Modern Ideology* (New York: Penguin, 1980), 58. On the struggles of archaeologists and archaeologists working on Jewish history in particular during this period, see M. Miller, *Archaeology in the U.S.S.R* (London: Atlantic Press, 1956), and, similarly, A. L. Mongait, *Archaeology in the U.S.S.R.* (Moscow: Foreign Languages Publishing House, 1959).

6. "The Black Sea and Danubian Regions and the Slave trade in Antiquity," *Klio* 40 (1962): 51–59.

7. "A Jewish or Gentile Prayer House? The Meaning of *PROSEUCHE*," *Tyndale Bulletin* 41 (1990): 154–59, and *The Book of Acts in Its Diaspora Setting*. The Book of Acts in Its First Century Setting, vol. 5 (Grand Rapids: Wm. B. Eerdmans, 1996).

mer Soviet Union. The lone prominent exception to this has been substantial contribution of Benjamin Nadel who wrote his 1947 Leningrad dissertation on these inscriptions and followed that up with numerous important articles.[8]

The Greek-style cities clustered around the shores of the Black Sea were sizable, cosmopolitan cities with well-established political organizations and processes, and trade centers between east and west. Strabo observed that when standing on the Crimea, people have Europe behind them and Asia in front of them.[9] In antiquity also this region was militarily and economically crucial, and a bridge between cultures and empires east and west. Chersonesus, for example, contains pottery from virtually all over the Roman empire. Athens, Cos, Pergamum, Rome, Alexandria and Caesarea Maritima were regular trading partners with Chersonesus.[10] And, as Rostovtzeff showed in his *Iranians and Greeks in South Russia,* commerce and culture from Asia were also features of Chersonesean and Crimean life in the Greco-Roman period. The Greek cities of the Bosporus contained most of the pagan cults one would expect to find in the Greek east, and during the first century these centers attracted the interest of Roman political plans and appetites. These were prosperous and lively economic and cultural centers during the first several centuries of the empire. It is not surprising, therefore, to find that along with the religious and cultural mix reflected in these Pontic cities, we should also find evidence of significant Jewish communities. The presence and impact of these communities are attested to by various material remains. Chief among these are the Pontic Jewish manumission inscriptions.

These Jewish manumission inscriptions comprise a body of approximately ten Greek inscriptions including the recently discovered example from Phanagoria published by Dan'shin.[11] In structure

---

8. A distillation of Nadel's dissertation can be found in *VDI* (*Vestnik drevnei istorii*) 1 (1948): 203–6. Also, "Actes d' affranchisement des esclaves du Royaume de Bosphore et les origines de la manumission in ecclesia," in *Symposion 1971: Vorträge zur griechischen und hellenistischen Rechtsgeschichte,* ed. J. Modrzejewski and H. J. Wolff (Cologne: Böhlau, 1975), 265–92. See also, "Slavery and Related Forms of Labor on the North Shore of the Euxine in Antiquity," in *Actes du colloque 1973 sur l' esclavage,* Annales littéraires de l'université de Besançon 182, Centre de recherches d'histoire ancienne 18 (Paris: Belle Lettres, 1976), 197–233.

9. Strabo's description of the region; 7.4.1–4.

10. The definitive English work on Chersonesus is E. H. Minns, *Scythians and Greeks* (Cambridge: Cambridge University Press, 1913).

11. See D. I. Dan'shin "The Phanagorian Community of the Jews," *VDI* 1 (1993): 59–73, and "The Jewish Community of Phanagoria," *Ancient Civilizations from Scythia to Siberia* (ACSS) 3 (1993): 133–50.

these inscriptions are quite similar. The vocabulary changes very little, and the legal form or genre is the same in virtually all inscriptions. They begin with the name of the ruler and some appellation with regard to the ruler, a date, the pronouncement or vow of release, which takes place in the *proseuchē*, notice that the slave is free from arrest, free from the former owner's heirs, and free to go wherever he or she wishes. Following this announcement a *choris* clause, or an exception, maintains that the freed slave must remain fervently attached to, or devoutly attend, the *proseuchē*. The translation of this particular phrase is notoriously difficult, and we will return to this shortly. The contract for freedom ends with the stipulation that the community of the Jews (*synagōgē ton Ioudaion*) will serve as the joint overseers of this agreement.

Before discussing these inscription in greater depth, it is important to note that other material evidence of Jewish communities does exist from this region of the Bosporus which certainly deserves further study and scrutiny. Many Jewish gravestones from Chersonesus, Panticapaeum, and other Pontic cities need to be catalogued and analyzed. The numerous *Menorot* in the museums of Chersonesus, Panticapaeum, and Simpheropol — which my colleagues, Robert Maclennan and Douglas Edwards, and I have seen and photographed — also deserve in-depth study, categorization, and analysis. This kind of material evidence, which has been largely overlooked or neglected for most of this century, bespeaks an established and extended Jewish presence in this region of ancient south Russia. For those interested in the subjects of diaspora Judaism, the relationship between Jewish communities and the dominant local or regional culture, or the relationship between the broader Roman world and these far-flung communities, the Crimea is a region containing considerable, unexplored, and important new data.

In addition to this, new opportunities now exist for research and cooperation with colleagues from the east which, if pursued, will most certainly lay bare new information about the life of Jews from the Roman and Byzantine periods. In this vain, new archaeological excavations did begin in ancient Chersonesus in 1993 focused on the question of Jewish presence there and the relations of that putative diaspora community with the surrounding diverse social world of that Greek Pontic city. After five years of excavation we can clearly demonstrate that a Jewish community with a synagogue did exist in this important ancient Greek city outside the modern city of Sevastopol dating from the second–fourth century c.e.[12] This presence significantly pre-dates the establishment of the Khazar kingdom of the eighth–ninth century in the Crimea. We have also conducted research in the archives of the Chersonesus museum where we found a plaster fragment with Hebrew writing. This plaster fragment contains the word *Jerusalem* in Hebrew.[13] According to the notes of one of the early excavators, G. D. Belov, and his successors, this fragment was found in association with the famous 1935 Basilica at Chersonesus, but in a locus that predates the sixth-century structure.[14] This so-called "Jerusalem inscription," together with the original archeological locus made clear from Belov's and other's fieldnotes, and two menorot from this area of the city, establishes a presence and a place for a Jewish community in Chersonesus which would very likely parallel the same diaspora communities in Phanagoria, Gorgippia, or Panticapaeum, the cities which produced the Bosporan manumission inscriptions.[15]

The location of the synagogue at Chersonesus is noteworthy. Like their contemporaries at Sardis in western Anatolia or Stobi in Macedonia, this diaspora community occupied a prime and prominent

---

12. See the article by D. R. Edwards in this volume on the synagogue at Chersonesus. See also a preliminary discussion of the Black Sea Project excavations by R. S. Maclennan, "In Search of the Jewish Diaspora: A First Century Synagogue in Crimea?" *BAR* 22 (1996): 44–51.

13. The Black Sea Project at Chersonesus, founded in 1993, has included both archaeological excavations and archival research and translation. Both have been vital in reconstructing the Jewish presence at Chersonesus. The staff and scholars at the Chersonesus Museum Preserve, and our colleagues Miron Zolotarev and Dimitrii Korobkov, the Museum Director Leonid Marchenko and the staff of the archives have generously and graciously helped open up the world of ancient Chersonesus to us.

14. The fieldwork around the 1935 basilica area and the mosaics and frescoes from the area which provide evidence of a synagogue and a "basilica-synagogue complex" was conducted by G. D. Belov intermittently from 1935 and several other archaeologists in this period; E. N. Zherebtsov, S. F. Strzheletskii, O. I. Dumbrovskii, and V. Borisova. Reports or folders #609 from 1950, 622 from 1949 and 1295 from 1952, stored in the Chersonesus Museum archives detail the initial excavation of the basilica-synagogue complex, though the excavators hardly recognized it as such at the time.

The Directors of the archaeological excavations at Chersonesus or, *The Black Sea Project,* are Miron Zolotarev, Douglas Edwards, Gary Lindstrom, Robert Maclennan, Jack Olive, and the author. Our excavations focus on the area of the Byzantine basilica. The excavations are under the auspices of Macalester College, Zaporozhye State University in Ukraine, and the Chersonesus Museum Preserve.

15. The Chersonesus "Jerusalem Inscription" has been reconstructed and translated by Esther Eshel for the Black Sea Project. See "A Hebrew Graffito from a Synagogue in the Crimea," *JSQ* 5 (1998): 289–99. She dates the inscription from the second–fourth century c.e.

place within the larger context of the city.[16] The synagogue was adjacent to a bath complex, positioned along the shore and close to the port. The Chersonesus synagogue was close to other substantial Roman period installations and thereby constituted an obvious architectural and social space and statement within that large and lively Greco-Roman city sometime between the second and fourth centuries. And these Jews remained at Chersonesus for sometime, for an intriguing legend comes to us through the ninth-century "Life of Constantine and Methodius." St. Cyril / Constantine was sent to the Khazars of the Crimea as an emissary from Constantinople. It was his task to "preach the holy trinity to these people." The *Life* says that Cyril went on his way, "after coming to Kherson he learned the Hebrew language and scriptures and translated eight parts of the grammar." Though legendary, this story, supported in an interesting argument by Minns, asserts a substantial history and continuity to this Chersonesan Jewish community.[17]

With this larger context and evidence for Jews in the Pontic region in mind let us return to the important Jewish manumission inscriptions. In the inscriptions the slave is released, but has the obligation to remain in or adhere resolutely to the *proseuchē*. The inscriptions conclude with the stipulation that the Jewish community will serve as the guardians of this agreement. Below two of the inscriptions, *CIRB* #70 and #71 are reproduced:

CIRB 70
βασιλεύοντος Βασιλέως Τιβε-
ρίου Ἰουλίου Ῥησκουπόριδος φιλο-
καίσαρος καὶ φιλορωμαίου, εὐσε-
βοῦς, ἔτους ζοτ΄ μηνὸς Περει[τί]-
ου ιβ΄, Χρήστη γυνή πρότε-
ρον Δρούσου ἀφείημι ἐπὶ τῆς π[ρο]-
σευχῆς θρεπτόν μου Ἡρακλᾶν
ἐλεύθερον καθάπαξ κατὰ εὐχή[ν]
μου ἀνεπίληπτον καὶ ἀπαρενό-

---

16. For Sardis see J. A. Overman and R. S. Maclennan, eds., *Diaspora Jews and Judaism: Essays in Honor of, and in Dialogue with, A. T. Kraabel*, University of South Florida Studies in the History of Ancient Judaism 41 (Atlanta: Scholars Press, 1992), 269–92. See the discussion of Stobi in A. T. Kraabel, "The Diaspora Synagogue: Archaeological and Epigraphical Evidence since Sukenik," *ANRW* 2.19.1, 494–97.

17. *The Life of Constantine and the Life of Methodius*, trans. with commentaries by M. Kantor and R. S. White, Michigan Slavic Materials 13 (Ann Arbor: University of Michigan, 1976), 21. And E. H. Minns, "S. Cyril Really Knew Hebrew," *Melanges P. Boyer* (Paris, 1925), 94–95.

χλητον ἀπὸ παντὸς κληρονόμο[υ
τ]ρέπεσ(θ)αι αὐτὸν ὅπου ἄν Βού-
λ[ητ]αι ἀνεπικωλύτως καθὼς η[ὐ]-
ξάμην, χωρὶς ἱς τ[ὴ]ν προσευ-
χὴν θωπείας τε καὶ προσκα[πτε-
ρ]ήσεω[ς], συνεπινευσάστων δὲ
καὶ τῶν κληρ(ο)νόμων μου Ἡρα-
κλείδου καὶ Ἑλικωνιάδος,
συνε[πιτ]ροπευούσης δὲ καὶ τῆ[ς]
συναγωγῆ[ς] τῶν Ἰουδαίων.

CIRB 71

———— ΚΑ ————
κου ἀφίημι ἐπὶ τῆς προσευ-
χῆς Ἐλπία[ν ἐμ]α[υ]τῆς θρεπτ[ῆς?]
ὅπως ἐστὶν ἀπαρενόχλητος
καὶ ἀνεπίλνπτος ἀπὸ παντὸς
κληρονόμου χωρὶς τοῦ προς-
καρτερεῖν τῇ ἐπι-
τροπευούσης τῆς συναγω-
γῆς τῶν Ἰουδαίων καὶ θεὸν
σέβων.

Several important if not problematic terms must be clarified before proceeding to the larger significance of these and other related
inscriptions for understanding the Black Sea diaspora communities.
Both CIRB #70 and #71 contain the terms *proseuchē* and *synagōgē*.
In the use of these two crucial terms we see highlighted an illustra-
tion of P. Jean-Baptiste Frey's observation that *proseuchē* almost
always refers to a building of Jewish meeting and prayer, while
synagōgē tends most often to refer to the community of people.[18]
There are some exceptions to this pattern, but with striking regularity *proseuchē* refers to a place or building of prayer for the *Jewish*
community.[19] A distinction between a building and the people who

---

18. See the comment by Frey in *CIJ* I in the Introduction LXX. "Dans les
inscriptions juives de Rome, le terme *sunagōgē* designe toujours la communauté, ja-
mais l'édifice cultuel; celui-ci est appelé proseucha." (New York: KTAV, 1975). See
also M. Hengel, "Proseuche und Synagoge: Jüdische Gemeinde, Gotteshaus, und
Gottesdienst in der Diaspora und in Palästina," *Tradition und Glaube: Das frühe
Christentum in seiner Umwelt*, Festschrift für K. G. Kühn, ed. G. Jeremias, H. Kühn,
and H. Stegemann (Vandenhoeck & Ruprecht: Göttingen, 1971), 157–84.

19. I. Levinskaia, "A Jewish or Gentile Prayer House? The Meaning of
Proseuche," *Tyndale Bulletin* 41, no. 1 (1990): 154–59.

gather in it is a fine one. The two terms are ambiguous and related concepts. However, in the reading of these inscriptions the nuanced distinction between the place *(proseuchē)* and the community as a political and corporate entity *(synagōgē)* does emerge. In these inscriptions, as is usually the case with manumissions, the vow of freedom is made in a holy place — the *proseuchē*. But the legally binding body and legal entity charged with oversight is the Jewish community or people.[20] The distinction between these two important terms prevailed in the Black Sea region in the first century of the common era. In *CIRB* #70 and #71 it appears that the freed person is expected to participate in, or frequent, the *proseuchē*. But the Jewish community, or the Jewish *politeis,* the *synagōgē*, has charge over the freed person's obligation with respect to the *proseuchē*. The manumitted one will be in, or attend, the *proseuchē*. The people, the synagogue, will guard the manumission and insure its integrity.

In these inscriptions the manumitted are not *douloi*. They are *threptoi*. This distinction is noteworthy and may shape our broader interpretation of the inscriptions. As A. Cameron, H. Raffeiner and others have pointed out, "slave," or "domestic / house slave" does not quite capture the sense of this term.[21] *Threptos* denotes a more personal than legal relationship.[22] As Cameron noted, this term suggests a range of nuances and relationships. But the force of the term, and what distinguishes it from *doulos, is* the personal relationship it suggests between servant and owner or employer. Those slaves being manumitted in the *CIRB* inscriptions are in close and perhaps *philios* if not familial relations with the owner and the owner's family.[23] Two inscriptions from the first and early second century, GV 476 and 1595, carry some sense of this personal, even intimate relationship between *threptos* and owner.[24] All manumission inscriptions from the Bosporus feature the term *threptos*.

---

20. *CIRB* 64, an early fourth-century inscription found at Kerch, is one of the Bosporan inscriptions to the Most High God and this speaks about building a *proseuchē*.

21. A. Cameron, "*Threptos* and Related Terms in the Inscriptions from Asia Minor," in *Anatolian Studies Presented to William Hepburn Buckler.* Manchester: Manchester University Press, 1939, 27–53. H. Raffeiner, *Sklaven und Freigelassene: Eine soziologische Studien auf der Grundlage des griechischen Grabepigramms* (Innsbruck: Universitätsverlag Wagner, 1977), 90–92.

22. Cf. the stimulating article by Z. Rubinson, "Saumakos: Ancient History, Modern Politics," *Historia* 29 (1980): 59.

23. Cameron notes this term can even signify Foster-Parent, Foster-Child, or adopted child, 27ff. *Threptoi* can be free or enslaved. *CIRB* 70 and 71 refer to *slave-threptoi* being granted their freedom *(eleutheron)*.

24. See Raffeiner, 92. See the second-century inscription GV 1595.

The term *proskartereseos / proskarterein* is an important term in the inscriptions and has been the subject of considerable debate. B. Nadel has done extensive and very important work on these inscriptions and this very phrase. Nadel takes *proskartereseos* to mean service. He understands this service in the sense of *Paramone,* as in the case of the well-known manumission inscriptions from Delphi.[25] Nadel concludes that the clause in which the term appears, beginning with *choris,* establishes the duty of the freedperson to perform economic service — especially agricultural labor — on behalf of the Jews of the *proseuchē.*[26] In these contracts the slave (usually *doulos*) was sold to a god, but required by the *paramone* clause to remain in service to his/her owner for a designated period of time. Nearly a fourth of the one thousand Delphic manumission inscriptions contain some kind of *paramone* clause. All but one contain the actual term *paramone.*[27] The work or obligation is usually stipulated in concrete and specific terms, as the survey of this material by Samuel demonstrated.[28] At least two manumission inscriptions from the Bosporus contain the term *paramone,* or some variant. They are *CIRB* 73 and 74. Both seem to stipulate that the *threptous/tos* are to remain (in service) until the owner's death. This is common among the *paramone* clauses of Delphi.[29] *CIRB* 73 and 74 are justifiably called *paramone* manumissions. However, the work or obligation pertains to the former owner and not the Jewish community. The term *paramone* almost invariably appears when the slave is granted freedom but retains some ongoing work or responsibility to the owner. The contracts are usually quite explicit about this stipulation and they note the time when the obligation or claim expires.[30] *CIRB* 70 and 71 do not appear as *paramone* manumissions. The term is not present, there is no clear obligation to the former owner, and no work is made explicit. The presence of the

---

25. See W. L. Westermann, "The *Paramone* as a General Service Contract," *JJP* 2 (1948): 3–50.

26. Nadel, *VDI* 23 (1948): 203–16. See the review by Falenciak, "A Survey of Soviet Juristic Papyrology 1946–1948," *JJP* 3 (1949): 195–97. Also, B. Nadel, "Slavery and Related Forms of Labor on the North Shore of the Euxine in Antiquity," in *Actes du Colloque 1973 sur L'esclavage,* 214–16.

27. Westermann, "The *Paramone* as a General Service Contract," 11.

28. A. Samuel, "The Role of *Paramone* Clauses in Ancient Documents," *JJP* 15 (1965): 256–84.

29. Samuel, "The Role of *Paramone* Clauses," 159. See GDI 2084 (185 B.C.E.). Also, and quite similar to the two *CIRB* inscriptions is GDI 1717 (160 B.C.E.) where there is a manumission with the obligation to remain for life.

30. W. L. Westermann, "Extinction of Claims in Slave Sales at Delphi," *JJP* 4 (1950): 49–61.

term in *CIRB* 73 and 74 only serves to punctuate the question about numbers 70 and 71. Why, if this is a manumission with obligation, is the usual term not present, as in the case of *CIRB* 73, 74, nearly all the Delphic inscriptions, and the various papyri also examined in the survey of the role of *paramone* in ancient contracts?[31] What then is *proskartareseos* and what is expected upon freedom?

I am aware of two other diaspora Jewish documents that use this term. Three instances of this term occur in Acts (1:14; 2:42, 46), and two in Romans (12:12; 13:6). Three of these instances occur together with *proseuchē* (Acts 1:14; 2:42; Rom 12:12). In Acts 2:46 the term refers to the apostles' regular attendance at the Temple "in one accord" *(homothumādon)*. In all instances, save Romans 13:6, the term *proskartareseos* refers to the devotion of the believers to the group, it is three times used in association with *proseuchē*, and once in association with the Temple in Jerusalem. The term lays stress on the community, their corporate harmony, and devotion, however idealized that may be in Acts. Each instance refers to corporate activity and practice. In light of the Black Sea inscriptions, and the affinity between *proskartereseos* and *proseuchē*, would not, "rejoice in your hope, be patient in tribulation, and hold devoutly to the *proseuchē*," be just as plausible a rendering of Romans 12:12 as the received translation that understands the term as referring to one's personal prayer and piety?[32] In light of this material, and the fact that *CIRB* 70 and 71 do not appear to be *paramone* clauses, as some seem to assume, we would take *proskartereseos/ein* to refer to adherence to the *proseuchē* on the part of the manumitted one, and not to labor that their owner still expects from them or for which they have been purchased by the *proseuchē* or anyone else. The adherence refers in some sense to participation or involvement in part of the life of the Jewish community. This understanding also helps make the most sense out of the unusual term *thōpeias*, which occurs along with *proskartereseos* in each of the manumission inscriptions where this formula occurs. The rare term suggests a kind of loyalty, flattery, adulation, or even devotion on the part of the one manumitted. This is also consistent with the far more intimate and even familial term applied to the slave, *threptos*.

Lastly, the term *sunepitropeuoúsās*, which occurs in *CIRB* 70, 71, 73, and the fragmentary 72, must be addressed. This term seems

---

31. A. Samuel, "The Role of *Paramone* Clauses in Ancient Documents," *JJP* 15 (1965): 256–84.

32. As in the case of the inscription from Rome *CIJ* I, 531.

to represent the legal or quasi-legal role played by the Jewish community in this agreement. It has been translated as "superintending" or "joint-guardianship." I am aware of only one example that hails from this period, involves a slave, and uses this rather rare term: POXY 265. This is a marriage contract, or rather extended prenuptial agreement, dating from 81 C.E. In it the term refers to one who helps to manage the estate and secure the fulfillment of the contract in the event of the death of the husband, Dionysus. The community (*synagōgē*) of the Jews (and "God-fearers" in *CIRB* 71) appears to serve a sort of civic and legal function in the Bosporus manumissions.

Of related interest here is POXY 1205, which is a manumission contract from the late third century (291 C.E.). The Jewish community (*synagōges ton Ioudaion*) has provided for the freedom of a woman and two children. In this inscription the price for manumission is stipulated. Moreover, the term *paramone* is twice used within the contract, it seems, as the name of the house servant (*oikogene doulen*) whose liberty has been purchased. This contract has been viewed as an example of an *eranos* type of corporate manumission, where a group or organization purchases a slave through loans that oftentimes had beneficial terms of repayment associated with them.[33] Such loans were not uncommon at Delphi.[34] J. A. Harrill has recently argued that *eranos* loans were dispersed in order to secure *paramone* services.[35] This contract confirms that corporate manumission was indeed practiced at times and certain places. This may be one way of approaching the Bosporus inscriptions, though the Black Sea inscriptions do not seem to parallel the Egyptian examples very closely. Having examined the text more closely we are in a position to try and interpret the inscriptions and ask what they may tell us about the diaspora Jewish communities of the Bosporus.

In trying to determine the substance of the Bosporus Jewish manumission inscriptions, B. Nadel's observation that only two of the manumission inscriptions from *CIRB* are not expressly Jewish is instructive.[36] That is to say, manumission on the part of the Jewish community was not an isolated instance. The diaspora communities

33. S. Bartchy, *First Century Slavery and I Corinthians 7:21*, Society of Biblical Literature Dissertation Series 11 (Missoula, Mont.: Society of Biblical Literature, 1973), 103ff.

34. GDI 2.1772, 1791, 1804, 1878, 1909, 2317.

35. "Ignatius, Ad Polycarp. 4.3 and the Corporate Manumission of Christian Slaves," *Journal of Early Christian Studies* 1 (1993): 118–19. I wish to thank Dr. Harrill for forwarding this important article to me.

36. B. Nadel, "Slavery and Related forms of Labor on the North Shore of the

of the Bosporus were involved in manumission on a regular basis. The manumissions in *CIRB* 70 and 71 are clearly formulaic and were reiterated in several other inscriptions. *CIRB* 70–73 and perhaps 985 have this formula and some apparently technical terms in common. We have enough of this evidence to be confident that this procedure was fairly standard within these Bosporus diaspora communities. Here a usual or common enough legal arrangement is being consummated. The terms we have reviewed are part of *Jewish* manumissions from the Bosporus. In examining manumission evidence from other parts of the empire, we have determined that the terms in these inscriptions are quite rare. They are part of the arrangement the diaspora communities in the Bosporus worked out with the owners of slaves and other civic authorities, if that became necessary.

Epigraphical evidence from other parts of the ancient world would lead us to expect a transfer of money, an arrangement of services, or some other kind of contractual agreement be made explicit in the manumission inscription, as in the case of POXY 1205 and numerous Delphic examples, if indeed they are *paramone* inscriptions. Yet there is no such explicit transfer of money or agreement for services in the Bosporan Jewish manumissions, and the crucial term itself is missing. There is scant evidence to suggest that in these inscriptions we see a corporate program to employ slaves and former slaves on the part of the Jewish communities. What then can we suggest is transpiring in these inscriptions and what do they tell us about Jews, slaves and the synagogue in the Black Sea region?

We do see in these Black Sea manumission inscriptions a distinction between the institution or structure called the *proseuchē* and the notion of a popular assembly of people or community referred to as a *synagōgē*. This is a distinction that is known beyond the Bosporus in the early Roman period.[37] In fact in these Black Sea inscriptions, similar to *CPJ* 138.I, we could speak of a *synagōgē* within a *proseuchē*. The building, place, or *topos*, here referred to with the familiar Jewish appellation of *proseuchē* is important, but it is the people, community or *synagōgē*, who assume the important legal responsibilities with regard to the freed slave detailed in the inscriptions.

The involvement of the Jewish synagogues of the Bosporus in the

---

Euxine in Antiquity," 214–15. Nadel states ten out of the twelve manumissions are Jewish.

37. D. Noy, "A Jewish Place of Prayer in Roman Egypt," *JTS* 43 (1992): 118–22.

process of manumission was fairly widespread. These inscriptions have been found in several Pontic sites. And there is a sufficient enough number of these inscriptions, of the very same or similar genre, that we can safely assume that this was a well-known practice or procedure for the Jews of the Black Sea region in the Roman period. The legal and basically civic role assumed by the synagogues in the inscriptions is an important one. Serving as the guarantor and overseer of the agreement reflects a significant social and political location for these Jewish communities. The synagogue not only insures that the exception clause to "hold fast to the *proseuchē*" is carried out, but they also insure the enduring freedom of the manumitted, as the repeated freedom from harassment, freedom of movement, and freedom from the heirs clauses make clear. The Black Sea synagogues were responsible for insuring the integrity and application of these manumission agreements. Within the context of the inscriptions these diaspora communities emerge as responsible, respected, and they engaged the broader legal and political life of the region. Beyond this legal role, however, a relationship or connection between the freed slave and the Jewish community persisted. This is the point of the exception, or *choris* clause in the inscriptions. The involvement of the synagogue appears to go beyond a juridical function in these instances.

We cannot claim to understand completely the relationship between the freed slaves and the Black Sea diaspora communities. The inscriptions simply do not offer that information. Why were the synagogues of the Black Sea region so clearly involved in the process of manumission on a fairly regular basis? We can say that the explanations that these are examples of *paramone* inscriptions, such as is common at Delphi, or that these diaspora communities were engaged in obtaining laborers or contracts for service with slaves or freedmen simply fall short. They leave too many vital questions unanswered, and the Jewish manumission inscriptions lack too many standard features of these types of inscriptions. So something else must be involved where these Bosporan Jews, slaves and synagogues are concerned.

It is not clear that these slaves were joining the Jewish community in the more contemporary sense of that notion. And there is no obvious indication that these slaves were becoming Jews, though that has been suggested.[38] There is, of course, ample evidence from this period that non-Jews were becoming interested in or associated

---

38. These interpretations are discussed in a 1997 dissertation by E. Leigh Gib-

with diaspora synagogues in many ways, short of conversion. As is well known, the Bosporan inscriptions to the "Most High God," which come from the very same locations as the manumission inscriptions, may reflect this kind of interest and involvement in the Jewish community on the part of some non-Jews. It should be noted, however, that whether or not these Most High God inscriptions in fact refer to Jews and Judaism in any way is a question which is far from resolved.[39]

But we are not dependent on the controversial "Most High God" inscriptions from the Bosporus to determine that in the diaspora non-Jews were involved in or attaching themselves to the synagogues in what were certainly varying degrees of interest or allegiance. This is one of the important features of the debate about the so-called God-Fearers. A. T. Kraabel and some others have raised the question as to whether an official or semi-official class of adherents in the synagogue called "God-Fearers" ever existed, or was this a term or category created by the author of the Acts of the Apostles?[40] But no one, including Kraabel, has argued that diaspora Jewish communities were not attracting attention from and engagement with non-Jews. On the contrary, the last decade of scholarship on Greek-speaking diaspora communities from the Roman period, such as those in the Crimea or Taman peninsula, has pointed to a far more lively engagement and interaction between Jews and their broader social and civic environment than previously imagined. This is part of what makes *CIRB* 71, with Bellen's reconstruction, interesting. In this instance, "the community of the Jews, and the *Sebōn*," a term with obvious connections to non-Jews engaged with the synagogue, are the ones who will have oversight of the agreement of manumission.[41] In light of this it is not utterly

---

son written at Princeton University, "The Jewish Manumission Inscriptions of the Bosporan Kingdom."

39. On the Cult of the Most High God in the Bosporus see; I. Levinskaia and S. R. Tokhtas'iev, "Jews and Jewish Names in the Bosporan Kingdom," in *Studies on the Jewish Diaspora in the Hellenistic and Roman Periods*, ed. B. Isaac and A. Oppenheimer (Tel Aviv: Ramot Publishing, 1996), 55–73. And I. Levinskaia's Leningrad dissertation from 1988, "Kul't Theos Hypsistos kak istochnik po etnokul'turnoj istorii Bospora v I–IV." For a dissenting view on this question see the recent excellent treatment by Y. Ustinova, *The Supreme Gods of the Bosporan Kingdom: Celestial Aphrodite and the Most High God* (Leiden: Brill, 1999).

40. Several articles on this debate, including Kraabel's original piece, "The Disappearance of the God-Fearers" have been collected in Overman and Maclennan, eds., *Diaspora Jews and Judaism.*

41. H. Bellen, "Die Aussage einer Bosporanischen Freilassungsinschrift (*CIRB* 71) zum Problem Der Gottfürchtigen," *JAC* 8/9 (1965/66), 171–76.

implausible that the freed slaves of the Bosporan manumission inscriptions were joining or becoming associated with the *proseuchē*
and the synagogue in it. But the inscriptions do not make such an
association explicit.

The relationship between the manumitted slave and the synagogue
rests somewhere between obligation and affiliation, though these are
not mutually exclusive. That is to say, the ongoing relationship between the freed slave and the synagogue in these inscriptions involves
a social and civic obligation assumed by the Jewish community, and
it may also reflect a degree of affiliation with the community assumed
by the former slave. Again, these are not mutually exclusive and a
kind of continuum between these options may exist, depending on
the slave and community in question. The ongoing relationship may
have been a result of the owner's interest, trust, or affection for the
proseuchē and the people in it. Consequently the owners inserted the
exception clause into the inscriptions. Also, the act of manumission
may have been provoked by some attachment to the synagogue on
the part of the slave. If so, then the owner freed the slave, but only to
the institution that would take on the responsibilities associated with
manumission. In either instance the owner or freed slave would have
been like other non-Jews in these Greek cities developing some connection with the diaspora synagogue. Upon manumission security
and support for the freed slave would have come from the synagogue
or Bosporan Jewish community. Or, finally, the Jewish communities
of the Bosporus may have been known as places and people interested and engaged in manumission and able to assume the subsequent
oversight required by the act of manumission. This would certainly
help explain the relatively high concentration of Jewish manumission
inscriptions in the rather defined region of the north and northeast
coasts of the Black Sea. In cases of need, hardship, or other threats,
there was a local, recognized institution to which owners could turn.
All three scenarios do justice to the language of intimacy and affection captured by both *threptos* and *thōpeias* and they provide an
explanation for the important but vexing *choris* clause found in all
of these inscriptions. Ongoing security and care are captured in the
obligation assumed by the synagogue for the freed slave. And all three
scenarios provide explanations which go beyond or are other than
either *eranos* or *paramone* models suggested by other scholars. The
Black Sea manumission inscriptions share too little in common with
either of these manumission genres. While these other manumission
categories provide helpful background and comparative material,
they are not analogous to our Black Sea manumission inscriptions.

In the important Black Sea manumission inscriptions we obtain a glimpse of a network of closely related diaspora Jewish communities from the northeast corner of the Bosporus. These synagogues were clearly engaged in the civic and legal life of their Pontic cities. They were respected and well enough known to have assumed important and substantial functions within the broader community. The language of the inscriptions highlights that role for the synagogues of the Black Sea region, both in terms of the admonition for the slave to remain strongly attached to the *proseuchē* and in terms of the constant oversight of the arrangement which was assigned to the synagogue. And given the number and uniformity of these inscriptions we can say that the Jewish communities of the Black Sea served these significant roles with regularity.

We can now add these diaspora synagogues of the Black Sea to our growing list of diaspora Jewish communities of the Greco-Roman world. There is much that we still do not know about the Jews and the synagogues involved with manumitting Bosporan slaves. As other scholars begin to take advantage of the opportunities and material available to them in this post-Soviet era, we will almost certainly learn more about these ancient Jewish communities which seem to have been quite well known, active, and respected along the Bosporus in late antiquity, but which today seem to us rather like a riddle wrapped in a mystery inside an enigma.

CHAPTER NINE

Jews and Christians
at Ancient Chersonesus
The Transformation of Jewish Public Space

Douglas R. Edwards
University of Puget Sound, Tacoma, Washington

Jewish diaspora communities played significant roles in the late antique period — both Roman and Byzantine. Communities of Jews at cities such as Stobi, Apamea, Sardis, Aphrodisias, and Ostia created architectural and symbolic expressions that illustrated the multifaceted webs of power within which they prospered.[1] Epigraphic evidence illustrates important local associations with pagan neighbors as non-Jewish patrons built buildings, or helped sponsor activities associated with the Jewish communities. The Aphrodisias inscription illustrates how close a connection such ties could become.[2] But Jews also had a religious or ethnic identity; that, in the fourth and fifth centuries of this era, became focussed on the sacred law and at times on the sacred language, Hebrew. These patterns are well documented for Asia Minor, Italy, and of course for Israel, but in the north Black Sea area, only faint hints of diaspora presence

---

The information offered in this essay could not have been assembled without the work and support of my colleagues: Drs. Miron Zolotarev, Robert Maclennan, J. Andrew Overman, Jack Olive, Gary Lindstrom, and Dimitrii Korobkov. The interpretation of the evidence is my responsibility.

1. For a useful overview, see L. M. White, *The Social Origins of Christian Architecture,* vol. 1: *Building God's House in the Roman World: Architectural Adaptation among the Pagans, Jews and Christians* (Valley Forge, Pa.: Trinity Press International, 1990).

2. J. Reynolds and R. Tannenbaum, *Jews and Godfearers at Aphrodisias* (Cambridge: Cambridge Philological Society, 1987). The resultant discussions of this important find are too voluminous to list here.

158

have surfaced. The reasons are complex, but most certainly are connected to the lifting of the Soviet curtain of silence — especially as regards Jewish communities in antiquity[3] and an increasing reawakening of scholars in the west concerning this important peripheral region of the Roman and Byzantine empires.[4]

Archaeological and archival work by members of the Black Sea Project has brought to light a new chapter concerning the diaspora presence in the north Black Sea, notably at the ancient site of Chersonesus, located on the outskirts of present-day Sevastopol. What follows here is a discussion of the rediscovery of a Jewish presence there, including a Jewish building — most likely a synagogue — which provides important evidence for understanding diaspora Judaism in this region, and its possible demise as the climate of tolerance changed in the sixth century c.e. This article is not the first presentation of this material,[5] nor is it intended as a final excavation report — which will be published by my fellow directors of the Black Sea Project. Rather this offers an initial foray into perceiving the presence of Jews at Chersonesus within the broader political and cultural climate of the late antique period.

Excavations of the Black Sea Project (BSP) began at ancient Chersonesus on the Crimean coast in July 1994. Five seasons of excavations and research in the museum archives have focused on the area around a famous basilica — it is depicted on the newly minted Ukrainian Hrevna banknote. The goal of the BSP was to obtain information about religious, social, and architectural transformations in that sector of the city from the Hellenistic through the Byzantine periods. Specifically, we sought information on (1) international trade relations, (2) evidence for religious groups and their civic interaction, (3) the role of ethnic and religious minorities — notably Jews — in the city, and (4) transformations that occurred during the key historical periods — the Hellenistic, Roman, and Byzantine periods.[6]

---

3. See the forthcoming article by James von Geldern and Robert Maclennan, "Excavation Archaeology in the former Soviet Union: Recovering the Past in Chersonesus."

4. See the reports on archaeology around the Black Sea region by J. G. F. Hind and others, especially J. Hind, "Archaeology of the Greeks and Barbarian Peoples around the Black Sea (1982–1992)," *Archaeological Reports* 39 (1992–93): 82–112; and Michail J. Treister and Yurii Vinogradov, "Archaeology on the Northern Coast of the Black Sea," *AJA* 97 (1993): 521–63.

5. Previous reports of the Black Sea Project's excavations at Chersonesus include R. Maclennan, "In Search of the Jewish Diaspora: A First Century Synagogue in Crimea?" *BAR* 22, no. 2 (1996): 44–51.

6. This entire program of research from the organization of work in the field

Chersonesus is on the southwest tip of the Crimean peninsula on the north coast of the Black Sea and the outskirts of modern Sevastopol, home of the Russian Black Sea Fleet and a closed military city until 1996. Consequently, those outside the former Soviet Union knew little of the scientific and archaeological research at Chersonesus. BSP was one of the first international archaeological teams from the west to conduct work in this sensitive area following glasnost. Cooperation and commitment of numerous Crimean and Sevastopol officials was necessary to insure success for this unique international endeavor.[7]

The BSP excavations began west of the sixth-century basilica and east of an area previously excavated by G. Belov — the first to dig there. We sought to link this area with region XXII to the west. From 1994 to 1997 BSP excavated seven 5 x 5 meter squares, running northeast to southwest and approaching the Black Sea. This largely unexcavated, centrally located, and transitional space has provided crucial information for the historical and cultural reconstruction of this area in the Hellenistic, Roman, and Byzantine periods.[8]

The Hellenistic and Roman Periods

Chersonesus was founded as a Greek city in the fifth century B.C.E. by settlers from Heraclea Pontica, although Greek connections may extend back to the sixth century B.C.E.[9] It flourished as an international trade and cultural center in the Hellenistic period. By the third century B.C.E. the city was embroiled in a series of conflicts

---

to the publication of reports was fully coordinated with the Crimean Branch of the Institute of Archaeology of the National Academy of Science of Ukraine and the National preserve of "Chersonesus Tavrian." The program resulted in a joint project between Macalester College, University of Puget Sound, and the Chersonesus Preserve now known as the Black Sea Project. The directors of the Project are Drs. Maclennan, Overman, Edwards, and Miron Zolotarev, and Mr. Jack Olive and Gary Lindstrom. As noted above, the principal area excavated was around the ancient basilica, the symbol of ancient Chersonesus.

7. Special thanks must go to the director of the National Museum Preserve, Leonid Marchenko, and to BSP codirector, Miron Zolotarev, whose hard work and support were essential for this project.

8. Excavation of this area enabled us to establish a fixed chronological sequence for the stratigraphic layers, and to apply that information to the much less precise earlier excavations by Belov and others to the west and east.

9. E. M. Minns, *Scythians and Greeks: A Survey of Ancient History and Archaeology on the North Coast of the Euxine from the Danube to the Caucasus* (Cambridge: Cambridge University Press, 1913), 515.

with Scythian forces in the region. Mithridates Eupator saved Chersonesus from the Scythians in the late second century B.C.E., and it survived for a time as one of the cities of the Bosporan kingdom. Remains from the Hellenistic period are evident in the area that we excavated. The artifacts from those earlier excavations are consistent with BSP artifacts from the same strata. Domestic remains — evidence of cooking and hearth-related material, jewelry, Greek graffiti on bowls, bronze keys, terracotta figurines, fish hooks, decorated loom weights — and a range of other finds consistent with residential space characterize the Hellenistic strata across the area. Belov, in excavations under the central nave of the Byzantine basilica, discovered the remains of four large Hellenistic houses — with courtyards, entry ways, cellars and cisterns, and commercial spaces connected to each house. This block of houses was bound by streets or paths, one of which was excavated by BSP. This part of Chersonesus was clearly domestic space in the Hellenistic period. Numerous stamped amphora handles found by BSP and by earlier excavators demonstrate the international trade network in which Chersonesus participated in the Hellenistic period — notably with Rhodes, Sinope, Delos, and other Hellenistic centers. Economic and cultural identity evident from items such as the Greek graffiti and Hellenistic figurines confirm the predominantly Greek affiliations.

Sometime toward the end of the second century B.C.E. many of these Hellenistic complexes were destroyed. A quantity of ash and charcoal was found throughout the area, and Belov argued that the buildings were ruined either by fires or by earthquake toward the end of the second century B.C.E.[10] BSP found confirmation of this destruction in portions of two separate destroyed Hellenistic buildings.

The Hellenistic city, therefore, established itself in the fifth century B.C.E., and began bringing the surrounding countryside under control, establishing rural farms and subdividing the *chora* by the fourth century B.C.E. By the late third and early second century B.C.E., trade with other Greek colonies was in full swing, as indicated by the stamped amphora handles and other imported wares. Excavations of farmsteads confirm a similar pattern as agricultural production and land use increased. By the mid-second century B.C.E., however, fortunes fell both in city and *chora*, such that by

---

10. G. D. Belov, *Report of the Excavations at Chersonesus, 1935–1936* (National Publishing House, Crimea, 1938); G. D. Belov, "Excavations in Chersonesus," 691/I, 1953–54.

the first century B.C.E. housing complexes in the city and the *chora* were destroyed. This devastation is probably the result of Scythian invasions, which destroyed nearly all the farms by the end of the second century B.C.E.[11] Rebuilding of the rural area, and possibly of the city itself, picks up again as a result of closer ties with and protection from the nearby Bosporan kingdom.[12] Jewish presence first appears within this environment.

The Hellenistic or Roman Menorah

On our initial visit to Chersonesus in 1993 my colleagues and I were shown two menorah.[13] One was roughly cut on a thin piece of limestone, which had barnacles on it, indicating that it had been under water for a time.[14] Reports of the Hellenistic necropolis excavations near the pottery shop in Chersonesus show the menorah upside down at the feet of a skeleton, which initially implied that it may have served at first as a kind of tombstone. A pottery kiln subsequently covered this Hellenistic graveyard. At a later period some form of reservoir or cistern was built, and it was then that the stone was re-used in the lining. According to the excavator's reports, the material remains in the cistern were from the early Roman period at the latest.[15] Thus the evidence indicates a Jewish presence at

---

11. S. Saprykin, *Ancient Farm and Land-plots on the Khora of Khersonesus Taurike: Research in the Herkaleian Peninsula, 1974–1990* (Amsterdam: J. C. Gieben, 1994), 95.

12. As Saprykin notes, "Khersonesus was the first of the Greek cities of the area to put itself under the power of the Pontic king; this happened as early as the end of the 2nd century B.C., and the situation persisted down to the beginning of the 2nd century A.D." (p. 26). He cites in particular Strabo 7.4.3; Phleg. Tral. xv. fr 22. Cf. also his comments regarding Chersonesus and Mithridates' rule: "So the revival of its [Chersonesus's] chora during the 1st century B.C. should surprise no one; it could either have happened before 80 B.C., when the Pontic king was pursuing a philhellenic policy and was supporting all the Greeks on the coasts of the Black Sea in particular, or later when he reneged on this policy and began to suppress the Greeks, turning instead to the barbaric tribes to thwart Greek separatism" (Saprykin, 96–97). Mithridatic soldiers posted in Greek cities, such as Chersonesus, were generally brought from eastern Asia Minor (97).

13. Dr. Miron Zolotarev showed the menorah to Robert Maclennan, J. Andrew Overman, Gennadii Toshchev (Professor of Archaeology and Ancient History at Zaporozhye State University), and me.

14. This submersion apparently occurred before the crudely cut menorah was made, since no barnacles appear to be over the scratch marks.

15. V. V. Borisova, "Report on the Excavations of the Necropolis near the Pottery Shop in Chersonesus." 730/2 (1956), photo 59 (museum archives); see also E. Solomonik, "On the Question of the Inhabitants of Tavrain Chersonesus" (1979), 8–9.

Chersonesus at least by the first century C.E. and possibly as early as the Hellenistic period, since the menorah was in a secondary use. This adds another city on the edge of the Roman Empire — or earlier — that included a Jewish diaspora presence. What does this tell us about the nature of the Jewish community at Chersonesus in this period? Unfortunately, very little. Clues to Jewish life in that period must come from contemporary evidence found in the surrounding region.

The evidence for Jews in the northern Black Sea area has been recognized for some time. The best summary is still the one by Fergus Millar.[16] All the inscriptions mentioned — with the exception of one from Olbia — represent communities east of Chersonesus, around the Cimmerian Bosporus. The manumission inscriptions are especially interesting, as are those that mention *theon sebon*. If one wants to get a glimpse into the nature of the Jewish community during the Roman period in the Crimea, the Bosporus kingdom where these inscriptions were found is a good place to begin. Many aspects of social life can be discerned, but here we examine only two details, using a manumission inscription dated to 67/68 C.E., which illustrates the type of networks within which Jewish communities operated:[17]

> To God the Most High, Almighty, Blessed, under the reign of King Rescuporis, loyal to the Emperor and friend of the Romans, pious. In the year 364, in the month of Daisius, I, Neocles, son of Athenodorus, set at liberty under Zeus, Ge, Helios [the slaves of . . . bred in my house?] . . . with the assent of Athenodorus son of Athenaios, my father. Wherefore they should be unharmed and undisturbed by all my heirs and may go where they want because of my valid order.[18]

The social act of freeing a slave is placed within the rubric of the Bosporan king, whose rule frames the action between the two parties. The association with Roman power within which the Bosporan

---

16. In Emil Schürer, *The History of the Jewish People in the Age of Jesus Christ*, revised English version, ed. G. Vermes, Fergus Millar, M. Black (Edinburgh: T. & T. Clark, 1979), 2:36–38.

17. J. B. Frey, *Corpus of Jewish Inscriptions* (*CIJ*), Europe, vol. 1 (New York: KTAV, 1975); *Corpus Inscriptionum Regni Bosporani* (*CIRB*), (Moscow, 1965). Cf. manumission inscriptions from Panticapaeum dated to 81 (*CIJ* 683; *CIRB* 70), and Gorgippia (*CIJ* 690b); Cf. D. I. Danshin, "Phanagorian Community of Jews," *Journal of Ancient History* 204 (1993): 59–72 (in Russian).

18. Lifshitz, Proleg., *CIJ*, 68.

king must — or chooses to — operate also frames the event. The divine realm is incorporated in two intriguing ways. First, the entire inscription itself is addressed to "the Most High God, Almighty and Blessed" — according to Lifshitz the latter two phrases are distinctly Jewish. Nothing stated thus far would be particularly unusual for any person emancipating a slave, with the exception of these opening remarks to the Most High God. The inscription, however, shows the explicit and implicit parameters that governed social discourse at this time. Jews had slaves; therefore they had to obey the rules established by the powers that allowed such social discourse. Such short vignettes as this epigraph give us a brief glimpse into the way persons construct their lives, the powers they acknowledge, accept, or tolerate, and the powers they do not. In this act of enfranchisement, Neocles acknowledges the powers of the Bosporus king and his allies, the Romans, who participate in this social act of emancipation.[19] The very act of inscribing it and presenting it publicly provides evidence for participation in the Roman social process. Neocles could have chosen not to follow this procedure. Presumably, he could have let the slaves go, or not had slaves, or revolted. Such legal and quasi-legal documents may not tell us how Neocles really *felt* about Roman or Bosporan rulers and their functionaries who made him go through this process. Nevertheless, regardless of his personal feelings, it identifies the power(s) he acknowledged. He and his pagan neighbors acknowledged the same powers — with one important exception: Neocles documented his action as taking place before the Most High God, presumably the most powerful player in the group.

This little exercise is intriguing because a Jew would not be expected to acknowledge such allegiances. Yet this stance toward the pagan power calls to mind the second-century letters and contracts of Babatha found near the Dead Sea in Israel. If, as most presume, Babatha died as a part of the Bar Kokhba revolt against Rome, it seems odd that she carried around a legal document — the deed to her property — which begins very much like the manumission inscription, though it lacks the divine address:

---

19. Coin evidence suggests that some of the Bosporan kings sought greater independence from Rome. See Nina A. Frolova, *Essays on the Northern Black Sea Region Numismatics* (Odessa: Polis Press, 1995; Russian ed., 1972), 130–50. Chersonesus was under the control of the Romans as early as the first century C.E., as indicated by the unsuccessful petition for liberty by Ariston, a local elite who died in Rome after six fruitless years. See Basil Latyshchev, ed., *Inscriptiones antiquae orae septentrionalis Ponti Euxini* (Petropoli, 1885–90), 1:423.

In the reign of Imperator Caesar divie Traiani Parthecia...I register what I possess.[20]

Babatha carried this legal document to her death even while attempting to overthrow the powers that legitimated the very document that guaranteed her right to the land. Perhaps she was simply hedging her bets. However, on one important level, she continued to acknowledge the power implicit in the legal Roman document. Such documents provide a glimpse into the rules and power persons implicitly or explicitly acknowledged, even though those rules may have contradicted others they held dear.

This leads to the second major point: the mention of Zeus, Earth, and Helios in the manumission inscription. As Fergus Millar and others have noted, the use of this phrase was widespread and long in use, going back at least to Homer. Stern saw it as so common that he compared it to a "dead letter" and assumed that it had little or no significance for those who used it. Nevertheless, though the phrase certainly has a formulaic character, a formula is more than a "dead letter." Granted that the persons who used such phrases may have thought little about their implications, their use presumes the pagan formula as a necessary feature of a social act. The underlying power networks that one presupposes when one does such "taken-for-granted acts" becomes clearest when the act is challenged. For most Jews, apparently, the sacrifices offered on behalf of the emperor in the Jerusalem Temple meant little: they were taken-for-granted acts. However, when such sacrifices were abruptly discontinued as part of the first-century Jewish revolt, the power networks implicit in such acts became clear indeed. In short, the manumission inscriptions show how much Jews were a part of the general social and political discourse in the north Black Sea region during the Roman period, as they negotiated and sometimes participated in the operative political, social, and cultural power networks. One can presume that Jews at Chersonesus in the first centuries C.E. participated in such networks — though without further direct evidence, this remains conjectural.

In order to appreciate fully the evidence for the Jewish presence at Chersonesus in late antiquity, one must be familiar with some additional background information. Chersonesus long had close ties to shipping and the sea, which was one of the reasons that

---

20. For a fuller discussion, see D. Edwards, *Religion and Power: Pagans, Jews, and Christian in the Greek East* (New York: Oxford University Press, 1996).

it remained so important an outpost for the Roman and Byzantine empires. The city came under Roman control largely after the Mithridates revolt was put down in the first century B.C.E. Roman troops were stationed in or near the city up through the third century. Not surprisingly, one finds a plethora of religious activity, not only in connection with many of the Olympian deities, including a monumental temple to Aphrodite — later incorporated into the Uvarov basilica[21] — and "the Maiden" (a form of Athena), but also the worship of the god Mithras[22] and — even more recently discovered — the goddess Isis.[23] Evidence of strong trade patterns with the Roman Empire shows that Chersonesus was economically active from the first through the fourth centuries. The city minted its own coins, had pottery kilns, including some for fine ware, and had the normal complement of public structures and facilities associated with a Greco-Roman City: baths, aqueduct, theater. With the exception of the menorah described above and possible third-century C.E. lamps, evidence for Jews is virtually nonexistent in the city until the fourth or fifth century C.E.[24]

The Presence of a Fourth/Fifth-Century Synagogue

Several clues indicate the presence of a synagogue immediately under, or in the vicinity of the sixth-century C.E. basilica. A semicircular structure was reexcavated by BSP in 1998. Preliminary findings date its founding to the fifth-century. Belov noted that this semicircular structure was covered by debris, including marble shavings and fragments he associated with the building of a nearby fifth-century C.E. basilica. The BSP also found similar marble shavings in Field 1 dating to the fourth / fifth century C.E. Parallels with

---

21. Minns, 525.

22. S. Saprykin, "A Head of Mithras from the Tauric Chersonesus," in *Ancient Civilizations from Scythia to Siberia* 1, no. 3 (1994): 324–33; M. I. Zolotarev, "Chersonesus Museum," *Ancient Civilizations from Scythia to Siberia* 1, no. 2 (1994): 220–23.

23. The numerous deities can be readily documented from the extensive epigraphic remains discovered at Chersonesus over the last century. For an earlier collection of the material see Latyshchev, *Inscriptiones antiquae septentrionalis Ponti Euxini* 1 (1885); IV (1901) and I, 2d ed. (St. Petersburg, 1916). More recent discoveries are described by E. I. Solomonik, *Novye epigraficheskie pamiatniki Khersonesa "Noukova Dumka,"* Akademika Nauk Ukrainskoi SSR, Institut Arkheologii (Kiev, 1964), and E. Solomonik, *Novye epigraficheskie pamiatnike Khersonesa. Lapidarnye nadpisi "Naukova Dumka"* (Kiev, 1973).

24. The lamps, to be published by Miron Zolotarev, parallel those discussed by Eric Lapp, "Zwei Spátantike Jüdische Tonlampen aus Kleinasien," *JAC* 34 (1991): 156–58.

the synagogue at Ostia suggest its possible use as a podium or the location of the Torah shrine. Leonard Rutgers has persuasively argued that an apse or aedicula that probably housed the Torah was a key feature added only after the third century C.E. to some diaspora synagogues.[25] Both the date and other finds lend added credence to this semicircle having served as part of a Jewish complex, probably a synagogue.

A lower apsidal building dating to the fifth century was located by Belov south of the sixth-century basilica. Abutting the complex (or less likely, serving as a southern addition) was a room with a mosaic floor[26] and nearby associated wall plaster fragments with inscriptions in Greek and Hebrew.[27] Strzheletsky, who carried out additional study of the basilica before its restoration,[28] dated the lower mosaic in relation to the lower basilica — fourth/fifth centuries — since two coins that he found in the makeup under the middle edge of the mosaic date to that period,[29] as reconfirmed by recent reexamination of the coins.[30]

The two coins, one of Valentinianus II (383–92 C.E.) and the other of Theodosius I (379–95 C.E.), confirm that the mosaic — and by implication the associated plaster wall — were installed no earlier than the late fourth century C.E. and more probably into the fifth century C.E., which is the approximate date of the lower apsidal building to the north.[31] The large chunks of plaster found clearly indicate that this plaster did not travel far, but were part of the wall plaster that came down when the building of which they were a part was destroyed. A sixth-century date for the destruc-

---

25. Leonard V. Rutgers, "Diaspora Synagogues: Synagogue Archaeology in the Greco-Roman World," in *Sacred Realm: The Emergence of the Synagogue in the Ancient World,* ed. S. Fine (New York: Oxford University Press, 1996), 67–95. Rutgers includes a picture of the aedicula at Ostia.

26. See Reports 609 and 2875. All reference to these archive reports is possible because of the excellent archival work done by Dr. Robert Maclennan and those who worked with him, notably Dr. James van Geldern of Macalester College.

27. See E. N. Zherebtsov, Report 734 (1957). The material discovered on the same site and in the same layer (see Reports 617–18 [1950], and 609, 1301 [1950]) was originally dated to a much later period (seventh or eighth centuries). But after additional study of the monument and the dating of the destruction of Basilica I, they can be dated no later than the sixth century.

28. Report 609, 39–40.

29. Report 609, 41.

30. I. A. Zavadskaya, "Problems of Stratigraphy and Chronology of the Architectural Complex, Basilica 1935, in Chersonesus," in *Materials in Archaeology, History and Ethnography of Tavria* (Simferopol: Tavria, 1996), 5:94–105 [in Russian].

31. Only two reports have been issued about these fragments, one published by E. N. Zherebtsov (p. 209) and another by E. Solomonik (p. 123).

tion seems plausible, since Belov found associated with the plaster seven coins dating to the fourth and fifth century and thirty-eight to the fourth. These findings gained even greater credence when similar wall plaster (unfortunately, with no writing) was found in our excavations associated with Late Roman pottery (dating up to the fifth century). Zherebtsov also notes that coins of the sixth century showing Anastasia and Justinian appeared in the so-called annex to the south, which also contained fragments of the frescoes.

Of particular interest is the plaster fragment inscribed with Hebrew. Professor Esti Eshel of Bar Ilan University (Israel) has analyzed the Hebrew inscriptions of Fragment No. 69, and offers the following translation:[32]

1. [. . .] the One Who chose Jerusalem [i.e., God]

2. [. . . will bless] Hanania from the Bosporos

3. [. . .] Amen, Amen, Sela

Eshel assumes that the phrase "He who chose Jerusalem" derives from the biblical text, Zechariah 3:2: " . . . may you be rebuked by the Lord who has chosen Jerusalem." Appeal to God as part of a blessing in a dedication is found in the Aramaic inscription in the synagogue of Jericho, which reads as follows: "The One Who knows their names . . . will inscribe them in the Book of Life." In the inscriptions in ancient synagogues sculptors tended to place an epithet (e.g., "the King of the World") rather than the name of God.[33]

Other important graffiti were found on fresco fragments 367 and 247.[34] These findings contain the Greek word *eulogia,* which may be linked to the Hebrew inscription (Fragments 267 and 269), because the Jews, both in Palestine and the diaspora, used the term as an equivalent to the Hebrew word *beracha,* "a blessing." The Hebrew fragment has important implications for our interpretation of the use of this space. First, because it was found in destruction debris and was part of a destroyed building in close association with

---

32. See E. Eshel's "A Hebrew Graffito from a Synagogue in the Crimea," *JSQ* 5, no. 4 (1998): 289–99. I thank her for providing a preliminary reading and analysis of the inscription. Earlier discussion of the fragment and its provenance are in Chersonesus Archive Report 1301, 57, 66; Report 609, 29; and Report 617, 16.

33. Seth Smith from the Jewish Theological Seminary (New York) suggests that in the inscription "Bosporos" indicates Hanania's place of origin.

34. See Report 1301, 56; Report 609, 29; articles by E. N. Zherebtsov (in 1963) and by E. I. Solomonik (in 1979), as well as the latter's recently published article in the journal *Krymskii Muzei* (Crimea Museum I, 1994).

a menorah, we can safely assume that at some period Jews used the lower building, probably as a synagogue. Second, the provisional dating of the inscription to the third or possibly early fourth century fits the archaeological context that we have uncovered in our current excavations. Third, it indicates that even if the reference is part of a biblical quote, Jerusalem is viewed as important by this diaspora community — or, taking a minimalist approach, by at least one Jew who inscribed an inscription on a plaster wall in the fourth or fifth centuries. The inscription parallels another Hebrew inscription found in the Crimea from roughly the same period, the bilingual Hebrew-Greek funerary inscription from Panticapaeum (*CIJ* 688) from the third or fourth century.[35]

The third piece of evidence for a synagogue appeared in 1957 when Zherebtsov, while working on the restoration of the Basilica 1935, came across a limestone block with a well-crafted relief of a menorah.[36] The block had been reused as construction material in the foundation of the apse of the sixth-century Christian basilica.[37] The nicely cut menorah has a lulab and shofar flanking it. The stone seems to have been part of a building for reasons outlined below. Hachlili observes that most menorahs flanked by ritual objects in the diaspora began to appear between the third and fourth centuries, and were generally associated with tombs. After the fourth century, they were associated with both funerary and nonfunerary arenas — a pattern that fits our archaeological context.[38] Apparently, the only shofar with holes similar to the Chersonesus example was one found at Beth Shean, which had three holes in the end,[39] and another from Ma'on with two holes.[40] Most do not have holes. Indeed, the Chersonesus shofar seems extremely atypical — perhaps integrating elements of a flute or pipe. In any case, the menorah's fine condition is a tribute to the hardness of the stone and the fact that it did not travel far.

The building with mosaic and the associated frescoes was a public building, dating to the late fourth or fifth century. The combination of the semicircle, the finely cut menorah, and the Hebrew

---

35. Schürer, 37.

36. See Report #734 (1957).

37. E. N. Zherebtsov, "Toward the Study of Early Middle Ages Monuments in Chersonesus," *Byzantine Chronicle* 23 (1963): 210 (Russian).

38. Rachel Hachlili, *Ancient Jewish Art and Archaeology in the Land of Israel* (Brill, 1988), 266–67.

39. Hachlili, 258.

40. Hachlili, 260.

inscription suggests that this public building was Jewish. The frescoes were on the north side of a wall buttressing — or less likely, connected to — the fifth-century apsidal building. The quality of the stone used, as well as the association with a monumental building, suggest that the Jewish community was well-entrenched in the city. Thus, like evidence from most of the rest of the empire, one community of Jews appears to have flourished during the pagan period into the fourth and fifth centuries c.e. Clearly, the apsidal building and the mosaic building complex changed the neighborhood substantially. Basing our judgment on the semicircle, the inscribed plaster, and the menorah, we may surmise that the mosaic building appears to have functioned as a synagogue, most likely from the late fourth / early fifth century to its sixth-century destruction.

The Byzantine Period

Christian presence first appears at Chersonesus only through late hagiographic sources. Trajan reputedly exiled St. Clement, the successor of Peter as bishop of Rome, there.[41] The sources report that he found two hundred Christians working in the marble quarry who needed to go long distances for a drink of water, whereupon Clement discovered a spring — à la Moses! His missionary activities were so successful that he gained five hundred converts and had seventy-five churches built — an obvious exaggeration.[42] Inevitably, the hagiographic sources observe that the authorities were so distraught that they threw Clement into the sea with an anchor tied around his neck.[43] A certain Theodosius from the west claimed to have visited St. Clement's venerated tomb in the first half of the sixth century — an item of potential significance for another discussion.[44]

Finally, a series of acts describing the martyrdoms of seven saints at Chersonesus (beginning around 300, during the reign of Diocletian) were probably recorded by writers from Chersonesus after Christianity was well-established there. A Jerusalem connection is reported in ancient sources: bishops from Jerusalem sent emissaries to Chersonesus to convert the heathen. For example, during

---

41. Christians were commonly exiled to Rome: Timothy, bishop of Gangrae, was exiled there in 460; Pope St. Martin died in exile there in 655; Justinian II was exiled there in 695. C. Walter, "St Clement in the Chersonese and the Iconography of his Miracle," in *Archeion Pontou* (Athens, 1978), 249; Minns, 531.

42. Minns, 530.

43. Walter, 246–60.

44. Ibid., 247.

the reign of Diocletian, the bishop of Jerusalem, Hermon, sent Basil — who became a martyr — and others to convert the barbarians.[45] Such sources, though late, provide important evidence for an animosity toward pagan culture that has some parallels in the archaeological evidence discussed below.

The Byzantine period brought dramatic changes to the landscape of Chersonesus.[46] Over two dozen churches and four major basilicas (including the one near which we excavated, and the Uvarov basilica, over fifty meters long) were apparently built during the subsequent four centuries.[47] New houses sprang up, pottery was prodigiously produced, numbers of Chersonesus coins from the period were found, and a great deal of material remains has been discovered.[48] Perhaps this period is the one actually reflected in the stories of St. Clement's great increase in converts. Although we are uncertain about the period of the actual establishment of some of the churches on the site, our excavations and those of Belov confirm at least one basilica — the 1935 basilica — where such vigorous growth and development took place. Apparently the builders not only reused a menorah stone in the foundation of the second basilica, but systematically hacked up second- to fourth-century sarcophagi from a nearby Roman necropolis, using some of those decorated with figures and inscriptions as part of the same foundation layer as the stone with the menorah.[49] At the least it was reuse of easy-to-get quality marble, at worst a crass disregard for the sacred character of the stones as originally placed. This action is no real surprise. In the fourth- or fifth-century fortress built by Christians after the destruction of Sepphoris in Galilee, the builders used Roman sarcophagi as the corner stones in plain view to the public. Furthermore, fourth-century synagogues at Stobi, Apamaea, and

---

45. Minns, 530–31; see C. Zuckerman, "Bishops and a Garrison in Cherson in the Fourth Century," *Materials in Archaeology, History and Ethnography of Tavria* (Simferopol: Tavria, 1994), 5:545–61 [Russian].

46. This pattern was reflected throughout the late antique world. See A. Cameron, *The Mediterranean World in Late Antiquity, AD 395–600* (London and New York: Routledge, 1993), 159–75.

47. Dating the building of particular structures is problematic. A careful reexamination of excavation reports, combined with select probes using more rigorous modern excavation techniques and the sharper understanding of ceramic typology, are needed — such as has been done by the BSP for the "1935" basilica, which clearly dates to the sixth century.

48. John Smedley, "Archaeology and the History of Cherson: A Survey of Some Results and Problems," in *Archeion Pontou*, 172–92, esp. 180.

49. Belov, *Report of the Excavations*, 40–58.

Gerasa were destroyed and replaced by Christian basilicas.[50] Such destruction was not systemic across the Byzantine Empire, as the continuation of the Sardis synagogue into the seventh century indicates.[51] However, such activities stemmed from the increasingly harsh strictures placed on pagans and Jews from Theodosius I (379–95) on, as evident from the destruction of the pagan temples in Carthage, Alexandria[52] and Aphrodisias, where the temple was converted into a church, probably in the fifth century.[53] The use of stones with pagan and Jewish symbols was more than simply reusing available building material: it represented a clear, albeit crude, signal as to where political and spiritual power now lay.[54]

In summary, recent evidence indicates that Chersonesus in west Crimea also had a Jewish presence in the form of a public building, probably a synagogue that existed from at least the fifth century C.E. In addition, at least one Jew at Chersonesus sought a connection to Jerusalem — even if it was only symbolic — which suggests that a desire for a common affiliation among Jews existed from even the farthest reaches of the empire. Moreover, the Hebrew inscription indicates an effort to express allegiance to the holy language — another important source of identity. The writer or dedicator apparently expected others to agree. The space of the lower basilica and the area with the mosaics and wall plaster was destroyed (or out of use) by the sixth century C.E. One monumental structure was replaced by another. Frank Trombley discusses "temple conversion," which he defines as "demolition or partial dismantling of a sacred edifice, and its modification into a church or martyrion."[55] Demolition of buildings was one way to make way for Christian basilicas, since most of the prime public space (agoras, council chambers, etc.) was already taken. Thus, for economic and — one must still suppose — theological reasons, such areas drew the bulk of attention.[56]

---

50. F. Millar, "The Jews of the Graeco-Roman Diaspora between Paganism and Christianity, AD 312–438," in *The Jews among Pagans and Christians in the Roman Empire,* ed. Judith Lieu, John North, Tessa Rajak (London: Routledge, 1992), 100–102.

51. Millar, "The Jews," 102.

52. Millar, "The Jews," 116.

53. Averil Cameron, *The Mediterranean World in Late Antiquity, AD 395–600* (London and New York: Routledge, 1993), 156.

54. Cf. the decree forbidding the rebuilding of destroyed synagogues by Honorius and Theodosius II in 423. A. Linder, *The Jews in Roman Imperial Legislation* (Detroit and Jerusalem, 1987), and F. Millar, "The Jews," 118.

55. Frank R. Trombley, *Hellenic Religion and Christianization c. 370–529* (Brill, 1993), 1:108.

56. *Ibid.,* 109–10; Friedrich W. Deichmann, "Frühchristliche Kirchen in antiken

Christian rebuilders had no qualms about re-using stones with clear pagan and Jewish symbols. At best this was benign indifference. How this destructive reconstruction was viewed at a later time at Chersonesus is less clear, and indeed the next generation would not necessarily know about the incorporation of such symbols into the sixth-century complex. Nevertheless, those who built the structure knew and didn't care! The lack of systematic desecration of the menorah or the portraits on the sarcophagi that occurred at Aphrodisias[57] suggests that arrogance or indifference rather than open hostility was operative. However, the re-incorporation of powerful religious and cultural symbols — one from a synagogue, the other from pagan graves — makes a key point as to where power now resides. This transformation of space provides yet more evidence that, as F. Millar has observed, Jewish communities had a period of prosperity during the second through the fourth centuries, but faced increasing persecution from the Christian church in the fifth and subsequent centuries, now the new power broker.

Heiligtumern," *Jahrbuch des Deutschen Archäologischen Instituts* 54 (1939): 105–36.

57. In Aphrodisias Christians went to letters inscribed on theater walls and semi-systematically crossed out the name of Aphrodite. In the seventh century the city's name was changed to Stauropolis, City of the Cross; see A. Cameron, *The Mediterranean World in Late Antiquity, AD 395–600, 156.*

Selected Bibliography on the Synagogue and Related Themes

Avi-Yonah, M. *The Jews of Palestine: A Political History from the Bar-Kochba War to the Arab Conquest.* New York: Schocken, 1976.

Collins, John J. *Between Athens and Jerusalem: Jewish Identity in the Hellenistic Diaspora.* Philadelphia: Fortress, 1983.

Chiat, M. J. S. *Handbook of Synagogue Architecture.* Brown Judaic Studies 29. Chico, Calif.: Scholars Press, 1982.

Grabbe, Lester H. *Judaism from Cyrus to Hadrian.* Vol. 2. Minneapolis: Fortress, 1992.

Gutmann, Joseph. *The Synagogue: Studies in Origins, Archaeology and Architecture.* New York: KTAV, 1975.

Hengel, Martin. "Proseuche und Synagoge: Jüdische Gemeinde, Gottshaus und Gottesdienst in der Diaspora und in Palästina." In *Tradition und Glaube: Das frühe Christentum in seiner Umwelt,* Festschrift für K. G. Kühn, ed. G. Jeremias, H. Kühn, and H. Stegemann. Göttingen: Vandenhoeck & Ruprecht, 1971. Repr. in J. Gutmann, *The Synagogue* [above].

Horsley, Richard A. *Archaeology, History and Society in Galilee: The Social Context of Jesus and the Rabbis.* Valley Forge, Pa.: Trinity Press International, 1996.

———. *Galilee: History, Politics, People.* Valley Forge, Pa.: Trinity Press International, 1995.

Kee, Howard Clark. "The Transformation of the Synagogue after 70 C.E.: Its Import for Early Christianity," *NTS* 36 (1990): 1–24.

———. "Early Christianity in Galilee: Reassessing the Evidence from the Gospels." In L. I. Levine, ed. *The Galilee in Late Antiquity.* New York and Jerusalem: Jewish Theological Seminary of America. Distributed by Harvard University Press, Cambridge, Mass., and London, 1992.

Kraabel, A. T. "The Diaspora Synagogue: Archaeological and Epigraphic Evidence since Sukenik," in *ANRW* 2.19.1, 477–510. Berlin: De Gruyter, 1979.

Levine, Lee I., ed. *Ancient Synagogues Revealed.* Jerusalem: Israel Exploration Society, 1981.

———. *The Galilee in Late Antiquity.* New York and Jerusalem: Jewish Theological Seminary of America. Distributed by Harvard University Press, Cambridge, Mass., and London, 1992.

Ma'oz, Zvi Uri. "Ancient Synagogues of the Golan." *Biblical Archaeologist* 51, no. 2 (1988): 116–28.

Meyers, Eric M., and James F. Strange. *Archaeology, the Rabbis, and Early Christianity.* Nashville: Abingdon, 1981.

Meyers, Eric M. "Synagogue." In *Anchor Bible Dictionary.* Ed. D. N. Freedman. Vol. 6. New York: Doubleday, 1992.

Neusner, Jacob. *Judaism in the Matrix of Christianity.* South Florida Studies in the History of Judaism 8. 2d printing. Atlanta: Scholars Press, 1991.

Saldarini, Anthony J. "Synagogue." In *HarperCollins Bible Dictionary.* Ed. Paul J. Achtemeier. San Francisco: HarperSanFrancisco, 1996.

———. *Pharisees, Scribes and Sadducees in Palestinian Society: A Sociological Approach.* Wilmington, Del.: Michael Glazier, 1988.

Schrage, W. *synagōgē.* In *Theological Dictionary of the New Testament.* Vol. 7. Ed. Gerhard Kittel and Gerhard Friedrich. Trans. and ed. G. W. Bromiley. Grand Rapids: Eerdmans, 1985.

Schürer, Emil. *The History of the Jewish People in the Age of Jesus Christ.* Vol. 2. Ed. Geza Vermes, Fergus Millar, and Matthew Black. Edinburgh: T. & T. Clark, 1979.

Shanks, Hershel, ed. *Christianity and Rabbinic Judaism: A Parallel History of Their Origins and Early Development.* Washington, D.C.: Biblical Archaeology Society, 1992.

Smallwood, E. M. *The Jews under Roman Rule: From Pompei to Diocletian.* Studies in Judaism in Late Antiquity. Ed. J. Neusner. Leiden: Brill, 1981.

Index of Ancient Texts

General Index